PRAISE FOR PEACE WITHIN

"*Peace Within* is an essential and generous gift for humanity, arriving at a critical moment in the evolution of consciousness on Earth. This remarkable book will support and empower you to embody your true nature through the wise full-spectrum teachings. Here is a beautifully-designed instructional manual and map that will enable you to engage with the magic of your life – body, heart, mind, and soul - through the power of the breath, radical self-awareness, emotional mastery, and compassionate love. DeMaria's uplifting work, encourages you to take a life-changing adventure, inspired by, and spurred on, by his own courageous and transformational personal stories. Prepare to wake-up to the startling simplicity of your own inner life in ways you never imagined possible."

-Chloe Goodchild, Voice Pioneer, Author, *The Naked Voice - Transform your Life through the Power of Sound*

"In *Peace Within*, Dr. Michael DeMaria offers a manual that can guide the reader toward the elusive peace and equanimity we all seek…Grounded in ancient and contemporary wisdom, DeMaria posits that we can find peace within wherever we are – peace within life, peace within relationships, peace within illness, and even peace within death. He offers clear and detailed practices to get us moving toward a more joyful and meaningful life. He does this with honesty, courage, and wisdom."

-Allan Lokos, founder and Guiding Teacher, Community Meditation Center in NYC; Author of *Pocket Peace, Patience, and Through the Flames*

"Dr. Michael DeMaria has assembled a unique and powerful workbook to help us find peace and healing, plus freedom from excessive negative feelings. He skillfully integrates practices he has developed over decades as a superior therapist, meditation teacher, yoga instructor, wilderness guide, and musician. With this wonderful manual one discovers ways to improve the health, effectiveness, and pleasure of body, mind, heart, self, soul, and relationships with others and the world.

-William Mikulas, Ph.D.; Professor Emeritus; author of *The Way Beyond* and *Taming the Drunken Monkey*

"Michael DeMaria is the best kind of teacher. His wisdom (and it is profound) comes directly from what he has suffered and learned himself, and his teaching is at once far-reaching, direct, and compassionate. With exercises that build on one another to inform every aspect of an individual's life, this book is an important guide to personal transformation."

-Trebbe Johnson, author of *The World Is a Waiting Lover* and *Aphrodite at the Landfill*

"In our chaotic and frightening world, finding peace and joy in our everyday lives seems increasingly out of reach. Yet, Dr. Michael DeMaria, through his incredible journey of spirit and life, has gifted us with this wonderful manual for finding the keys to *Peace Within*. The Māori koru is a perfect symbol for this work, representing the dynamic spiral of life unfurling, ever changing, yet maintaining the core of peace at its center. In his new book, Dr. DeMaria has shared deeply of his own personal journey, while delivering a practical set of modules for bringing us back to what is real: our own individual journeys to the spiral's center.

-Martha Sarasua, M.D., Ph.D., Psychiatrist, Consciousness Researcher & Author *Healer's Journey*

"Dr. DeMaria combines his superb credentials, expertise and compassion to make this an essential book for those looking for inner peace. It has practical advice in each module to help you reconnect with your soul. I recommend it to my friends and my patients, and if you are on the path of healing, you owe this book to yourself."

-Jorge M. Peláez, MD, *Neurologist, Functional/integrative Medicine, and Fellow in Anti-Aging & Regenerative Medicine*

"Through *Peace Within*, Dr. Michael DeMaria shares his compassionate heart, his wisdom and his vulnerability, in being human. For those who are truly ready to begin living a life filled with deeper peace and compassion for themselves and others, *Peace Within* is a practical, creative and scientifically sound blueprint which has the potential to serve as a timeless resource for one's life's journey.

    -Cindy L'Abbe, MSW, CFMN, ACC, *Therapist, Meditation Teacher, Educator*

"Dr. Michael DeMaria takes you on a courageous journey sharing his darkest moments. It's a rare professional that can share so deeply and publicly of him or herself to bring you a clear and well-constructed guide to your own journey within. I cried. I pondered. I meditated. *Peace Within* is for everyone whether suffering from PTSD or just finding your way in a busy over-stimulated techno world.

    -Elise Treff Gordon MD, *Captain, Navy Medical Core, flight surgeon*

"In the world of personal enrichment resources, everyone wants to show you a path. In this overcrowded world, it is difficult to give a sterling recommendation. *Peace Within* is truly one of those great resources. Dr DeMaria provides a guiding hand, but one that subtly reinforces the deep knowledge that we already know what we need to make our lives whole. As with Dr. Spock, who tapped the intrinsic knowledge of mothers in the 1950's, providing the catalyst for a change from regimented child rearing methods to a freer and more compassionate approach, DeMaria draws upon the same deep knowledge we all have to bring about our own transformation. Where many teach self-knowledge, DeMaria emphasizes self-compassion, while providing a set of extremely well-developed exercises to carry you thru the process that he knows so well.

    -Clint Goss, Ph.D. *Author, Researcher and Recording Artist*

"This is a beautiful book, written from the heart. It's also a practical and user friendly guide of how each and every one of us can heal ourselves, our communities, and the world. I recommend it very highly!"

-Bonnie McLean O.M.D., A.P., M.A., B.S.N., *Acupuncturist, Author, and Healer*

"Dr. DeMaria comes from an exquisitely sensitive place, offering the benefit of both his professional expertise and personal life lessons learned. The result is a book filled with profound wisdom and practical exercises to remind each of us who we really are and how to stay connected to that genuine source of Peace Within - the only place it can truly be found."

-Dave Berman, Certified Hynotherapist, Laughter Ambassador, and Author of *Laughter for the Health of It*

"*Peace Within*, is a unique step-by-step guide to experience peace, healing, health, and wholeness. DeMaria's book helps you create a personal growth retreat, in the comfort of your own home, by giving you tools and practices that help you find *Peace Within* your body, mind, heart, and life. I love this book and highly recommend it to everyone who is seeking inner peace."

-Ann McIndoo *CEO/Founder and Bestselling Author*

"*Peace Within* is an encouraging, life-altering work, helping you discover that no matter what life throws at you, you can claim the subtle river of peace that is already flowing deep within you. Allow this book to be your inspiration and motivation to seek a happier, healthier life, inside and out, by grasping the peace that is yours for the taking, despite any circumstances you encounter."

-Autumn J. Conley, Editor

PEACE *Within*

Clear Your Mind, Open Your Heart, Embrace Your Soul, and Heal Your Life

Michael Brant DeMaria, Ph.D.

*To my mother,
Jacqueline
for the ever present gift of life;
whose deep love is with me,
in each beat of my heart
and breath I take…*

*and to my father,
Francesco
in deep appreciation of
his greatest gift to me,
the love of life itself.*

*Thank you both…for your love,
and spirit which transcends
life and death…*

Copyright © 2016 by Michael Brant DeMaria.

All Rights Reserved. No part of this book may be reproduced in any written, electronic, recording, or photocopying without written permission of the publisher or author. The exception would be in the case of brief quotations embodied in the critical articles or reviews and pages where permission is specifically granted by the publisher or author.

Although every precaution has been taken to verify the accuracy of the information contained herein, the author and publisher assume no responsibility for any errors or omissions. No liability is assumed for damages that may result from the use of information contained within. All information is meant for educational and entertainment purposes only and not as medical advice. Please consult your physician before beginning any exercise program.

Ontos World Press
512 E. Zaragoza St.
Pensacola, Florida 32502
www.ontosworldpress.com

Library of Congress Cataloging-in-Publication Data

DeMaria, Michael Brant
Peace Within: Clear Your Mind, Open Your Heart, Embrace Your Soul and Heal Your Life
Printed in the United States
ISBN: 978-0-9802196-5-4 First Edition 2016
Library of Congress Control Number: 2016910190
Ebook First Edition ISBN: 978-0-9802196-9-2

First Edition

The author can be reached at michael@michaeldemaria.com
and www.michaeldemaria.com

Contents

ACKNOWLEDGEMENTS 15
THE SPIRAL KORU 19
PRELUDE 21
INTRODUCTION 23
HOW TO USE THIS BOOK 25
CONTRACT 25
CORE PRINCIPLES 26
MY STORY 27
THE PEACE WITHIN PROCESS 33

1: The Peace Within Process   36

THE EMOTIONAL CIRCULATORY SYSTEM 37
THOUGHTS, FEELINGS AND SENSATIONS 38
THE CORE TOOLS 42
YOUR PEACE WITHIN SPACE 43
YOUR PEACE WITHIN JOURNAL 43
BREATHWORK 46
BELLY BREATHING 48
BELLY BREATHING EXERCISE 51
MINDFULNESS 53
COMPASSIONATE AWARENESS 54
MEDITATION 56
MODULE 1 – MAIN POINTS 58
MODULE 1 - PEACE WITHIN PRACTICES 58

2: Peace Within Your Day   60

THE JOURNEY WITHIN 62
THE CENTERING BREATH 63
CENTERING BREATH EXERCISE 67
FINDING YOUR CENTER 68
CLOSING YOUR EYES 70
RELEASING INTO THE NOW 72
RELEASE INTO THE NOW EXERCISE 73

- FINDING YOUR GROUND 76
- GROUNDING EXERCISE 79
- MODULE 2 – MAIN POINTS 81
- MODULE 2 - PEACE WITHIN YOUR DAY PRACTICES 81

3: Peace Within Your Body 84

- COMING TO YOUR SENSES 86
- FIVE SENSES MINDFULNESS PRACTICE 87
- MINDFUL HEARING 88
- MINDFUL SEEING 89
- MINDFUL TASTING AND SMELLING 92
- MINDFUL TOUCH 96
- CARING FOR YOUR BODY 99
- FULL- BODIED BREATHING 101
- SMILE POWER 103
- SMILE PRACTICE 106
- YOUR SMILE PRACTICE 107
- HEARTFELT BELLY LAUGHTER 109
- LAUGHTER YOGA EXERCISES 110
- LYING DOWN MEDITATION 110
- PEACE WITHIN YOUR BODY JOURNALING 116
- MODULE 3 – MAIN POINTS 118
- MODULE 3 - PEACE WITHIN PRACTICES 119

4: Peace Within Your Mind 120

- YOU ARE NOT YOUR THOUGHTS 123
- THE PAST AND FUTURE 126
- BOATS ON THE RIVER MEDITATION 129
- CLOUDS IN THE SKY AND FISH IN THE SEA 132
- PEACE WITHIN YOUR MIND JOURNALING EXERCISE 134
- MODULE 4 – MAIN POINTS 135
- MODULE 4 - PEACE WITHIN PRACTICES 136

5: Peace Within Your Heart 138

- THE HEART 142
- FEELINGS JOURNAL EXERCISE 143

NOT RESISTING, NOT PUSHING 145
FOUR STEPS TO PRPCESS EMOTIONS 149
EMOTIONS AND ATTACHMENT 156
THE RAPIDS OF GRIEF AND THE WHIRLPOOL OF SHAME 159
NAMING YOUR FEELINGS MEDITATION 162
THE THERAPEUTIC LETTER 163
EMOTIONAL WEATHER PATTERNS 166
PEACE WITHIN YOUR HEART JOURNALING 168
MODULE 5 – MAIN POINTS 169
MODULE 5 - PEACE WITHIN PRACTICES 171

6: Peace Within Your Self   172

SELF-COMPASSION 174
SELF-TALK 178
SELF-COMPASSION EXERCISES 180
EMBRACING THE UNIVERSE 181
VARIATIONS: 182
COMPASSIONATE AWARENESS 183
SELF, SOUL AND EGO 184
PEACE WITHIN THE SELF EXERCISE 191
MODULE 6 – MAIN POINTS 191
MODULE 6 - PEACE WITHIN PRACTICES 192

7: Peace Within Your Soul   194

THE ROAD HOME 198
OUR FIRST TEACHER 200
INNER CHILD EXERCISE 201
FIRST LOVE 203
ACORN THEORY OF THE SOUL 208
WHAT KIND OF TREE ARE YOU? 210
SOUL WORK AND SURVIVAL WORK 211
WRITING YOURSELF TO TEARS 213
CHILD WISDOM EXERCISE 215
DREAM LIVES EXERCISE 216
TUNING INTO THE SOUL 217
THE EMOTIONAL CIRCULATORY SYSTEM 2.0 217

EARTH, SEA, SKY MEDITATION 219
THE CAPTAIN (SOUL) AND FIRST MATE (EGO) 222
MODULE 7 – MAIN POINTS 225
MODULE 7 – PEACE WITHIN PRACTICES 226

8: Peace Within Relationship 228

SELF AND OTHER..230
WHEN TWO CENTERS MEET 232
KEEPING YOUR WALLET 238
TAKING BACK YOUR WALLET EXERCISE 242
REFLECTIVE LISTENING EXERCISE 243
EMOTIONAL QUICKSAND 243
HEAL THYSELF 245
THE SEARCH FOR THE MAGICAL OTHER 247
TWO EMPTY GLASSES 248
MODULE 8 – MAIN POINTS 251
MODULE 8 - PEACE WITHIN PRACTICES 253

9: Peace Within Life 254

DEEP LISTENING 259
IN THE FLOW 261
DEEP LISTENING EXERCISE 264
THE HARDENED HEART..266
FORGIVENESS..268
FORGIVENESS EXERCISE 271
FORGIVING ONESELF...275
FROM SHAME TO REGRET..277
FROM HARD HEART TO WHOLE HEART 278
VULNERABILITY AND SHAME 279
PLEASE BE PATIENT WITH ME; GOD ISN'T
FINISHED WITH ME YET 280
FORGIVING LIFE..281
EXPECT NOTHING, BE READY FOR ANYTHING 283
THE HEART WARRIOR..288
MODULE 9 – MAIN POINTS 291
MODULE 9 - PEACE WITHIN PRACTICES 292

10: Peace Within Death — 294

- THE STARS WITHIN MY HEART — 295
- DEEP STILLNESS — 297
- THE OCEAN OF PEACE — 301
- REST IN PEACE — 204
- DYING WITH PEACE — 206
- DEATH LODGE — 208
- THE TWO LIGHTS — 211
- INNER LIGHT — 213
- DEEP GRATITUDE — 314
- DEEP SLEEP PRACTICE — 315
- MEDITATION FOR DEEP SLEEP — 317
- PEACE WITHIN MORNING PRACTICE — 318
- EXERCISE — 318
- CREATIVE INFINITY — 320
- SONG OF THE SOUL — 323
- DEEP PEACE IN DEATH — 326
- MODULE 10 – MAIN POINTS — 329
- MODULE 10 – PEACE WITHIN DEATH PRACTICES — 330
- POSTLUDE — 332

Peace Within Notes — 343

ACKNOWLEDGEMENTS

There is no way to thank everyone who has contributed to the birth of this work, but I will do my best. First and foremost, I sit in deep and profound gratitude to my mother who not only gave birth to me, but carried me when I was unable to carry myself. Mom, although you have left your physical body, I now know, more than ever, how deeply you are the wind beneath my wings – as I feel you in each breath and beat of my heart. I love you dearly and your love and unwavering belief in me weaves in and out of every word of this work.

To my dad and brothers, thank you for putting up with me, and keeping me humble, honest, and remembering that I am all too human. I love you.

To my wife of 34 years, and partner of 39, Kathleen *'jelly bean'* Kies, you stood by me during that painful, difficult, and overwhelming year of 2004 when I often felt I could not go on. I am so grateful for the grit and grace you bring to my life. Danielle Christina DeMaria, my precious, creative, brilliant, and huge hearted daughter – you are my greatest teacher and I would not be here today if it was not for you. There are no words to express the depths of love, care, and genuine affection I have for you, and the way I sit in awe of all of who you are and what you teach me daily.

To the amazing Jennifer Brown and Tami Simon, of Sounds True.

The many soulful and heartfelt conversations I had with each of you over the years helped shape this work and bring it into focus in a way I could not have done without you. Truly, thank you!

To Ann McIndoo – you helped me distill 30 years of ideas into a coherent vision and helped me dig deep and find the story that was inside me waiting to be birthed. Truly I could not have structured this work the way I did without your sage advice, guidance and belief in me and this work!

To Mahala Church, you saw the work when it was so crude and rough and gave me such wonderful support, hand-holding and encouragement as we further sculpted what Ann and I began, and encouraged me to find the spiral Koru and add so many loving touches to the feel and overall structure. I will always be grateful to you for helping me polish the diamond in the rough it was when we first started working together.

To Lynn Lauber, you helped me grow as a writer and human being. You took me to the next level in weaving my own story into this work, while holding my feet to the fire to make sure I didn't shrink back from fully showing up and being real. I deeply admire your authenticity as a writer. You've been a true gem in my life as I continue to hone the art of writing from the heart.

To Autumn Conley, your copy editing at the last hour even with both of our life challenges was able to bring this beast into its final form, and polish each facet one more time. Thank you for your attention to detail and helping me smooth and craft the final product.

To Vanessa Maynard, my amazing graphic artist for the interior layout. We went through quite a journey! Thank you for continuing to believe in my vision and helping me bring this work into the world. I could not have done it without you!

To Rupa Limbu, who created the amazing cover art for this work. We had over 630 designs submitted by 60 designers in the contest and you nailed it! I so love what you created! A big thank you to you AND all those around the world who voted!

A huge thank you to the inaugural class of the *Peace Within Process for Integrative Wellness* who met every other week for the first six months of 2016 and help me vet this whole book and program. You guys so showed up and touched my heart in so many ways. I bow to all of you!

Although I thank them throughout the text I have to once again thank my dear teachers and mentors, Dr. Bill Mikulas, Dr. Bill Plotkin, and David Darling, who literally at times walked me through this healing journey and were always genuine guides by my side.

A special thanks to Team Ontos – Margeaux Donovan Gibson, my stellar, superstar intern who has been a dear friend and fellow heart warrior for 20 plus years and who gets this work at a deep level. To Katie Leigh not only a dear soul friend, and fellow heart warrior, but an integral part of Team Ontos handling so much of the social media and helping bring the mission and vision of Ontos and the *Peace Within* process out in the world.

I'm not sure where I'd be without my dear soul sister Laura Colo, whose friendship, care, editing, and unwavering belief in the importance of this work and following one's heart. Our soul friendship over the last 17 years has been a priceless gift. A thousand thank yous for always believing in me and kicking my butt to get it out there.

A thank you to my lifelong soul brothers, Bill Schulz, Bob Brennen, Jon Windley, David Walden, Clint Goss (and soul sister Vera Shanov!), Richard Sneider and Dan Fitzsimmons. You are always there even when not physically! Thank you for the gift of your friendship which continues to be a great blessing in my life.

Any omissions, errors, inconsistencies, are purely my fault and I apologize for any oversights that the astute reader might find. In true organic fashion if you do find any and let me know, they will be corrected in future editions.

THE SPIRAL KORU

Since childhood, I've drawn spirals. It has been one of the constants in my life. Whenever I was stressed, bored, or lost, I would spontaneously draw these shapes, which would evolve, grow, and eventually take over the whole page. I did this quite subconsciously until in graduate school when I began reading about the archetypal meaning of spirals. I discovered that there are five ancient petroglyphs found throughout the world, but the spiral is the only one found in every continent of the ancient world. Not only that, but it's widely considered the archetypal symbol of the soul's journey.

Many years later, when I was going through a very difficult period in my life, I had a dream where I 'heard' a voice telling me to paint spirals. So I did. Since then, I have painted spirals of all types, in all colors and shapes and sizes. These have played a crucial part in lifting me whenever I fall into darkness and putting me back on the road to light heartedness again.

When I began working on this project I wanted a symbol to express the simplicity and depth of the *Peace Within* process. I finally settled on an image inspired by the Koru spiral of the New Zealand Māori people. It is at once a spiral, a circle, a wave and the image of growth, birth and new life. The spiral shape is inspired by the first stages of the unfurling of the silver fern frond. It symbolizes new life, growth, strength, and peace. The spiral, enclosed within a circle, also expresses the idea of perpetual movement, while the inner coil suggests a constant return to the point of origin.

In this way, it is also a fractal for me—an infinitely complex, never-ending pattern. I always liked the way my early drawings also resembled a fern perpetually growing, one frond after another — beautiful, changing, while its essence remains the same. For me, this is also how the breath works: a perpetual movement, with a constant return to a center of peace.

The Māori Koru image highlights key points throughout the book, and at the introduction of each chapter. I'm thrilled to have it featured so prominently in this work and to share its deep meaning with you.

The Māori Koru represents peace, tranquility, personal growth, positive change, new life, and harmony. My prayer is that these blessings will come your way.

PRELUDE

In 2004, at the age of 42, I found myself plunged into a spiritual and emotional emergency, an all-encompassing dissolution that impacted every area of my being. My life as a successful author, teacher, and psychotherapist seemed over. I didn't know where to turn for help. I thought I'd hit rock bottom, and then the waters came. A hurricane slammed into our Gulf Coast town, and a fifteen-foot wall of water engulfed our neighborhood and destroyed most of what my family and I called home.

I'd dedicated my life to helping others, but none of my experience or degrees were of any help to me. Within hours the flood had come and gone, leaving in its wake the devastated rubble of my former existence.

As I surveyed the ruins, I was unsure whether I'd ever be able to rebuild my life or regain the peace I'd lost even before the storm's devastation. But, as I was to discover, breakdowns often lead to extraordinary breakthroughs.

***

Everything flows. From the smallest sub-atomic particle to the largest galaxy whirling through the vastness of space, all is in motion. In our daily lives, we encounter what appear to be solid objects, but are, in fact, configurations of energy. Our very earth spins at an incredible speed, yet appears to be perfectly still. Ancient cultures understood this fluidity of reality through the simple process of meditation and the close observation of consciousness.

The health of our bodies also depends on a constant circulation of blood and air in order to maintain balance and health. Our emotional and physical selves are a sublime arrangement of thoughts, feelings, and sensations. We become ill when we resist or become attached to these emotions instead of allowing them to flow through our consciousness. This simple principle has informed my personal and professional life.

The best way to tend to our bodies, minds, and hearts is not by trying to control their innate wisdom, but by trusting it. In this way, we unite the components of ourselves in an elegant, orchestrated microcosm — just as the dance of Earth, water, sky, and sun converges to produce life on our planet.

While everything flows, life also grows, transforms, then dies, like the life cycle of a butterfly or the endless seasons of the year. We move through ever-unfolding stages of growth, shedding what no longer serves us. We go within to transform, then reemerge—renewed, wiser, and more compassionate. Eventually, we're ready to take flight—freeing our minds, opening our hearts, and flowing with the music of all creation.

This was what I had to learn all over again.

INTRODUCTION

The source of peace resides within each of us. The great struggle and tragedy of modern life is that we continually seek outside of us instead.

Our culture perpetuates the great lie that peace can be found elsewhere. The seduction of the outside world is greater than ever before, with smart phones, cars, and televisions. Our lives are so fast paced, hectic, and overwhelming that we suffer from future shock, data smog, and information overload.

"The only journey is the one within."

~Rainer Maria Rilke

We repeatedly seek, search, and hope that perhaps this time, this job, relationship, home, or experience will bring us the lasting peace we need; yet these devices and possessions only distance us and keep the focus outside of ourselves.

This has been the core dilemma faced by most of the people I've worked with over the last thirty years, from every walk of life. However, there is an antidote: *Turn within*, for that is where the path to true peace abides.

I have also struggled deeply with letting go of the cultural conditioning that told me peace had to be created on the outside. However, time and self-compassion eventually renewed my connection to the deep, inward ocean of peace I had thought was lost.

How do we journey to the source of peace that is available to us each moment of the day? This is the question I have heard from clients and students for over three decades. It is the question I had to once again ask myself, and I had to rediscover the answer one step at a time.

This is the reason I'm writing this book and sharing some personal accounts of my own journey. I know the most deeply personal often resonates with what is most universal. My hope is that these will serve as touchstones to your own journey.

I am honored to share my path with you. Come take the most amazing, most adventurous journey of your lifetime and explore the ocean of peace that lies within *you*!

HOW TO USE THIS BOOK

I have used the term *module* instead of chapter to reinforce the fact that this is a hands-on guidebook. You may start anywhere within it, anyplace you desire.

Although working through the modules sequentially is recommended, each can be explored individually, depending upon the issues you are confronting. Perhaps you're struggling in a relationship and are drawn to Module 6, on *Peace Within Your Relationship*. By all means, jump in and start there! As you work through, make a concerted effort to eventually complete the other modules as well.

Modules may also be completed at your own pace so you can fit them into your life in a way that works for you. It is possible to spend a week, two weeks, or even a month on the practices within each module. At the very least, I suggest that you allow a week per module. It takes about thirty days for something to become a habit, and my hope is many of these practices will stay with you for the rest of your life. I ask you to make a commitment to your health and well-being by making a contract with yourself to try these practices and complete the program and see what a difference they can make.[1]

CONTRACT

I _____ make a commitment to myself to do the exercises, readings and meditations on a regular basis for the duration of the *Peace Within Program*.

In order to maximize the *Peace Within Program* and healing process, I commit myself to self-nurturance and care through adequate sleep, healthy diet and exercise.

_____   _____

(signature)   (date)

_____

(completion date)

CORE PRINCIPLES

The Core Principles of the Peace Within Process that follow are the essence of the program. Keeping them in mind will help you maneuver through the details of each module and exercise. These serve as the foundation of the journey to find and experience peace in each moment. I'd like you to read them each day during your self-paced *Peace Within Program* and see how your understanding of them grows and develops over the next three months.

1. Peace is our natural state and our true nature.

2. We lose our connection to this natural state through living in a world of duality and polarization (culturally and socially).

3. This natural state of peace remains, like a hidden underground sea, beneath conditioned thoughts, feelings and beliefs inherited from culture, family, and society, as well as from trauma and wounding.

4. This natural indwelling peace is as dynamic and fluid as water and has the character of energy that animates the body.

5. We can't will ourselves to experience this natural indwelling peace, but we can create the conditions where it arises, like a spring in the desert.

6. This natural state is very similar to a childlike openness to what is present in each moment and has the quality of curiosity and compassion (receptivity, openness, and welcoming).

7. Peace dependent upon external circumstances is fleeting.

8. Peace grounded from within (arising from knowing and connecting to our natural state) is freeing and healing and helps us discover who we really are.

9. The breath is a river that we can travel at any time, back to the ocean of peace, which is its source. This is experienced as a deep sense of interconnection and love for self, others, and life at large.

MY STORY

At the age of 42, my life began coming apart at the seams: personally, professionally, and emotionally. From the outside, I appeared to be the model of success. I had a thriving psychotherapy practice, a lovely wife of 22 years, an amazing 17-year-old daughter, and a beautiful home on the Florida Gulf Coast.

I'd grown up a whiz kid who loved an intellectual and physical challenge: I earned two B.A. degrees in philosophy and psychology by the age of 20, a M.A. in psychology at 21, and a Ph.D. in clinical psychology at 25. I was also a black belt who taught martial arts and meditation.

The middle of three sons of an immigrant father and a mother who'd grown up in foster homes, I was definitely my father's son. He was an Italian overachiever who'd survived World War II, dodging bullets, bombs and starvation before finding his way to America—his life-long dream—at the ripe age of 19. Arriving in Brooklyn, barely knowing English, he sold rags on the streets to survive, and in nine short years had earned a Ph.D. in chemical engineering. He was my hero and role model.

I'd also been on a spiritual path for as long as I could remember, eventually working with indigenous and spiritual healers from around the world. Despite this, in midlife, my life had begun crumbling from within and I seemed unable to stop it.

I faced a number of painful challenges that year, but the main cause of my descent was a knee and back injury that required surgery and triggered unresolved trauma from surgeries I'd had as a young child.

I had often been ill as a boy, including undergoing several surgeries that terrified me. Back then, doctors felt it was better *not* to tell a child he was having an operation until the day of the procedure. So, whether it was for a tonsillectomy or abdominal surgery for a double hernia, I was picked up at school by my mother, only to find that she'd packed a bag and we that were headed again to the hospital.

I have vivid memories of moments before the abdominal surgery, of being left on a cold metal gurney outside the operating room, all by myself and feeling as though I was about to die. Masked figures appeared and pressed a mask over my mouth and nose as the noxiously sweet smell of ether poured into my lungs. They asked me to count backwards from ten. I struggled not to take a breath, and felt sure I was dying.

Suddenly, I disappeared into a terrifying vortex and felt the sensation of leaving my body and going off to another world – a near-death like experience. When I awoke, I was in a recovery room, surrounded by screaming children, and in terrible pain. These events all had a profound, traumatic effect on my highly sensitive nature.

Those feelings of panic and dread returned, in the form of a full-blown post-traumatic stress reaction as I approached new surgeries as an adult.

After spending so much of my life specializing in the area of trauma and loss, here I was experiencing it myself, losing control of my mind and emotions. Depression, fear, and anxiety: I felt them all again. Images of clients I had worked with who'd 'lost it' filled my mind as I found myself whirling into the same abyss. It was like being trapped waist deep in quicksand: The harder I struggled, the deeper I sank.

It felt as if my mind, heart and life had turned against me. I struggled to find some solid ground, some sure footing, but I continued spiraling down.

Since the age of 18, I'd practiced a type of meditation to calm my mind and help me deal with dark times. I had created a beautiful meditation space in my home, a large walk in closet with important images and objects from my life journey, as well as my beloved meditation cushion. Unfortunately, my injuries made it impossible for me to sit in my meditation space and on my cushion. So, I simply stopped meditating, which only aggravated the situation.

In the span of a year, I experienced more loss than I had in the previous forty-two years of my life. The year that changed me forever began when a client of mine committed suicide, an experience that shattered me emotionally. Within a few months, a business associate, professional colleague, and friend who had worked with me for close to a decade was arrested. Their crimes, which I'd known nothing about, were suddenly very public and put my professional reputation, livelihood and family in jeopardy. A few weeks later, I suffered a knee and back injury, which made it very difficult for me to work and required surgery.

Then, one by one, my associates began to leave the large group practice I managed, eventually leaving me alone with my office manager. The day before my surgery, my office manager informed me that she would also be gone when I returned.

I felt completely lost and alone. I didn't think it could get any worse, but it did.

As I began my painful postsurgical rehabilitation, Hurricane Ivan roared up the Gulf Coast. My family had already survived two previous hurricanes, but this was the most devastating: Swirling debris, a tower of water, and winds that sounded like a freight train. The hurricane decimated our entire neighborhood. My family was forced to move into the back rooms of my office downtown. As insurance claims poured in from the disaster, our insurance company fell into bankruptcy. I felt defeated.

My greatest pain during this battle was feeling exiled from the inner peace that had always been readily available to me. I had dealt with plenty of adversity and outward struggle in my life, but my saving grace was that I could always retreat and rejuvenate through meditation, yoga, and time spent in nature. Now, though, with my injuries and post-traumatic stress, I simply could not find my way home to myself.

In the modules that follow, I'll share the steps I took that eventually led me back from the brink to the meaningful, peaceful life I thought I'd lost forever. I share my story, not because I think it's important, but to illustrate how each of us can be undone by events we never imagined possible. Most of all, I want you to see that, we can return to our deep selves again, no matter the trauma and tragedy we have encountered, if we have a way forward.

I'd utilized the core principles I present here many times in the past, but now I had to relearn them, again, in an even deeper way. I also had to come to terms with central components of my own life's traumas, embrace my heart's deepest calling, and heal my life.

As I struggled each day over the next four years, I reevaluated everything about my work and my understanding of who I was. Most importantly, I began to let go of my expectations and beliefs about myself, others, and reality. My pain, grief, and despair eventually led to a powerful transformation.

I experienced blinding moments of insight and awakening over the coming weeks and months, as well as painful setbacks and new challenges. Through it all, something new grew within me. I truly felt like the proverbial caterpillar being turned inside out and upside down in a chrysalis, to finally reemerge, transformed, stronger, and more whole than before.

Although I'd experienced inner peace before, this time was different. Instead of occasional moments of it, I discovered a pathway to an endless ocean of peace. It stretched into infinity and could be visited at any time.

Within you also lies such an ocean. No matter what you are struggling with, your life has a stillness and silence beneath the chaotic surface. No matter how hectic your world, this ocean of peace is always there to refresh, revive, and nourish you – if you take the time to discover it. Sometimes it begins as a small trickle of water in the desert, but if you are persistent, take your time, and practice – you, too, will discover it. It's truly as natural as breathing, and breath is the river we travel down to merge once again with that endless ocean of peace.

THE PEACE WITHIN PROCESS

What do I mean by *Peace Within*? Although it refers to what most people think of as inner peace, there is a difference. For many, inner peace involves getting *away from life:* going on a retreat, escaping to a mountain getaway, or an ashram, monastery, or yoga class. Although all of these can help us become acquainted with a taste of peace, what I'm referring to by *Peace Within* is finding peace wherever you are: *Peace Within life*, within relationships, within the workplace, within illness, within struggle, and even *Peace Within death*. This is the vision that grew in me and has become my practice with each breath.

In my 30's, I'd guided wilderness-based vision fasts, retreating into the wilderness in order to escape the noise and clutter of the outside world, and guiding others there as well. These journeys were valuable, important and some of the most powerful work I've ever done. However, after going through my transformation and awakening, I found I could discover the same peace everywhere I turned. There is no need for me to hike miles into the wilderness or to fast; this peace is available everywhere once you tune your mind, heart, and soul to its current.

Peace Within is an inner state that is not dependent upon external circumstances. Because life is always changing and moving like a river, *peace within* is actually a dynamic process that requires improvisation and skillful maneuvering through the rapids of life.

This comprehensive, integrative process addresses mind, body, heart, and soul. Unlike many other approaches it merges Eastern and Western practices.

Each module of the book deals with a different dimension of being human and finding *Peace Within:*

The Peace Within Process	*Peace Within Your Self*
Peace Within Your Day	*Peace Within Your Soul*
Peace Within Your Body	*Peace Within Your Relationship*
Peace Within Your Mind	*Peace Within Life*
Peace Within Your Heart	*Peace Within Death*

As you read the text and practice the exercises, remember that *Peace Within* refers to a dynamic, living, integrative peace that grows from the inside out. In time, your inner peace will become less and less dependent upon external circumstances; rather, it will grow from the inside-out emerging from the great ocean of peace that is always available to all of us, if you know how to access it.

My journey from despair to awakening and living in deeper alignment with the ocean of peace that informs my life, day in and day out, has been nothing short of amazing! In the following pages, I have refined the essential elements of what I discovered on my journey into a format that I hope will resonate with you and help you find your *Peace Within*.

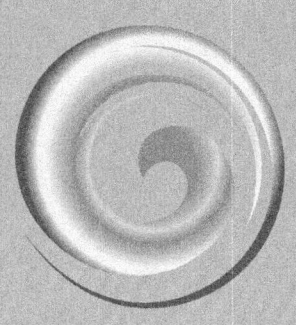

MODULE I

This module introduces you to the main concepts in the peace within process, core principles, core tools – and an overview of the modules and how best to work through them. You will learn about the emotional circulatory system, and the dual components of deep breathing and compassionate awareness to bring more peace into your life and relationships.

1: THE PEACE WITHIN PROCESS

I was born in the wilds of southwestern Connecticut, an hour out of New York City by train, but surrounded by deep, dense woods that could have come straight out of *The Last of the Mohicans*. Ancient fruit orchards, brooks, and boulders provided fertile ground for my explorations. I left the house for the woods whenever the world became too much for me.

My inner life was always more compelling to me then the outer one. As a child, I often experienced feelings that seemed too large and deep for words. Maybe that's why I didn't speak until I was nearly 3.

During these treks in nature, I sensed something great and ancient around me: I felt connected to a nameless, palpable presence. My breathing slowed, and my heart opened; I was filled with joy and contentment.

In the intuitive way of a child, I was involved in the major components of the *Peace Within* practice— a deep, relaxed breath, a state of meditation that quieted my mind in focus and contemplation, and a mindfulness that allowed me to experience whatever was before me: a maple tree, a singing bird, or the cloud-filled sky.

It is this deep, joy-filled peace that I want to help you cultivate in your own life – a peace and presence closely akin to the wonder, awe, and mystery we experienced as young children.

THE EMOTIONAL CIRCULATORY SYSTEM

The *emotional circulatory system* is a concept I've coined to describe the *Peace Within* process at work. The great enemy of inner peace is not emotions themselves, but the way we deal with them. Emotions come and go constantly all day, like the weather. When the emotional circulatory system is working well, we can allow the emotions to move through us, without repressing them or acting them out. The emotions themselves are less the issue than our reaction to them. As the saying goes here on the Florida Gulf Coast, "If you don't like the weather, just wait a minute."

In life, *time* is often all we need to *feel better*.[1]

In this module, I'll provide an overview and road map for the practices we'll be going into more deeply as we explore the emotional circulatory system.

Module 2, *Peace Within the Body*, will focus on working with sensations; Module 3, *Peace Within the Mind*, will focus on working with thoughts in the emotional circulatory system; and Module 4, *Peace Within the Heart*, will explore working with feelings.

THOUGHTS, FEELINGS AND SENSATIONS

In the human cardiopulmonary circulatory system, there are two main components: the heart and lungs. I like to think of the emotional circulatory system in a similar way. Instead of pumping blood, we are pumping experiences. Instead of oxygenating the blood, we are bringing compassionate, heart-centered awareness to our experiences.[2]

Just as blood is made up of three main components—plasma, red and white blood cells, and platelets—so also are experiences made up of three parts: *thoughts, feelings and sensations*. All you experience and all that passes through your consciousness can be categorized into one of these.[3]

Our physical circulatory system is in constant motion. The rhythm of the heart and lungs circulates in a beautifully orchestrated rhythm. Our lives are also based on flow and circulation. Movement *is* life. It's when we become stuck in one idea about who we are, where we are, and what is happening that we suffer. In order to remain vitally alive, and healthy we must let these elements flow through us.

In meditation, we call becoming stuck *attachment*. Whenever we become attached to an idea, feeling, person, object, or drug we cease to flow. Then the emotional circulatory system becomes unbalanced, and suffering ensues.

Compassionate awareness is like oxygen for our emotional hearts and souls. The root of the *peace within process* is learning to move from the imbalance and suffering that occurs from a dysfunctional relationship with your consciousness towards a healthy, natural, regulation of it. This occurs when you learn to allow your feelings, thoughts, and sensations to circulate naturally and effortlessly, while resting in compassionate awareness.[1]

How do we draw oxygen into the blood in order to nourish the constant stream of life? The breath! It is the same with the emotional circulatory system. Deep diaphragmatic breathing helps bring compassionate awareness to our experiences and their accompanying thoughts, feelings, and sensations.

In this way, the two main components of the emotional circulatory system are *compassionate awareness* (the heart of the system) and *diaphragmatic breathing* (the lungs of the system)*(See Diagram 1)*.

Throughout the modules, I'll introduce you to practices that help the emotional circulatory system run smoothly. There are micro-meditations and exercises, as well as longer guided and unguided meditations. The micro-meditations and exercises can be done at any time and are meant to punctuate your day with moments of peace.

These practices provide you with immediate tools to quickly quiet the mind, open the heart, and allow experience to flow through you. A quiet mind and open heart in this context does not necessarily mean there are no thoughts or feelings present – only that you are not *attaching* to them and are allowing them to move through you.

As you understand more about how the emotional circulatory system works you'll begin to realize how everything is ceaselessly arising in awareness, passing through it, then dissolving or dropping out of consciousness. This occurs just as the breath rises and falls, the day turns to night, and the seasons of the year come and go. When you begin to focus on the rising and falling and less on the contents of consciousness, you begin to experience the *natural state of peace* that resides within, not the drama the mind creates. Once this has happened, the journey has begun.

EMOTIONAL CIRCULATORY SYSTEM

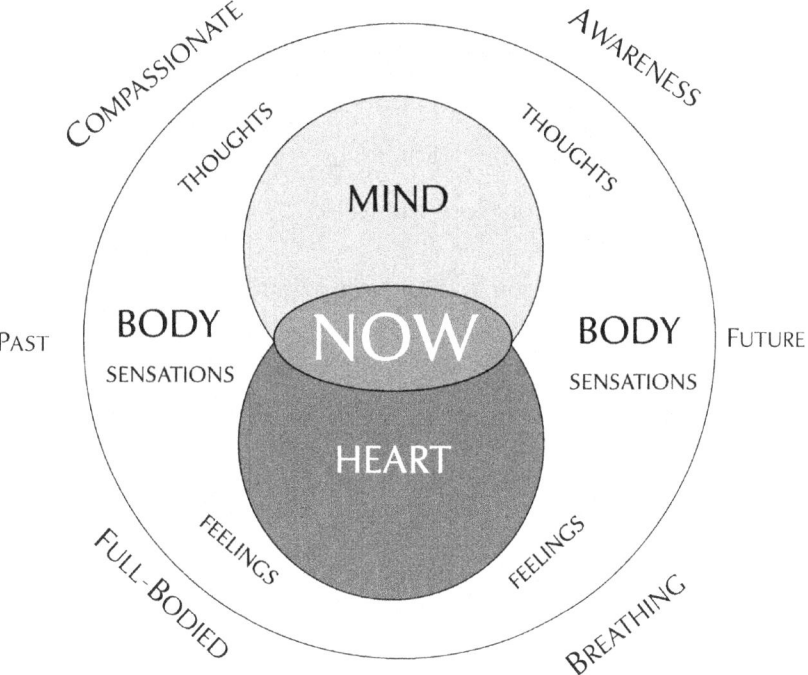

The emotional circulatory system improves when we bring compassionate awareness and full-bodied breathing to our moment to moment experience without pushing away the unpleasant, nor clinging to the pleasant.

DIAGRAM 1

THE CORE TOOLS

Although our goal is to experience a deep inner peace that is not dependent on external circumstances, we initially need to cultivate these practices in a place that helps induce this state. Once we become familiar with shifting our consciousness, becoming mindful and self-compassionate in a quiet, safe space, we can then carry these skills out into the world.

Your *Peace Within* journal and your *Peace Within* space are two core tools in this process.

One way I like to think about this is that before you embark on open-water diving, you typically practice and learn about diving in a shallow swimming pool. In this way, you can become acquainted with the tools of diving, such as the breathing apparatus, the regulator that allows you to breathe underwater, the weight system, and buoyancy control.

The *Peace Within* process 'pool' creates a safe, sacred space where you can practice meditations, breathwork, mindfulness, and journaling in a relaxed, safe, and focused way. This is also a place to digitally detox by moving away from your computer, digital tablet, and smartphone. My *Peace Within* space is a walk-in closet, but it could be the corner of a bedroom, or even something portable, such as a yoga or Pilates mat.

YOUR PEACE WITHIN SPACE

Find a place where you can practice the exercises in this book, as quiet and out of the way as possible. Although a room dedicated to this is ideal, for many this may be unrealistic. The size is less important than having a regular place where you can retreat from the world to practice.

Essential elements include:

1. *A cushion, bolster, or meditation bench for sitting meditation*
2. *Yoga or Pilates mat for lying-down meditation*

Optional elements are:

3. *Objects important from your life journey: photographs, drawings, writings, etc.*
4. *Candle (Be careful with open flames!)*
5. *An MP3 player for playing guided meditations*
6. *Eye pillow or mask to block out light and soothe eyes*

YOUR PEACE WITHIN JOURNAL

The *Peace Within* journal provides a foundation for your journey and a log of your progress. Reverting to our diving analogy: A diver's 'log' is an indispensable part of training, so the diver can record her progress as she learns to dive deeper, and use different equipment. It also serves as a priceless personal document.

A typical dive log notes the date, time, number, and location of the dive, the conditions, what equipment was used, depth of the dive and any personal experiences. All of this can be written in your *Peace Within* journal; however, your writing here will be much more than this, because the journal exercises themselves *are* dives!

In fact, the word *journal* comes from the root word *jour,* the same used in journey and French for "day." At its best, a journal is a journey within. Just as I had people journal when I guided them on vision quests deep into the wilderness, this process is also a journey into your inner nature. You will truly discover who you are beneath conditioned thoughts, and culturally conditioned emotions that come from a lifetime of exposure to mass media, advertising, and corporate culture. At times, you might feel overwhelmed, or disoriented, but the journal will help keep you on track as you document your journey.

The journal will also be a place where you can explore spontaneous, unedited, uncensored writing in exercises to help you identify your own process and let go of emotions. For me, the journal is a critical component of coming to realize you are not your thoughts, feelings, or even the stories you tell yourself. You are the flow itself.

First, you need to acquire an actual journal that appeals to you, one you'll feel comfortable writing in. It could be as simple as a black composition book, or you may prefer a beautiful leather-bound journal. Whatever you choose, listen to your heart; it will be a wonderful touchstone for you as we journey together.

If you're a techy and want to keep your journal on your computer, that's fine, though it is best to password-protect it. Some people find writing longhand works better for them, particularly when journaling about their meditation practice, but this isn't necessary.

Essential elements include:

1. *Acquire an appealing journal.*

2. *Keep a number of writing utensils handy with your journal for whenever you might feel like writing.*

3. *Write your intention in the front of the journal, then sign and date it. You might even make a copy of your 'commitment contract' and place it in the front of the journal.*

4. *Optional – You might want to decorate the inside or outside of your journal in a way that is pleasing and meaningful to you.*

Both the *Peace Within* space and journal help you create the proper mindset to approach this journey. In doing so, you are honoring your experience and yourself in a way that promotes and fosters your personal healing and growth through this process.

BREATHWORK

Breath forms the foundation of our lives. It is the first thing we do when we come into the world and the last thing we do before we leave it. In most cultures, breath is synonymous with the soul, as in the words spirit (English) *qi/chi* (Chinese), *prana* (Sanskrit), *psyche* (Greek), *mana* (Polynesian), and *ruach* (Hebrew).

Still, when I first heard the word *breathwork* at the age of 18, it sounded strange. "Isn't breathing involuntary, the most effortless act in the world? Why should anyone work at it?" I asked myself. As my first meditation class taught me, although we all breathe without thinking about it, few of us breathe correctly. I soon realized how powerful exploring my breath could be. Over the decades, I have learned the extraordinary varieties of breath exercises.

The breath is the intersection of the body and mind.

Thich Nhat Hanh

It is important to begin to develop an ongoing practice of breathwork that helps you breathe deeply and enriches your body with nourishing oxygen. Learning to breathe effectively, will take some effort. Becoming conscious of how you breathe and developing healthier breathing practices helps you take care of your body, while deepening your experience of inner peace.

We all arrive in the world breathing well and deeply. Watch an infant, cat, or dog; they instinctively use a natural, deeper form of respiration called abdominal, diaphragmatic, or belly breathing.

However, once we start school, and spend our days sitting at desks, focusing on our minds, we begin shallow breathing. We become divorced from our natural full-bodied respiration and begin to breathe from our chests. By adulthood, our stress-filled lives have fostered chronic, chest breathing. The good news is that by practicing breathwork, you can train your body to breathe properly through the abdomen.

This kind of work involves waking up to the moment-to-moment miracle of breathing. This includes simple breath awareness, deep diaphragmatic breathing, and any other practice that focuses primarily on breathing. Breathing is the one bodily function that is both under voluntary and involuntary control. Its ceaseless contraction and expansion beautifully mirrors the balance that we find throughout nature and our lives—night and day, birth and decay, waking and sleeping, life and death.

Breathing well and mindfully is always the river that takes us back to the ocean of peace that lies inside us. We will explore this in great detail throughout our journey together; however, because it is the epicenter of the *Peace Within* process, it is important to emphasize it from the very start.

As you breathe in at this moment, I want you to be aware of the fact that you are getting to know a bit more about who you really are with each inhale and exhale. What if you were not your body, but the breath that animates the body? How differently would

When you own your breath, nobody can steal your peace.

Unknown

you explore, touch, connect, and be invested in breathing deeply, well and fully? It is said indigenous people around the world feared white conquerors because they seemed completely unaware of their breathing; that meant they were disconnected from their environment, hearts, and souls. I continue to find this to be true. Many people come into my office or my meditation and yoga classes, and it amazes me how few are really present in their breathing.

Although I'll be guiding you through meditations to formally practice at different times of the day, it's just as important to be aware of your breath and the rising and falling of the belly at all times

BELLY BREATHING

Belly breathing, also known as abdominal or diaphragmatic breathing, is the way to optimize breathwork and facilitate the proper functioning of both the cardiopulmonary and emotional circulatory systems. The natural present moment awareness we had as children was accompanied by belly breathing—our natural breathing style.

The diaphragm is a large, dome-shaped muscle that lies just below the lungs, the most efficient muscle used in respiration.

Breathing from the chest is a very shallow form of respiration in which we only use the top portion of our lungs. Most of the blood vessels that provide oxygen to our bodies are in the neglected bottom half of the lungs, so chest breathing takes in less oxygen. This makes us breathe more rapidly and increases the body's stress response. Chest breathing also upsets the body's blood oxygen/carbon dioxide balance and can actually lead to all sorts of physical symptoms, from headaches and fatigue to anxiety and even panic attacks. During my many years of meditating and playing indigenous flute, I have frequently experienced the stress reducing, energizing, and healing power of belly breathing.

Deep breathing encourages complete oxygen exchange. As a result of filling the bottom third of the lungs, which often fail to fill in shallow chest breathing, deep breathing encourages complete oxygen exchange. This outflow of carbon dioxide and inflow of oxygen slows the heart rate and reduces or stabilizes blood-pressure. It also interrupts the body's flight-or-flight response, induces natural relaxation responses by turning off the sympathetic nervous system (the body's accelerator), and engages the parasympathetic nervous system (the body's brake).

As a culture we revere 'six-pack abs,' the 'washboard stomach,' which restricts breathing from the belly. The result of all this shallow breathing is increased stress, tension, and anxiety.

Unfortunately, most people I work with only breathe shallowly, particularly those who have been traumatized or who experience chronic anxiety and stress. Deep breathing, our most natural self-healing technique, simply feels unnatural.

We literally tighten the belly to keep ourselves from allowing feelings to move through us. When we repress feelings and strong emotions, we subconsciously breathe shallowly or, even worse, hold our breath.

One of the primary reasons deep breathing seems so unnatural is the cultural message that we should 'bottle up' emotions – particularly strong ones. Women are taught not to express or show anger, and men are often instructed to bottle up grief and to never cry.

This was certainly the case in my own family. My father seldom cried, and could not only be stubborn but also launch into frightening rages that I later understood were related to PTSD from his years at war. Although, he was not supportive of my creative interests, I was always involved in music and particularly enjoyed singing in the church choir. The music director chose beautiful songs for us right out of the early Gregorian chants. I loved this ethereal music, so other-worldly while also touching the heart and the soul.

I was excited about the first concert we were to give to the congregation. It was a mystical night, with the sanctuary lit only by candles giving it the feel of a medieval monastery. As we began singing, I saw my father's face in the front row streaming with tears. Of all the things I had ever done, he'd never had that reaction before.

After the concert, his eyes were still moist as he gave me one of the biggest hugs I could remember. He told me he was proud of me and how the singing brought back memories of his childhood in Italy before the war. I felt something deep within me open and breathe in pleasure and relief.

That encounter told me a great deal about him and what innocence he had lost through the war and his move to a new country. I saw that under his rages lay a tender heart, full of great love and feeling. Healing happened for both of us that evening, through the breath and by allowing the tears and feelings to flow freely between us. It was also one of many instances in my life where music served as the midwife for healing.

BELLY BREATHING EXERCISE

Find a relaxed, quiet, and peaceful place where you can either sit or lie down without being disturbed.

Place one hand on your chest and one on your belly. I like to put my right hand over my heart and the left hand over the belly, but do whatever feels most comfortable *(See Diagram 2)*.

Breathing in through the nose, imagine the air coming into your nose, traveling all the way down into your belly and expanding it like a bellows. As you do so, feel the hand on your belly rise. Then breathe out through your mouth or nose, whichever feels more comfortable, and feel the bellows empty and the belly fall. Continue to breathe in this way, then alternate with shallow breathing just from the chest. You'll notice how the shallow chest breath will feel constricted and tense, while belly breathing brings a deep state of relaxation.

Breathing deep, full bodied belly breaths is a wonderful practice to do before any formal meditation, before sleep, or upon awakening. Throughout this book, whenever I refer to taking *deep breaths* or *breathwork*, I am referring to techniques based on this basic component of diaphragmatic breathing.

DIAGRAM 2

You are now ready to move onto the second major component of the emotional circulatory system: *mindfulness*.

MINDFULNESS

Mindfulness has been my central practice for the last three decades. Even as a child, I practiced it, though I wasn't aware that there was a name for this activity.

As a boy, I was a highly sensitive dreamer, quiet and introverted. My parents used to say I would sit so intently, silently gazing out at the woods and nature, that they would make jokes that I was watching the grass grow. I remember long hours beholding the world from my favorite maple tree that grew in our front yard. I retreated to her (I always thought of this tree as female) whenever the adult world became too much.

Today, the practice of mindfulness is a topic of interest in fields ranging from physics to psychology, even making the cover of *Time Magazine* in February, 2014, which declared the birth of "The Mindful Revolution." Science has revealed how extremely effective mindfulness is in in alleviating many physical and emotional disorders, from anxiety and obsessive-compulsive disorder (OCD) to depression and drug addiction. I was fortunate to be introduced to the practice in 1980 by one of the world authorities on mindfulness and meditation, Dr. William Mikulas.[5]

Simply put, mindfulness is non-judgmental, present moment awareness of what is. Where meditation usually involves focusing on an object of attention to develop concentration, mindfulness is simply being present to whatever emotions, thoughts, and sensations are passing through consciousness without judgment. Like breathwork, we will be going into this in greater detail throughout the book. Each practice has a mindfulness component. The more you practice and experience the power of mindfulness, the more you will organically and naturally foster a deep connection with the natural state of peace that is your birthright and truest nature.

COMPASSIONATE AWARENESS

There is an additional component to mindfulness that is often missing in most discussions today: *compassionate awareness*.

In our culture I find it's crucial to include this heart dimension in order to experience a deep well of peace. The Chinese character for mindfulness is actually made up of the character for 'now' and 'heart-mind':

Because Western culture and languages are primarily thinking oriented, we don't even have an adequate word to capture the depth of the original meaning of mindfulness. So much of meditation and mindfulness practice tends to be thought-based and intellectual, with the heart left out of the equation. One of the major reasons I wrote this book is to include this heart dimension. In fact, as we progress, you will find that it is the heart dimension, that opens us most readily and directly to the ocean of peace that lies within. In fact, one way to practice compassionate awareness is to say the mantra to yourself: *"Heart-Mind-Now"*.[6]

There are few approaches that deal with our emotional lives, which I believe are at the root of so much violence on the planet. We are not taught in school how to deal skillfully with difficult emotions.

It is my hope that a *Peace Within* process of some kind that incorporates breathwork, meditation, and mindfulness, will one day be an essential part of every child's education—as important as reading, writing, and arithmetic.

Perhaps in this way as humanity becomes more skillful at cultivating *Peace Within*, we can one day also experience true, genuine, and lasting peace-without.

MEDITATION

Peace is the absence of conflict. In a world defined by duality, it's a precious commodity. In helping people deal with inner and outer conflicts for over thirty years, I've found that the power of meditation helps bring a deep experience of inner peace, which is also healing to the mind, body, and soul. Modern science has finally discovered what ancient cultures have long known: Meditation can literally change you.

It turns out that the brain isn't a static organ stuck in early adulthood; rather, it is a muscle that never stops changing or losing the ability to form neural connections. Research shows that meditation can change the physical structure of the brain.

Eileen Luders, a researcher at the University of California, and her colleagues compared brain scans of meditators and age-matched non-meditators and found that meditators possessed more gray matter in regions of the brain that are crucial for attention, emotion regulation, and mental flexibility.[7]

When neuroscientist Richard Davidson first began studying compassion, it was with long-term meditators who were monks. The instrument of measurement was an electrode EEG cap. When the monks saw that this cap was to be placed on the head, they all began to chuckle. The researchers believed it was because the cap looked odd, with so many long electrode wires that resembled wild hair, but that wasn't the reason. Finally, one monk explained what they found so funny: It was that everyone knows that compassion doesn't come from the brain, but the heart.[8]

In many ways, my life has been a meditation on the experience of peace, and how to achieve it, even during the darkest of times. In my work, I have also witnessed individuals, couples, and groups struggle to find serenity within themselves and their relationships. In observing them, I've found that it's the power of meditation that has helped them bring about a deep experience of inner peace, which is healing to mind, body, and soul.

In the next module, I'll put together compassionate awareness with breathwork practices to introduce you to a whole host of meditations—from brief micro-meditations to longer formal meditation practices that are done seated, lying down, standing, or walking. I'll also include suggestions as to how you can utilize music with many of the meditations as you deepen your practice.

The micro-meditations cannot only be used to reset the emotional circulatory system throughout the day to keep it flowing, but they can also be used before each of the more formal meditation and journaling exercises. You will find they will help keep you present, as well as more creative and skillful.

MODULE 1 – MAIN POINTS

To summarize the main points in Module 1: The *Peace Within* Process.

1. The emotional circulatory system functions much like our physical circulatory system and is made up of sensations, feelings and thoughts flowing through our awareness.

2. The two components of the emotional circulatory system are the breath and mindfulness.

3. The emotional circulatory system is optimized through practicing deep belly breathing and compassionate awareness of what is present in the moment.

4. The Peace Within process is a set of practices to help keep the emotional circulatory system running smoothly through breathwork, mindfulness practices, meditations, and journaling exercises.

MODULE 1 - PEACE WITHIN PRACTICES

1. Be mindful of your breathing. Encourage yourself to belly breathe whenever you notice yourself becoming anxious, frustrated, or distracted.

2. Set up your Peace Within space.

3. Acquire your Peace Within journal and begin the first entry.

4. *Journal about why you are embarking on this program, what you are getting out of it and mark on the calendar when you will finish.*

5. *Print out the core principles and look at them each day and notice how your understanding and feelings about each principle evolves and changes.*

6. *Sign your peace within contract.*

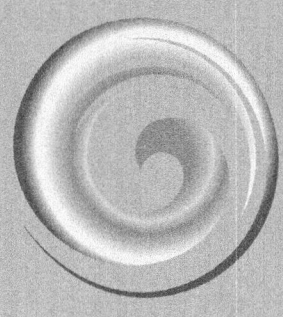

MODULE 2

This module builds on the basic concepts and core tools by introducing you to four easy, accessible and effective self-care practices (the centering breath, finding your center, releasing into the now and grounding) that are like micro-meditations to help you punctuate your day and will also be the starting point for journaling exercises and longer meditations to come.

2: PEACE WITHIN YOUR DAY

It's no accident that I work daily to help people breathe from the abdomen, considering that as a child the most significant trauma I experienced was abdominal surgery that left me with over 200 stiches inside and out. It was this trauma in my belly that led me back to my belly years later.

I'll never forget the terror that overcame me before that surgery when I was 7, as the doctors and nurses placed the ether mask over my face. I felt I was suffocating. I was sure these were the last breaths I would ever take.

Then I fell into a kaleidoscopic delirium; strange sounds and images twirled by me as my mind plunged into some strange other world. Alternatingly beatific and horrific, I felt the sensation of falling, then flying.

The next thing I remember was staring at the ceiling, with children screaming all around me. My belly and pelvis felt like they had been run over by a truck, and stitches covered my abdomen. I felt lost and alone. Later in life, I learned from my martial arts and chi kung practice that this area is called the *dan tien* – or *hara*, and it is the very core of our being. It's the place of grounding, of feeling connected to the Earth and our own power. This center of mine had been severely compromised and injured as a child.

I was relieved to see my parents, and they tried to comfort me, but I felt a strange sort of alienation from my body and life itself. I know now I was in a dissociated state and, from that time on, I realized I was different.

This experience increased my sense of isolation from the outside world. I spent long hours reflecting on this strange sense of separation that I felt from everything around me. Death had become a reality for me. From that day forward, death lived over my shoulder as I realized I might be whisked from the face of the Earth at any moment. It was a strange sort of fascination with death on one hand and fear of it on the other. Even though I was only 7, in some sense, I no longer was a child.

In other ways, though I know now that this experience was also a kind of soul initiation into the mysteries of life and death. I woke up at a young age, and my powers of concentration were actually deepened because of this experience. In fact, this ended up benefiting me later in my adult work as a teacher and therapist.

THE JOURNEY WITHIN

Every week as I sit with clients I hear a common refrain: "No one seems to struggle like I do." At least once a week, I respond with the following, "You're comparing your *interior* to everybody else's *exterior*."

Peace comes from within, do not seek it without.

Buddha

The great struggle of the modern age is that we live in a culture that distracts and conditions us with unrealistic, impossible, and even toxic messages about who we should be. What's more, we aren't even taught in school who we really are. Instead, we are graded, evaluated, sized up and down from the outside by how we perform on a test, in a sport, or in social situations. We become alienated from the most sacred relationship of all: *with our soul*. In fact, most of us grow into adults without ever really discovering what lies within us.

The journey within is a process. The good news is it feels very natural once you begin. You already possess the ultimate tool of the universe within you that makes you uniquely qualified for this journey — *awareness*. This will be your guiding light, your friend and ally as we travel this journey together.

Let's use a simple example. Imagine your awareness is a flashlight. Whenever you look at something, it's as if you're shining a light onto it. Now, it's this page of paper and the words you are reading. Take a moment to look around the room you're in.

Imagine, as you gaze around, that everything you set your eyes on is lit with the light of awareness.

When we begin the journey within, we are allowing our awareness to settle on those things closer to us, such as our breath and body. Let's begin with the breath.

 PEACE IS OUR NATURAL STATE AND IS FOSTERED BY CENTERING OURSELVES WITH BREATH AND BODY AWARENESS PRACTICES IN THE HERE AND NOW.

THE CENTERING BREATH

During my many years as a wilderness guide, one of the first things I learned in survival training was the rule of threes. We can survive three weeks without food, three days without water, but only three minutes without air. When we stop breathing, carbon dioxide levels builds up in the blood, leading to overwhelming air hunger. It only takes minutes for the body's internal oxygen levels to drop dangerously low. Nevertheless, for the most part, we live horribly unaware that our lives hang by the thread of our next breath.

When we don't breathe deeply and properly (diaphragmatically, from the belly) one-third of the oxygen in our lungs is not expelled. What's more, our emotional circulatory system suffers as we get lost in thoughts, negative self-talk, and emotions that slowly and insidiously cut us off from our emotional hearts and eventually from ever experiencing *Peace Within*. In fact, as you work on becoming aware of your breath, your mind will wander ceaselessly. We talk of this wandering as 'the drunken monkey of the mind.' We must learn to breathe again by cultivating breath awareness.

Breath is the life-giving river that runs through our bodies. When we ride this river, it connects us to all living things from the algae, trees, and plants that have filled our atmosphere with oxygen for the last 3.5 billion years, for every land dwelling ancestor who has lived since the first breath was taken on land some 395 million years ago. If we allow it, this river will guide us to the ocean of peace that lies within. The river of your breath is always a sure path to the ocean of peace.

When you spend time reflecting on and exploring your breath, amazing things will happen. I first learned about belly breathing at the age of 18, fresh from experiencing a deeply disoriented extreme state of consciousness.

When I went to college, my father wouldn't support my desire to study music and poetry. I ended up in a pre-med program, focusing on science and technology, but my heart and soul were far away from those subjects. This created a great conflict in me. When

> *Each one has to find his peace from within. And peace to be real must be unaffected by outside circumstances.*
>
> Gandhi

my father chastised me for sleeping through my organic chemistry mid-term after he paid for a personal tutor, I exploded at him for the first time in my life. I also dropped out of the course and underwent a general unraveling, a kind of spiritual emergency.

BREATHING CONNECTS OUR INNER AND OUTER WORLD AND IS THE HEART OF OUR EMOTIONAL CIRCULATORY SYSTEM. THE BREATH IS LIKE A RIVER AND IS OUR PATH TO THE OCEAN OF PEACE THAT LIES WITHIN.

Gradually, I began to explore my own psyche and the world of psychology. At that point, I had the good fortune to take a meditation class with Dr. William Mikulas, the world renowned meditation teacher and authority on Buddhist psychology, whom I mentioned before. Not only did he teach me how to meditate, but he also became a lifelong teacher, colleague and friend.

Part of our meditation class included journaling our experiences. I remember being amazed with how little I knew my own body and breath; not scientifically, but experientially. As I began to practice deep breathing from the belly, I quickly noticed how intimate breathing really is. I learned how the steady, rhythmic rising and falling of our lungs is an extremely sensuous experience that we all but ignore, at least most of the time. Drawing the air deeply into our innermost core, while pushing out carbon dioxide created by biochemical processes within every cell of our body, is life affirming and incredible.

I had underestimated the power of my own breath because it is an autonomic function that feels, as ordinary as sneezing or scratching my arm. Still, it was my breath that sustained me, and it was especially crucial in this stressful period. I realized that my breath is my best friend. This breathwork helped me find my way back to myself.[1]

Over the years, I came to see that my father hadn't been all wrong. The truth of my path was learning that life is not climbing a mountain, but flowing down a river with many twists and turns.

At 18, I wasn't ready to embark on a purely creative career, wandering the world with my music and poetry. In the end, I found a way to become a "creativity doctor", artist and musician at the same time. I could honor my heart as well as my father's dreams for me.

The self-discovery I learned through the power of meditation and breathwork was a crucial part of my eventual awakening.

If there is only one thing you take away from this book to change your life for the better, I hope it is that you become profoundly aware of your breath, and regard it as your trusted ally, one you can always rely on, even during the darkest of times.

CENTERING BREATH EXERCISE

DIAGRAM 3

This centering breath exercise is a simple one. The key to the centering breath is breathing deeply from the diaphragm.

Position yourself comfortably, sitting or lying down. Place both hands on your belly button (See Diagram 3). You will notice warmth developing between your hands and your belly, which results from the dual circulation of the hands and belly reinforce each other. This is a self-soothing exercise, which provides self-nurturance during times of stress or anxiety. I liken this to giving yourself a hug.

Take a deep, cleansing breath, breathing in through your nose and out through your mouth. Focus on pushing your hands upward on your belly as you breathe deeply. This first breath should be a particularly deep one as you breathe in through your nose and out through your mouth.

Take ten deep, slow breaths in this way. To ensure that your breaths are slow, rhythmic, and deep, count to four as you breathe in and count to four as you breathe out.

Inhale: One, two, three, four...

Exhale: One, two, three, four...

This is your basic breath, the root of all breath practices to follow. Deep breathing and the centering breath are at the heart of your emotional circulatory system.

As our journey together continues, you will see how the breath is at the center of quieting the mind, opening the heart, and developing a better relationship with yourself and others.

FINDING YOUR CENTER

Breath awareness is followed by body awareness. As we move from being more aware of our breathing, we begin to also become aware of the body. I'm not speaking of a conceptual understanding, but an actual first-hand experience of connecting to our body: our felt center.

The Creek Nation's name for the Creator, *Esaugetuh Emissee*, translates to "The Master of the Breath." The breath connects our interior with our exterior. It connects us to the life around us, to each other, and, most importantly, to our felt center.

Following is a very simple exercise that can help you find this felt center.

First, find a quiet, safe place where you won't be disturbed. Second, read through the following exercise. Third, give yourself the gift of actually doing the exercise before reading further.

Begin by closing your eyes for a moment and take three slow, deep breaths, breathing in through your nose and out through your mouth. Notice how differently you feel in your body by simply closing your eyes and breathing deeply. Focus on the points of contact between your body and whatever your body is touching: feet on the floor and, body lying on a couch or sitting in a chair (See Diagram 4).

Allow your attention to scan your body from your head to your feet, tuning into sensations as they flow through you in this moment, in this place, and time. Notice how your bodily sensations increase simply by focusing on them.

Taking another, nice, deep breath, put your hands on your belly as you continue to breathe deeply. Focus on breathing from your belly, noticing your abdomen rise and fall as you do. Now imagine breathing up from your feet, all the way to the top of your head. As you breathe, imagine you are drawing your breath from your feet, through your legs, trunk, arms, neck, and all the way to the top of your head. Now imagine breathing down the same way, from the top of your head, scanning your body with your awareness all the way down to the soles of your feet. Do this three times. You may experience tingling in different parts of your body, warmth, lightness, or heaviness. Whatever you experience is fine; you can't do this wrong. Now, bring your awareness and attention to your abdomen, focusing on the warmth generated by your hands on your belly. This is your felt center.

Slowly open your eyes. As you orient yourself visually to the world of objects and light, try to keep a bit of the centeredness and softness you felt during the exercise.

When you first try this exercise, you may feel foolish, confused or nothing in particular. This is a practice and a process; there is no right or wrong way to feel. In your journal, write exactly what you experienced. By the end of the program, your experience will have changed, sometimes radically so. It is like taking your blood pressure and heart rate at the beginning of starting an exercise program. This journal entry will simply tell you how in touch you are with your body in the present moment.

CLOSING YOUR EYES

We are so visually oriented in our culture that we don't allow ourselves to close our eyes during the day for any length of time, much less tune into our bodily sensations in the present moment. By quieting the mind and centering in the present moment, we immediately reduce our brain activity by as much as 60-70 percent. The simple act of closing our eyes immediately reduces stress on our bodily functions. It takes exponentially less brainpower to process auditory information than it does to process visual information.

Throughout most of our days, there are ample opportunities to close our eyes for a few moments, breathe deeply, and drop into the ocean of peace that lies within. Depending on how restless your mind is, it may require more than simply closing your eyes, but it is still a powerful beginning.

I encourage you to find your felt center on a regular basis. You may say, "I'm stuck in business meetings and lunches or classrooms all day. I never have the privacy and time to do this!" Realistically, there are many opportunities to take a moment for this micro-meditation. I do it in the bathroom between clients. You can do it sitting in a car before a trip, in your office after lunch, or whenever you have few uninterrupted moments.

THE SIMPLE ACT OF CLOSING YOUR EYES AND TAKING A DEEP BREATH IS A NATURAL, SIMPLE, AND EASY WAY TO REDUCE STRESS AND QUIET THE MIND.

RELEASING INTO THE NOW

Learning to close your eyes and breathe deeply is a good beginning; however, most of us live with such endless chatter in our heads, much more is needed to bathe our minds and hearts with peaceful waves of breath.

Fortunately, there are many ways to come home to our natural state, which is literally always right where we are standing. One

DIAGRAM 4

of my favorite ways is releasing into the now.[2]

THE CENTRAL PRACTICE OF THE PEACE WITHIN PROCESS IS TO ALLOW THE EMOTIONAL CIRCULATORY SYSTEM TO CIRCULATE, ALLOWING ALL THOUGHTS, FEELINGS, AND SENSATIONS TO COME AND GO WITHOUT PUSHING THEM AWAY OR ATTACHING TO THEM.

Release means "to liberate, surrender, and let go." As you will find in the following modules, so much of our inner unrest comes from holding onto and replaying endless stories in our minds about ourselves, each other, and our lives, instead of allowing the thoughts and feelings of the emotional circulatory system to flow freely.

Imagine, for a moment, that all the stories you tell yourself are like so many waves on an ocean. Beneath the surface of your life stories and the churning chatter of your mind, lies a deep, endless ocean of peace. Unfortunately, you're probably so busy focusing on the surface—on boats, islands, and changing weather patterns—that you forget the peace that lies beneath the surface.

Each time I do my micro-meditations or formal meditations, I imagine myself diving below the surface of the water to discover the deep still ocean of peace below.

RELEASE INTO THE NOW EXERCISE

The next micro-meditation is what I simply call a release. It is central to my own life – and it is usually the very first thing I teach. It's as powerful as it is simple!

Once again, I'd like you to read through the exercise first, then do the exercise before reading further.

Stand with your about shoulder-width apart, with a slight bend in your knees. Remembering your centering breath exercise, put your hands over your belly and begin to

DIAGRAM 5 - POSITIONS 1 & 2

rock your body from side to side and front to back. Then begin to make slow circles until you establish your center point and felt center. You'll know when you're there: when you stop the gentle rocking motion and find yourself still equally weighted on both feet.

Take a nice, deep breath. Shake up and down gently a few times to get the blood flowing. Now, with feet about two shoulder-widths apart, and your knees slightly bent, bend your arms slightly and turn your palms inward and upward at the waist (See Diagram 5, position 1). Now, at waist level, begin to raise the palms of your hands skyward, fingertips facing each other. Breathe in and slowly raise your palms toward the sky (See Diagram 5, position 2) When your palms reach your neck, rotate your forearms and hands so they are still facing skyward (See Diagram 5, position 3). Raise your hands (still finger tips pointing at each other) over your head until your arms are outstretched straight upwards. Continue breathing deeply this whole time. Gently straighten your legs. At the very top of your inhalation, your arms and legs should be outstretched.

Breathing out with a sigh, begin dropping your arms outstretched at your sides, your palms now facing the Earth (See Diagram 5, position 4). As you lower your arms, breathe out, accentuating the "ahhhh..." sound of your sigh. Continue as your arms fall to your sides and your legs relax with a slight bend in them once again.

When you breathe in, raise your arms and slowly straighten your legs, as though you're inflating yourself like a balloon. The key is to do this whole sequence slowly.

2: PEACE WITHIN YOUR DAY

As you approach the apex of the release, allow yourself to let go of all thoughts. In fact, let your entire past go and release into the now. Do this at least three times. Close your eyes and notice how different you feel in your body.

This release into the now exercise allows you to access your felt center in the here and now and prepares you for any activity where you need to focus, de-stress, and re-center. I encourage my clients and students to do a release whenever they are stuck in an activity and feel fatigued, stressed, or overwhelmed.

The release incorporates a centering breath with a centering exercise, and adds the dimension of deep release and becoming more present and focused in the now. Try it. You'll like it!

DIAGRAM 5 - POSITIONS 3 & 4

FINDING YOUR GROUND

> *The world cannot be discovered by a journey of miles...but only by a journey of one inch...by which we arrive at the ground at our feet, and learn to be at home."*
>
> ~Wendell Berry

When God said to Moses, "Cast thy shoes from thy feet," He helped Moses wake up to the miracle of being present in the here and now.[3] I have always loved this image, because I love to 'cast my shoes from my feet' wherever and whenever I can. Becoming grounded in our bodies in the present moment is greatly aided when we can feel the earth under our feet. When I speak of having a first person experience of grounding, I am referring to listening to the truth that your blood whispers to you through the language of sensation.

Most stress comes from being lost in thought, which perpetually transports us into the past and future. We spend our precious moments regretting the past or being anxious and fearful of the future. In the process, the emotional circulatory system stops flowing because we forget where we are, in the here and now. We have all experienced driving somewhere and not remembering how we got there or going into a room to get something and forgetting what it was. When lost in thought, we are not present in the moment. Presence is a quality of mindfulness.

In order to experience what is real, we must drop out of our heads and into our bodies. We must experience the place upon which we stand at that moment as sacred. This is grounding and centering ourselves. God's words to Moses make sense!

 SENSATION GROUNDS AND CENTERS US IN THE HERE AND NOW AND TRULY HELPS US COME TO OUR SENSES ON THE INNER ROAD TO PEACE.

When was the last time you took off your shoes and stood on the grass or the bare earth? When was the last time you took a barefoot walk and felt the different sensations under your feet? Because we grew up in a culture that shields our bare feet from the ground, they are not only tender but also have little ability to feel and experience the earth.

There is a movement with growing scientific evidence for what is called *earthing* or *grounding*. Humans carry a positive electrical charge, and when we walk barefoot or go into the ocean or take a shower, we actually discharge that electrical charge. In our modern digital world, where we perpetually coexist with electronic devices, the problem is even more severe. The positive charge builds even higher, which increases cortisol levels and other stress related metabolic factors.

In stress reduction and trauma treatment, grounding exercises prevent people from being pulled into the past through flashbacks of early trauma. This is called *somatic mindfulness* and has become the treatment of choice for those suffering from PTSD (post-traumatic stress disorder).

One of the best ways to ground yourself is to simply go outside, and walk barefoot on the earth. Really take notice of the amazing sensations beneath your feet as you feel the different textures of grass, earth, or rock.

Yoga is another powerful grounding activity, allowing us to "grasp" the earth with feet and toes the way our ancestors did and a variety of animals still do.

This is one of the reasons I like to hold some of my meditation and yoga classes at the beach or in other natural settings. People immediately feel the power and effect of the earth on their practice and how they more easily and effortlessly drop out of the head and into the body.

If you can't go outside right now, perhaps there is a window you can look out. Notice all the colors you see and trace the outline of the shapes of objects in your visual field. If you don't have a window, close your eyes and listen to the sounds in the room. If you can't close your eyes, simply tune into the sensations in your body – particularly the tips of your fingers and toes. Grounding is about being present in the here and now and tuning into your senses without commentary or judgment.

Our ancestors experienced the world through their feet, which helped them feel and sense vibrations, changes in temperature and moisture as they maneuvered through harsh, challenging, and difficult environments. We know that even elephants can "hear" through their feet, which provide them with a vast world of information, sensations, and experience that alerts them to danger.

GROUNDING EXERCISE

Please read through the exercise, then practice it before reading further.

DIAGRAM 6

Begin by "casting thy shoes from thy feet". Stand with your feet a shoulder width apart. Breathe deeply from your diaphragm. Your legs should not be locked, but slightly bent, and your spine nice and straight.

Locate your felt center, as we did in the previous exercises, placing your hands on your abdomen and rocking back and forth and side to side, then slowly in circles until you come to a grounded, resting center point.

Now imagine a string attached to the top of your head, pulling you skyward while gently allowing your shoulders to melt down your back. Remove your hands from your abdomen and let them hang loosely on either side of your body (See Diagram 6).

Extend your arms downward, while spreading your fingers apart and stretching them downward.

Pull in your abdomen, imagining your navel pulling toward the spine and engage your quadriceps, pulling up your kneecaps. Breathe from the tips of your toes to the top of your head. Now, imagine breathing from the soles of your feet, drawing the energy from Earth, up through the front of your body, over your head. Then, breathe out, down your back, toward Earth.

If you haven't already, close your eyes. Now, imagine you are a mountain that has seen endless seasons come and go. Imagine the ageless weather patterns you have experienced over eons: winter to spring, spring to summer, and summer to fall, over and over again. Imagine the civilizations that have come and gone, the snowy winters and scorching summers. Through it all, you held fast, stood steady, and remained strong, still, and peaceful. Take your time. When you have experienced the mountain's sense of stillness through the endless changes, open your eyes on your next breath.

Notice how you feel and write about it in your journal.

MODULE 2 – MAIN POINTS

To summarize the main points contained in Module 2:

1. *Lasting peace can only be found by journeying within.*

2. *This inward journey begins with grounding in the here and now which is greatly added by the following exercises:*

    a. *The Centering Breath*

    b. *Finding Your Center*

    c. *Releasing Into The Now*

    d. *Grounding Practices*

MODULE 2 - PEACE WITHIN YOUR DAY PRACTICES

1. *Journal on each of the exercises: What did it feel like? What did you get out of it, if anything? Were you able to tune into the sensations in your body?*

2. *Explore beginning and ending the day with each of the exercises for a week.*

3. *Pick your favorite exercise (journal about why it's your favorite) and do it several additional times each day. Then use that one as your daily and nightly ritual.*

In the upcoming modules we will deepen this practice with other ways to quiet your mind, open your heart, and help you find your flow through the rapids of modern life. Before going on to the next module, close your eyes, take a deep breath, and feel the points of contact between your body and whatever part of Earth you are sitting, lying, or standing on.

Enjoy the journey!

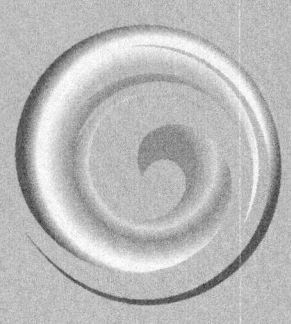

MODULE 3

In module 2 we move from basic breath and body awareness practices that can be done at any time anywhere to deeper meditations that are more powerful and time intensive. Where compassionate awareness is the heart of the peace within process, and breathing is the spine, these meditations are putting flesh and bones to the practice.

3: PEACE WITHIN YOUR BODY

I gazed up at the ceiling, feeling defeated, lost, and alone. The post-surgical pain in my knee did little to drown out what had now become a familiar, dreaded ache at the base of my spine. Even worse, my mind kept taking me back to past traumas and tossing me around in a whirlpool of negative self-talk: "You're weak. Your life is over. You've failed everyone," it whispered.

"Have you noticed you're barely breathing?" Jessica, my physical therapist, interrupted my thoughts to ask me. "I want you to take a good, deep breath."

I followed her suggestion, albeit grudgingly.

She watched me with a strange look on her face. "What happened to the Michael I know, the one who always has a smile on his face? When you breathe, I want you to smile."

"I don't feel like smiling," I muttered.

"That's the most important time to smile."

Of course, I knew she was right, so I struggled to give her a half-hearted smile.

"Michael, that's completely pathetic."

Unable to hold it back anymore, I wept. I had resisted crying in front of anyone for so long, that finally letting out the pain was a great relief.

Peace begins with a smile.

~Mother Teresa

"You don't understand, I hurt everywhere," I managed.

It wasn't simply my physical self – my knee and back—but also my emotions that hurt. I literally felt as if my heart hurt, that my life hurt.

Jessica let my words slowly sink into the silence before she continued. "Everywhere? Do your ears hurt?"

With that comment, I spontaneously smiled and let out a small laugh, something I hadn't done in months. "No."

"It's very common for chronic pain patients to obsess and hyper-focus on their physical pain, so I want you to do your best to focus on the parts of you that aren't in pain at the moment."

Although I had heard that advice before, something about the way Jessica spoke allowed her thoughtful words to touch me. I began to note the many places in my body that didn't actually hurt. Slowly and steadily, I started focusing on them.

In this way, through her compassionate awareness, Jessica helped me return to my senses. She helped me focus on the array of sensations that existed in my body and to break free from the whirlpool of negative thought that had entrapped me for months.

COMING TO YOUR SENSES

Few of us have lost our minds, but most of us have long ago lost our bodies.

Ken Wilbur

The grip of trauma has the power to yoke us to the past and make living in the present virtually impossible. In fact, all kinds of past conditioning, painful and difficult experiences, or negative thoughts can cycle through our minds and remove us from our bodies. Our obsessions are driven by the thoughts and stories we tell ourselves, instead of the simple miracle of moment to moment present awareness.

I may have had physical pain, but the real battle I fought was not in my body but my mind. To be completely honest, I wasn't even in my body; I was lost in thoughts from the past, in victimhood. In many ways, I'd lost my hold on reality and begun to act and think irrationally. I was truly lost.

We use the phrase "coming to your senses" to refer to seeing clearly in the present moment and acting sensibly after a period of confusion. We've all seen movies where someone who is acting hysterically is slapped and jolted back to reality. It's as if they are being called out of their thought trance into the here and now.

We all need this kind of wake-up call at various times in our lives. In fact, how often are we truly in the moment, fully present in our senses? Yet these senses are the royal road back to discovering our bodies and reclaiming our natural sanity in the moment.

 Tuning into our senses (hearing, seeing, touching, smelling, and tasting) is a simple and easy way to become more present in the here and now and thus, embark on the road back to peace within.

FIVE SENSES MINDFULNESS PRACTICE

The five senses mindfulness practice helps you move from one sense to the other – and realize the amazing lights, sounds, touches, smells and feelings that are always operating, but usually subconsciously. Tuning your consciousness into each of the senses immediately brings you into the present moment, and facilitates *Peace Within* the body.

Initially, this practice is best performed in a quiet place, such as your *Peace Within* space. Later, you'll want to practice out in the world, whenever you have the chance. You can also schedule times to practice five senses mindfulness in nature, at the supermarket, or in the car. The beautiful thing about this practice is that it can be done any point in the day and will gradually help you develop a meditative/mindful attitude.

I suggest exploring each sense one at a time, for at least five minutes or more, then journaling about the experience. You can visit each sense in different sittings, or you can do them one after the other. If five minutes feels too long, try at least three minutes on each sense. Notice which senses you prefer 'tuning into' and which are most difficult.

Wherever you have chosen to practice first do your *centering breath* and *releasing into the now* warm-ups as you bring yourself into the present moment.

MINDFUL HEARING

We'll start by closing our eyes and tuning into the sense of hearing. We begin with hearing because it so readily lends itself to discovering and connecting to the present moment and the ocean of peace. Concentrate for a moment on how natural and effortless hearing is. Notice its constant presence, even though we seldom tune into it. I like to start by saying silently to myself, "Thank you for my ears, so I can hear. Thank you for the gift of hearing." This helps engage the heart and moves us toward not simply mindfulness, but also compassionate awareness.

Now, take another deep, cleansing belly breath as you settle in more deeply into mindful hearing. Begin to notice the sounds arising and passing through your consciousness. Notice any droning sounds that are continuous, such as the humming of an air conditioner, fan, or appliance. Let go of any judgment. There are no good or bad sounds; they simply exist. In fact, droning sounds like white noise can be calming when you simply notice them without judgment and tune into them. What sounds do you hear off in the distance? What are the closest sounds you can hear? Can you hear your own breathing? Your heartbeat?

As you settle even more deeply into mindful hearing with compassionate awareness, notice any sounds beneath the sounds, perhaps sounds within the body itself or, the sound of silence. Notice the silence; become aware of it.

Now, notice how differently you feel in your body. Note how your mind has naturally quieted, just by practicing a few minutes of mindful hearing. Take out your Peace Within journal and make an entry about your hearing practice. What was it like for you? What did you learn? What did you experience? Did you notice sounds you never heard before?

The more you practice mindful hearing, the more extraordinary it becomes. This is by far my favorite mindfulness practice, which probably has something to do with my being a musician and composer. Much of the inspiration I receive for creating my healing/meditation oriented music is from the mindful hearing meditations. It is also the fastest way for me to shift my consciousness into the now and experience myself more as a wave of energy – like a sound wave – as opposed to a physical body.

MINDFUL SEEING

Next we move to mindful seeing —the sense we rely upon most to maneuver through the world. We read with our eyes. We visually recognize objects and shapes. It may be difficult to mindfully see as you did as a child, but it's a powerful practice to begin by simply noticing shapes and colors the way you did in childhood.

Begin cultivating some compassionate awareness by saying either silently or aloud, "Thank you for my eyes, so I can see. Thank you for the gift of seeing." Try to spend time imagining you have been blind all your life and now have the opportunity to see for the first time. Appreciate the miracle of seeing and how extraordinary it is! Notice how light filters through wherever you are sitting or notice any reflections, shadows, or images in the room.

Now, trace the outline of what you see in front of you as if you are creating an imaginary sketch around everything you see in your visual field. Sketch from left to right. Notice the colors of each object in your visual field and say each color quietly to yourself. Continue labeling colors without judgment, just noticing and labeling those you are aware of in your visual field.

Now, notice the depth between objects and the space around them. Be aware of the space around your body and between your body and the room you're in. Noticing the 'negative space' is a powerful way to begin to wake up to the amazing nature of the now. As your mind becomes aware of space around you, it also has the effect of creating more space within (between thoughts, feelings, and sensations).

After noticing shapes, colors, and space, take note of the texture of objects in the room. Are they smooth or rigid? You can even label the materials they are made of, such as wood, plastic, granite, or concrete. Next, note the texture of the floor. If you are outside, note the texture of the earth. Is there grass, dirt, rocks, or trees? Again, say each of the textures. You can also label the color and object together; green bottle, burnt orange lamp, black and white painting, green grass, etc.

As you practice mindful seeing, it's important to keep working on your belly breathing. Notice how judgments arise in your mind, such as, "I hate that lamp," or, "I love that painting."

We are not stopping the judgment but simply noticing it and not identifying with it. Mindful seeing is difficult because so much of our time is spent judging and discerning, whether it's arranging a room, picking out what we are going to wear or, separating people into good and bad, based on physical appearance. The other difficulty is that objects often transport us into memories, daydreams, and stories that take us out of the moment.

The good news is that mindful seeing allows you to watch the judging mind at work and notice ways that the drunken monkey of the mind takes you away from the moment in powerful ways.[1]

Once again, take a deep cleansing breath and say to yourself, "Thank you for my eyes, so I can see. Thank you for the gift of my eyes." Now take out your Peace Within journal and write on the following questions: How was this exercise for you? How did you feel before the mindful seeing exercise, and how did you feel during it and after? Do you notice any changes in your body, mind, or heart? What are some unique places or ways you could practice mindful seeing?

MINDFUL TASTING AND SMELLING

As humans, our senses of taste and smell are utilized much less than seeing or hearing. Although we can explore one or the other separately, they are so interconnected that I like to introduce people to mindful tasting and smelling together, as part of a mindful eating practice.

In the *Peace Within* process, I recommend trying to eat at least one mindful meal a week. Over time, cultivate a certain amount of mindful eating into each meal. This is easier said than done. Eating is a deeply instinctual activity that is rooted in the earliest stages of biological life on the planet; It's literally welded into our DNA. It's easy to become eat mindlessly. Try not to beat yourself up about this. Simply bring compassionate awareness to your mindful eating practices. For example, when you notice yourself wolfing down food, simply take note, inhale deeply, and try to bring mindfulness into what you are smelling, tasting and eating in the moment.

A favorite practice in many mindfulness-based programs is simply eating one raisin or almond with great attention to all the subtleties of the experience. When I first practiced this, at the age of 18, in my first meditation class with Bill, I was literally overcome, with tears in my eyes. It was as if I had never eaten anything before. My tears came from both joy at discovering the miracle of being so exquisitely present, but also a sense of sadness about how mindless I had been most of my life about eating. It's a shame that we don't teach mindful eating in our schools, and I hope that will change one day. For all our talk about dieting, once you start mindfully eating, you will truly be much more conscious of what you are putting in your body and that will be healthier for you overall.

For example, I have done mindful eating exercises with students who were blindfolded. I've asked them to eat an orange and a small cookie mindfully and to notice the different sensations going on in their bodies, taste buds, and smells. They are always amazed by how rich the experience of eating the orange is on all levels, compared to the dull, bland experience of the cookie. Often, we are not eating the food, as much as we are devouring the ideas about food that we carry in our heads. We eat compulsively and unconsciously instead of being present in the daily miracle of nourishing our bodies.

Decide whether you would like to work with a raisin or an almond. Find a quiet place, like your Peace Within space, to practice this mindful eating meditation. Place the almond or raisin on a saucer, plate, or napkin. Do a 'release into the now' and take three deep, cleansing, centering breaths with your eyes closed. Slowly open your eyes and spend some time mindfully seeing the almond. (I'll use an almond throughout the rest of the exercise.) Slowly and mindfully pick up the almond and examine it thoroughly, noticing its color, shape, and texture. Spend time smelling it and rolling it around in your fingers. This is a chance to practice mindful touch as well – noticing the subtle sensations at the tip of your fingers and how the almond feels.

Take another deep, cleansing breath and slowly bring the almond to your mouth. Begin by just touching it to your lips and tongue. Do you notice any taste or smells? Do you note any changes inside your mouth? Are you salivating yet? Can you sense the anticipation – how your taste buds are being triggered? Notice everything you can about how your body is responding to this very simple act of taking an almond and lifting it to your lips and tongue. Now put the almond down and notice again any reactions, feelings, or sensations throughout your body.

Take another deep, cleansing breath. This time, take the almond to your mouth and allow yourself to take a small bite. Put the rest of the almond down and notice all the many sensations coursing through your mouth, tongue, and taste buds. What do you taste? What do you smell? How is your body responding? Isn't it amazing how this one small, micro-bite of food lights up your system? Perhaps there are other sensations and responses. Is your mind making judgments? Are you remembering the past or anticipating the future? Just notice all the thoughts, feelings, and sensations present, not trying to stop them or push them away – but not following them either.

If you find yourself getting carried away or lost in thought, simply bring yourself back to your breath by taking a nice, deep breath again, then returning to the act of eating and tasting the almond. Repeat this with each successive small bite, until the almond is gone.

Now, take out your journal. Note your experience and answer the following questions: What was it like for you? How was this experience different or similar to mindful hearing and seeing? Which sense are you most drawn to? What would your life be like if you ate all of your meals more mindfully?

What do you feel your greatest challenges and obstacles will be in eating more mindfully in the future? What are some things you can do to overcome these obstacles? Plan a meal to eat mindfully in the coming week and note it on your calendar.

MINDFUL TOUCH

Humans have an amazing sense of touch. Without fur or scales, we have developed this sense in remarkable ways. Touch is the primary way we connect in intimate relationships through hugging, consoling, comforting and the act of making love.

Today, many people are either touch deprived or have experienced severe trauma from inappropriate sexual or violent acts that make them feel alien in their bodies. What amazes me is that even though we are wired for loving and affectionate touch, many of us suffer from fears and touch avoidance. This leaves us alienated and estranged, not only from our own bodies but from other people.

Mindful touch can begin the healing process by helping you find safe, relaxing ways to reconnect with this power in the here and now, without the fear of being hurt. I often prescribe massage therapy to those who have been traumatized. Therapeutic massage can be deeply healing for the mind, body, heart, and soul. For many, though, even this is too threatening. That's why I recommend taking a mindful shower as a first step.[2]

A shower is one of the most powerful healing acts you can do for yourself each day in the Peace Within process. Unfortunately, most people rush through bathing quickly and obliviously, thinking about all the things they have to do in the day ahead. As a result, the healing power of the water and mindfulness is lost.

Find a time when you can take a mindful shower, without being disturbed or in a rush. Once you have chosen a time for your mindful shower, create a peaceful environment. You can do this by lighting a candle, burning incense, or putting on quiet, relaxing music.[3] Turn on the water and, as you wait for the water to warm, release into the now and do your three, deep centering breaths. Feel the earth under you and listen to the sound of the water. Notice any temperature changes in the room as the water warms. Notice any anticipation or feelings you have about getting in the shower. How does the air feel on your skin?

Notice any hesitation, feelings of discomfort, or self-consciousness. Remember to, just note these feelings, thoughts, and sensations without repressing them or pursuing them.

As you test the water temperature with your hand, say to yourself, "Thank you for my hands, so I can touch and be touched, so I can feel the healing power of this water." When the temperature is just right, step into the shower. Do so mindfully, noticing the touch of your feet against the floor of the shower. What is the texture and temperature? How does it feel against your feet? Also notice all the sensations flowing through your body as you step onto the tile.

Your body is being massaged by a current of water that is not only washing away dirt, grime, and sweat but also shifting the ionization (electrical charge) of the body that helps ground and foster a feeling of relaxation and peacefulness.[4]

Allow the stream of water to move from one body part to the other and bring awareness to the experience. As the water cascades over your head, say simply to yourself, "Water against my head. Warm water against my head." Then, move to each shoulder. Say, "Warm water flowing on my shoulder." For many indigenous people, water is a true, living presence, with the capacity for intelligence, healing, and love. They encourage talking to it like a healing presence. Continue this for each body part, until you finish with your feet.

After you've massaged every part of your body with the cascading water, place your entire body under the shower and say, "Body being massaged by warm, flowing water. Body being massaged, cleansed, and renewed by warm, healing, flowing water."

> *Take care of your body. It's the only place you have to live.*
>
> *~Jim Rohn*

Two optional compassionate awareness practices to end with are saying to yourself, "Thank you for my body. Thank you for the gift and miracle of my body." You can also thank the water itself: "Thank you for your healing touch against my body." Feel a sense of gratitude in your heart for the healing water. Next, take three, deep cleansing breaths before turning off the water. Notice the difference in how you feel compared to how you felt when you first entered the shower.

As you mindfully dry off each body part, note how the touch of the towel feels different from the touch of the water. Explore the textures of the towel and how your body feels after the shower. Notice the temperature of the air. As you dress or put on a robe, notice the texture of your clothes or the robe touching your skin. Then do a release into the now, paying special attention to the following questions: What was the mindful shower like for you? What did you discover about the sense of touch? What did you particularly like about the experience? Was there anything you disliked about it or would do differently next time? How would your life be different if you practiced mindful showering every day? What can you do to facilitate more mindful touch and showers in your life?

Although I encourage using a shower for this mindfulness of touch practice, some people prefer to take a bath. The principles are the same. and either can be a wonderful form of self-care.

CARING FOR YOUR BODY

As you begin to live more fully in your body through the *Peace Within* practices, you'll develop the natural desire to take better care of yourself. Our bodies are our truest home while we inhabit this planet, and caring for ourselves physically is central to finding *Peace Within*. If we don't take care of our bodies, our bodies won't take care of us.

Regular exercise, good sleep, and proper nutrition keep the physical circulatory system running in optimal shape. They are also critical for keeping our emotional circulatory system operating well. I often tell people that if they are only going to make one change in their lives, they should start exercising. When we begin to exercise regularly everything improves: we sleep more soundly, crave healthier food, our minds naturally quiet, and our overall emotional and physical health receives a wonderful boost.

Our bodies have an appetite for exercise just like we have for food and sleep. Exercise truly is a fountain of youth, one that also helps you nourish the river of breath coursing through your body, which ultimately feeds the ocean of peace that lies within. Deep breathing exercises the lungs and feeds our body life giving oxygen and nourishment. Exercise is also one of the most efficient ways to detox your body – through the breath and perspiration. Exercise gets rid of energy cobwebs created throughout the day.

The best exercise of all is walking. Studies have shown that those who walk at least twenty minutes a day are more likely to stick to their walking routine and see more weight loss after a year than those who do vigorous exercise and burn out. Exercise doesn't have to cost a fortune or take hours a day. The key is to find what works for you and what you enjoy doing.

If you are someone with a strong spiritual side and identify more with your soul than your body, you can think of your body as your Earth suit. Perhaps you can identify with Shakespeare's poetic metaphor that our bodies are a garden entrusted to us, and it is our job to tend the garden well.[5] Or Yogi Vishvketu, an Indian sage, once said, "Your body is like an apartment. You take care of it, you stay long time. If you don't, you get evicted."[6]

Now that we have explored the benefits of deep belly breathing and mindfulness practices, including compassionate awareness, I'll introduce you to another way to work with both components of the emotional circulatory system. This method is fun and easy and will deepen your experience of *Peace Within* the body.

FULL- BODIED BREATHING

There are many breathing techniques from different traditions around the world. Most fall into what is known as four-fold breathing, such as, *4-2-4-2* controlled breathing. The first number represents breathing in a count of four. The second refers to holding the breath for a count of two. The third refers to breathing out a count of four, and the fourth means pausing for another count of two until you take your next in-breath. This type of breathing is a particularly powerful and effective technique to quiet the mind, reduce stress, and bring calm into the moment.[7] I have worked with this practice personally and with students for many years, with great results. Many have used it to deal with everything from panic attacks to anger and stress.

However, I've also found that many people have difficulty with counting their breath or feel the counting actually gets in the way. Some feel the two-second pauses are too long and interfere with a more fluid breathing rhythm. As I developed the concept of the emotional circulatory system, I imagined breath and mindfulness to be combined. Just as the lungs and heart pump to every part

I love to breathe. Oxygen is sexy!

—*Kris Carr*

of the body, I also began to visualize breathing in from the tips of my toes to the top of my head and breathing out from the top of my head down to the tips of my toes, tracking the sensations as I breathed up and down.

This method closely followed breathing in to a count of four and breathing out to a count of four, without having to actually count. Tracing the entire body with the breath, while also noticing sensations moving through the body as you do, has been an extremely effective way of practicing breathwork for my clients, students, and myself. This method can be done sitting, walking, standing, or lying down before sleep or upon awakening. Over time, you can condition yourself to do this anywhere, at any time. It keeps your breathing deep and smooth, and your mind focused as you sweep the body with breath and awareness. It's an ideal way to keep the emotional circulatory system running smoothly *(See Diagram 7)*.

FULL-BODIED BREATHING PRACTICE

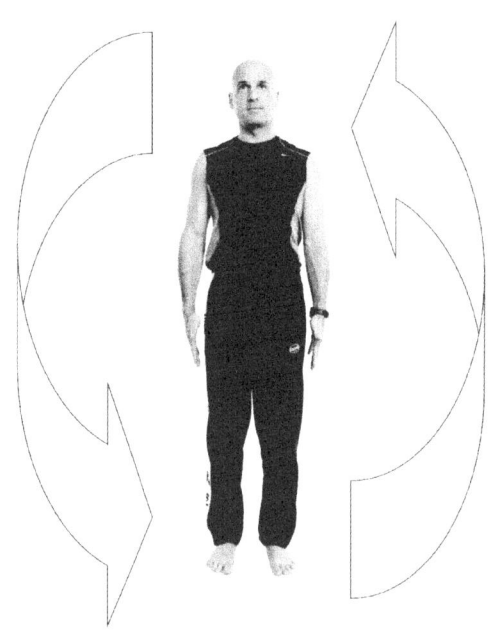

As you breath in, imagine breathing from the tips of your toes up to the top of your head. As you breath out, imagine breathing from the top of your head down to the tip of your toes.

DIAGRAM 7

SMILE POWER

"The smile is a candle in the window of the soul, indicating the heart is at home." I've always loved this anonymous quote, which is full of such universal truth. If the eyes truly are the windows to the soul, the smile is a beautiful candle we can light any time of day,

> *I have many problems in my life, but my lips don't know that. They always smile.*
>
> ~Charlie Chaplin

reminding us and those around us that our natural state is peace.

In my yoga classes when we breathe in, I always encourage everyone to smile. It's actually difficult to get adults to smile, and some students are so lost in negative thought loops they completely ignore me when I say, "Breathe in and smile." In fact, I find myself reminding clients and students to smile almost as much as I remind them to breathe, but, when you put these two actions together, amazing things can happen! Don't believe me? No matter how down, busy, serious, depressed, anxious, tired, frustrated, or angry you are, take a nice, deep, cleansing breath. As you do, smile. Just feel a sense of joy as you literally breathe in the smile. As you breathe out, relax into an even deeper smile. If you don't feel like smiling, that's even more reason to do so.

The act of smiling affects us physiologically and psychologically, fostering happiness. Back in graduate school, my area of specialization was human emotion. It was in those studies that I first became acquainted with the research on smiling, and it amazed me. Smiling is the most universal human gesture that cuts across all boundaries of language, ethnicity, race, gender, age, and class. It's perhaps the only true universal symbol among all humans. Scientists like Andrew Newberg have also found the smile to be the symbol that was rated with the highest positive emotional content. Here are some facts from the research that will convince you that smiling is one of the most direct, easiest ways to find

Peace Within:

1. *Studies have shown that those who smile live longer and reported happier lives and relationships (as many as seven years longer).[8]*

2. *It takes twenty-six muscles to smile, and sixty-two muscles to frown.*

3. *Smiling creates a neuro-emotional feedback loop that creates a positive cascade of feeling.*

4. *Children smile 400 times a day on average, while most adults smile on average only 15 times per day*

5. *Smiles are evolutionary and contagious, and we carry an innate drive to smile.*

6. *Smiling stimulates the brain's reward mechanisms in a way other pleasure-inducers, such as chocolate, winning a game, or receiving money, cannot match.*

7. *Smiles reduce stress hormones, much like deep breathing and sleep.*

8. *Smiling is an inexpensive way to improve your appearance.*

9. *A smile is an inexpensive way to brighten someone's day and your own.*

10. *When you smile at the world, it smiles back.*

What is more amazing is that although smiling induces positive results, the more we smile and cultivate smiling, the more our brains change overtime. Through this powerful positive feedback loop of smiling and the neuro-chemistry of the brain, these 'smile pathways' become stronger and more developed.

A warm smiles is the universal language of kindness

~William A. Ward

During the months in 2004 when I suffered my PTSD episode, and was consumed by suicidal depression, I remember how people steered away from me. For most of my life, I've been blessed with a smile on my face, but during those months, I wore a constant frown that expressed my fear of the world and my own self-hatred. I remember people moving to get out of my way, frowning, and grimacing when they looked at me. I finally realized that they were simply mirroring my facial expressions. This realization was startling and became seared into my mind and heart. It was a profound lesson I hope I never forget. That is why I challenge myself every day to smile for myself, others, and a world that is in desperate need of more genuine, heartfelt smiles.

SMILE PRACTICE

Do you feel smile challenged or deprived? The good news is that smiling can be learned or, more accurately, relearned. Genuine smiles, what I call *soul smiles*, are actually physiologically discernible. We want to practice the *soul smile*, not the *social smile*.

There are two muscles involved in smiling: 1) the zygomaticus major, which activates the corners of your mouth; and 2) the obicularis occuli, which encircles the eye sockets. Our social smile appears when we only engage the corners of our mouths, whereas when our eye muscles are involved, scientists call this a genuine or sincere smile.

One of my favorite things to do is watch adults with infants and young children. Adults, natural smile-avoiders, will do all kinds of goofy things trying to get a baby to grin or giggle. Suddenly, when the connection is made, there is an amazing back-and-forth exchange, like a playful, musical dance of smiles. We do this because it feels good, and releases feel-good chemicals and hormones like oxytocin in the brain and body. More importantly, we experience an immediate connection to the present moment and to our hearts.

Every smile makes you a day younger.

~Chinese Proverb

YOUR SMILE PRACTICE

Here are a few of the reasons smiling is such a great way to practice self-care and mindfulness:

1. *A smile costs nothing.*
2. *A smile requires no special equipment.*
3. *You can do it anywhere, at anytime.*
4. *It feels good.*
5. *It helps you befriend yourself and others.*
6. *It is a wonderful, simple mindfulness practice.*

Here are a few simple ways to practice smiling more:

1. *Each time you take a deep breath, add a smile.*
2. *Practice your genuine smile in a mirror, then a fake smile. Go back and forth and notice how differently you feel inside.*
3. *Practice smiling in the car.*
4. *While meditating, develop the habit of wearing a gentle, sincere smile. This is the smile you see on many Buddhist statues. Imagine smiling within and having a sense of humor about yourself and your practice.*
5. *Try to smile to at least five people a day, such as the clerk at the grocery store or gas station, a co-worker, or someone you walk by on the street.*
6. *Take some 'selfies' while experimenting with a sincere, heartfelt, genuine smile and develop the habit of imagining yourself with that smile.*
7. *Make a point of always returning a smile when someone smiles at you.*

To practice bringing more depth and genuineness to your smile, close your eyes and spend some time imagining someone in your life who brings a great deal of warmth and love to you, a person you feel a heart connection with, someone who gives you a sense of joy. Now, take a deep breath in. As you do so, imagine drawing the breath and that feeling into a full-bodied, soul smile.

Notice how you feel and write about it in your *Peace Within* journal.

HEARTFELT BELLY LAUGHTER

Although my physical therapist, Jessica, helped me smile again and begin to heal myself by getting out of my head and into my body, it was many months before I learned to laugh again. A smile, I discovered, is a wonderful prelude to a laugh.

We know smiling is a simple, yet very powerful form of self-care and a way of finding *Peace Within* our bodies. The same is true for laughter. In fact, there has been a global movement in the last twenty-five years called Laughter Yoga, a method that informs much of my own work and teaching.

Laughter Yoga was developed by an Indian physician, Madan Kataria in the mid-nineties.[9] Many studies have shown the value and power of laughter for decreasing adrenal and cortisol levels in the body, while increasing feel-good neurotransmitters like serotonin. It has been shown scientifically that the body cannot differentiate between fake and real laughter, and that both provide the same physiological and psychological benefits.

In addition to smiling, children frequently laugh. It's estimated that 4 year olds may laugh as often as 300 times a day. In contrast, there are times adults may go days or weeks without laughter when feeling deeply depressed or emotionally numb.

You don't stop laughing because you grow old. You grow old because you stop laughing.

~Michael Pritchard

You don't need to become a swami to learn Laughter Yoga or even go to a retreat or study with a teacher. All you have to do is laugh! The difficult part is giving yourself permission. Here are some of my favorite laughter exercises that you can do on your own:

LAUGHTER YOGA EXERCISES

1. *Santa Laughter: Simply laugh from the belly, just like Santa, with a series of deep breaths from the belly saying, "Ho! Ho! Ho!"*

2. *Fake Laughter: Try to make the most obnoxious sounding fake laughter you can.*

3. *Vowel Laughter: Laugh in each of the different vowel sounds: "Ha, Ha, Ha..."; "He, He, He..."; "Hi, Hi, Hi..."; "Ho, Ho, Ho..."; "Hu, Hu, Hu..."*

4. *Cell Phone Laughter: Imagine you are on the phone with the funniest person you know, the one who can always make you laugh. Now, imagine she just told you the funniest thing you have ever heard. Now laugh, and try to keep laughing for a whole minute. Be sure to take nice, deep breaths when you run out of air.*

LYING DOWN MEDITATION

It's time to introduce you to our first formal meditation practice, a guided, lying down meditation. Although Buddha himself said there are four basic postures—sitting, lying down, standing and walking – most people imagine meditation as sitting quietly on a cushion, with your legs crossed, gazing at your navel. Sitting meditation was my practice for twenty years before I began to take lying down meditation seriously, out of absolute necessity because of my injuries.

Not only did lying down meditation work almost immediately for me, but I found that over time, my meditation practice opened up and accelerating in ways I'd never imagined.[10] As a result, for the last ten years, lying down meditation has become my favorite form of daily practice, although I still do meditation sitting, walking and standing as well. Lying down meditation is often the first practice I introduce to my students. This fundamental practice has given me the ability to dive deeply into the ocean of peace more easily, even in times of physical pain, emotional trauma, or sensory overload.

There are many reasons to begin with guided, lying down meditation, including the following:

1. *Easy for beginners to learn*

2. *Less strain on joints than sitting*

3. *Allows the mind to relax*

4. *Encourages shift in brainwave activity more readily*

5. *Easier to do abdominal breathing*

A main drawback of lying down meditation is that you may fall asleep. It's not unusual for beginners to drift off or lose acute awareness of the process. In my opinion, this only means you are not as practiced at diving down with your awareness into these deeper states. With time and patience, you'll be able to do so.

I'd like you to read the following exercise, then have someone read it to you while you are lying down. You can also read it into a voice recorder (most smartphones have this capacity), then play it back so you can hear it as you do the exercise.

Begin by finding a quiet, comfortable place to lie in a reclined position, with your face toward the sky, your body lying flat on the Earth. Whether you are on a bed, carpet, couch, or outside on the grass, it is still part of the Earth, the gravity of which allows you to stay firmly held.

Lie in a way that allows your body to be in alignment, left to right. Your feet and arms should be a comfortable distance from your body. Your head, neck, shoulders, trunk, and pelvis should all be aligned left to right.

Whether or not you use a small pillow to support your neck is up to you. Some people find they go deeper without it, while others like to roll up a small towel and place it just under the nape of the neck. Experiment to discover what feels most comfortable to you. You can also place the palms of your hands facing up or down, whichever is more comfortable. Hands up can help you stay awake.

Now, begin breathing in a relaxed fashion, with a deep, long, cleansing breath, breathing in with your nose and out with your mouth. On the out breath, make the sound of, "Hah..." Do this three times, and imagine releasing all the physical, mental, and emotional tension you've been holding. After these three deep, cleansing breaths, move your hands to your sides, a comfortable distance from your body.

Imagine every breath you take to be a wave of relaxation flowing over your body, washing away worry and tension. Imagine breathing in from the tips of your toes all the way to the top of your head. As you breathe out, imagine breathing the energy from the top of your head, back down to the tips of your toes. We call this full-bodied breathing. This kind of breathing helps deepen and smooth the breath and induces a deep state of relaxation. Continue breathing in this way for a few more rounds.

If any thoughts come into your mind, imagine them as clouds floating by. You are not pushing thoughts away, nor are you pursuing or entertaining them; you are simply cultivating a deeply receptive, open, and welcoming attitude toward whatever thoughts, feelings, or sensations arise, without judgment. Some people prefer the image of boats on a river. In this image, imagine putting any thoughts that arise into the boat and allowing the boat to float down the river of your consciousness.

Breathe, relax, and let go, simply and naturally. Continue your breathing with nothing to do and experience simple, pure being…here and now…present and relaxed…letting go. As I mention each part of your body, bring your attention to it and breathe into it as you let go of any tension. Notice the waves and pulsations of sensation ever flowing throughout your body.

Bring your awareness to the top of your head. Become aware of sensation in the top of your head. As you do, you may even begin to experience tingling on the top of your head – even becoming aware of the follicles of hair on your head. Next, begin to release and relax your forehead, your eyebrows, and eyes. Release and relax all the muscles in your face, your cheeks, and your cheekbones.

Release and relax your jaw, tongue, and entire mouth and lips. Release and relax the temples, sides, and back of the head as you feel all the tension in your body melt away. Release and relax the neck and throat, imagining breathing in and out of the throat. Release and relax your shoulders, shoulder blades, and even allow all the muscles within the shoulders to soften, melting away any tension.

Coming to your upper arms, imagine releasing and relaxing all the tension in your upper arms, elbows, and lower arms. Your wrists, palms, and the backs of your hands are released and relaxed, as well as your fingers and the tips of your fingers. You may even feel your arms, hands, and fingers to be like rivers or streams of sensation, allowing all the physical, mental, and emotional tension to flow out of your body and down into the earth.

Bring your awareness to your chest and feel your heart open and soften, releasing and relaxing the entire chest area, the rib cage, lungs and upper back. Let go of the tension in the sides of your body, the mid and lower back released and relaxed, and even the belly softening and opening to the waves of relaxation that course through your body with every breath. Release and relax the waist, hips, and hip joints. Feel the entire pelvic bowl release and open – releasing and relaxing the sides, back and front of the pelvis. Now, coming to the legs, feel the upper legs release and relax, the knees soften, melt, and open. The muscles in the calves and shins release and relax. Feel the ankles soften and open, even the heels, arches, and soles of both feet. Feel the balls of both feet release and open as even the toes and tips of the toes relax and let go. Feel both legs, feet, and toes as streams or rivers of sensation, allowing all the tension — mental/physical and emotional — to flow out of the body and down into the earth.

Be aware of the whole body now, glowing with sensation, pulsing with a flow of warm, relaxing, peaceful, and subtle energy. Be aware of the stillness of Earth as She supports you, the smoothness of the breath flowing through you and how the mind has become more quiet, and the sense of spaciousness now present. Whatever thoughts arise, simply allow them to pass through your consciousness like clouds floating by…clouds floating by…

Now, pause in stillness for ten minutes, simply resting in peaceful, quiet awareness.

On your next inhale, bring your arms around your body and give yourself a hug. Cross your ankles if you choose to and, ever so gently, rock side to side. We call this 'hugging the universe,' or 'embracing the mystery.' You are a universe, infinite and inexhaustible, a microcosm of the macrocosm. Take a moment now to feel a sense of awe at the miracle of this your life, a never-to-be-repeated moment in the entire history and unfolding of the cosmos. There will never be another you in all of space and time. Make a vow to be more loving, accepting, and nurturing to yourself, now and always. When you're ready, slowly roll to your right or your left, bringing your knees in and using your hands as a pillow as you take a moment to slowly come out of your inner lying down meditation journey. Notice how differently you feel in your body from when you first lay down. Breathing simply and easily, give yourself a moment to slowly open your eyes and come out of the meditation, feeling more centered, grounded, and peaceful.

PEACE WITHIN YOUR BODY JOURNALING

Find a quiet place where you won't be disturbed. Take out your Peace Within journal and a pen or pencil. Do three deep, cleansing breaths. Find your felt center and release into the now to prepare yourself for the journaling portion of this module. Remember, this is unedited, uncensored writing. Let go of worrying about grammar, spelling, or sentence structure and – just let it flow!

1. *How do you experience your body in this moment? (hungry, full, tired, energized, cold, hot, sore, comfortable, stressed, relaxed, etc.)*

2. *Are you preoccupied with one part of your body more than others? If so, which part?*

3. *What part of your body do you like the most?*

4. *What part do you like the least?*

5. *If you could change anything about your body, what would it be?*

6. *How attached are you to your body?*

7. *Do you live as if you are your body, or as if you have a body? What*

do you believe is the difference between these two?

8. *What beliefs and expectations would you have to give up or let go of to find Peace Within your body? For example, is there an ideal weight you are always striving for, one you never reach or maintain for any length of time? Is there something you fear, such as losing your hair? Do you feel that if there were something different about your body you'd finally feel good about it, such as being taller or shorter?*

9. *Imagine what it would be like to be completely at peace with the way your body is right now. Write about what it would be like to accept your body as is. Perhaps you have chronic pain. What if you allowed yourself to accept that you might always have this pain, but make peace with it? How would that feel differently inside?*

After you've finished journaling, put down your writing utensil, release, then close your eyes and take three deep breaths as you notice how it feels to have explored this relationship with your body. Now say the following mantra three times: "I am not my body. I animate this body. I am at peace with my body."

MODULE 3 – MAIN POINTS

To summarize, the main points contained in Module 3, *Peace Within the Body* are:

1. Senses bring us into the here and now.

2. Mindful hearing, seeing, eating, and mindful activities like showering help us practice being present and peaceful throughout the day.

3. Practicing full-bodied breathing helps us:

    A. Get out of our heads and into our bodies

    B. Practice deep belly breathing

    C. Smooth and deepen our breath

    D. Practice mindfulness of body (somatic mindfulness)

4. Care of our body is accomplished through proper sleep, nutrition, and exercise.

5. Smiling and laughter are part of bodily self-care.

6. Peace Within lying down guided meditations helps with deep healing.

7. Journaling exercises can help you examine and explore your relationship with your body.

MODULE 3 - PEACE WITHIN PRACTICES

1. *Continue to practice mindful breathing with the addition of full-bodied breathing throughout the day. Make sure you begin the day and end it with each of the exercises.*

2. *Be mindful of your smile and laughter quota for the day and week. Notice how you feel before, during, and after laughing or doing soul smiles.*

3. *Do at least one sitting meditation for seven minutes daily (To get started, see my 7x7 Meditation Challenge at www.youtube.com/mbdemaria) and one guided lying down meditation weekly.*

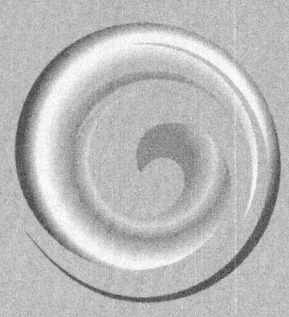

MODULE 4

This module builds on the previous mindfulness of body and breath practices to mindfulness of thoughts and thinking (thought awareness). As we move from breath and body awareness to thought awareness we begin to learn to quiet the mind through stepping back from our thoughts and allowing them to float by like clouds in the sky, boats on a river, or fish in the ocean.

4: PEACE WITHIN YOUR MIND

We all are faced with dark nights of the soul. We all experience suffering. We all encounter loss, illness, and eventually death. This is part of the human condition. Even though I realized all this, for some reason, I couldn't find inner peace myself. Although my 2004 surgery had fixed my knee, my mind remained trapped in a negative maelstrom of circular thinking from my past traumas. Fortunately, I finally worked up the courage to call my good friend and meditation teacher, Dr. William L. Mikulas.

Bill had blessed my life beyond measure as my teacher, colleague and life-long friend but it had been a long time since we talked. I had actually avoided him because I felt I had 'failed' as his student by falling so deeply into my own depression and inner abyss. It's hard for me to admit, even now, but I was so suicidal at the time that I had to carry my daughter's photo in my pocket and look at it throughout the day just to remind myself why I couldn't follow give in to the overwhelming desire to kill myself.[1]

Finally, feeling at the end of my rope, I called and told Bill I really needed to talk. As usual, he graciously agreed.

Whenever Bill and I get together, we spend time with our eyes closed, sitting in silence. Usually, this time is rich, deep, and still, but that day, even in his presence, which normally brought me centeredness, I struggled with my thoughts. I was in physical pain and unable to even sit cross-legged as usual. The fact that he could only made me feel more separate, self-conscious and disconnected. My body felt awkward and painful as if I were on an alien planet.

When we opened our eyes, mine were filled with tears. I poured out my pain, frustration, struggles, and, above all, my fears. My business was in shambles, my body diminished, and my future felt bleak and hopeless. How could I ever help others again when I could no longer find equilibrium and inward peace myself? Bill listened, nodding a few times to acknowledge my words. Sweat poured from my neck and down my back. I expected him to chastise me for being so lost, for abandoning the many lessons he had taught me.

Instead, when I finished, he took a deep breath and nodded his head again.

"Hmmm…well, you're doing a lot of thinking, aren't you?" he said.

A big belly laugh burst from me, something I had not experienced in so long. It felt good. He continued, "There's nothing wrong with reflecting on this present state of affairs you find yourself in, dealing with your physical injuries, and getting your life back together, but hyper-reflection, overthinking is not so good. You need to set aside a bit of time, perhaps an hour every week, to research and explore what you can do to heal your body and deal with the financial and business challenges ahead of you. Then, put it aside and make room for stillness and silence. That's where real healing will come from."

I recognized these words, I had even spoken a version of them to others and myself, but I needed to hear them from someone with a compassionate, wise presence, someone who cared about, knew, and respected me.

I nodded in understanding and acknowledgment.

 "Remember that all this thinking you're doing is just that, thinking, which is taking you into the past, through regret, or into the future, creating fear. Most of all, remember that you are not your thoughts. Your thoughts are not reality."

His words struck like an arrow in my heart. I repeated them quietly under my breath, like a mantra, with my eyes closed, letting them sink deeply into my soul: "I am not my thoughts. My thoughts are not reality."[2] Those words came to me like a brilliant shaft of sunlight shining through what, just moments before, was a stormy sky. Saying the words to myself, like a sacred mantra once again, I felt the sky open and clear. Everything I was thinking was not me, not reality.

For the first time in months, I stood back from my thoughts and watched them pass like clouds floating by. I nodded my understanding, and this time, the tears in my eyes were of gratitude.

Bill, my friend and teacher, smiled. We spent some time in silence, and I was able to still my mind, even in the presence of physical pain. I smiled as I followed my breath and listened deeply to the silence and stillness in the room. My physical pain began to recede.

I still had a long way to go, but for the moment, I drank from an inner oasis of peace. My eyes and heart swelled with a sense of hope. Although I didn't know it at the time, it was also a seed that would germinate, grow, and become the taproot that would reach down into that ocean of peace that was waiting within me.

You are like the man in the cinema house, laughing and crying with the picture, though knowing fully well that he is all the time in his seat and the picture is but the play of light. It is enough to shift attention from the screen to oneself to break the spell.

~Nisargadatta

YOU ARE NOT YOUR THOUGHTS

"You are not your thoughts" may sound odd and inaccurate, since in modern Western culture, we so completely identify with our minds. It's hard for us to imagine ourselves being anything other than our thoughts. This is a common delusion, an optical illusion of consciousness. Telling someone in the Middle Ages that the Earth moved and not the sun, might have been enough to spawn a stoning. At the very least, you would have been labeled ignorant, delusional, and a heretic. Before you toss aside the idea that we are not our thoughts, I would like to introduce you to a metaphor I call 'the film projector of the mind' (See Diagram 8).

A film is a collection of thousands of images set in motion when a projected light source creates the illusion of motion.

Imagine that your mind is a film projector. Now, imagine each discrete image on the filmstrip as one of your individual thoughts. When the thoughts (images) are shown together (stream through your mind), they create stories—a never ending commentary and narration on your life: *the contents of your consciousness.* This is not who you really are. Who you really are is the pure light of awareness. Consciousness is the light source illuminating your thoughts and feelings, not the contents of consciousness.

If you've ever meditated or done concentration or attention exercises, you probably noticed the large number of thoughts constantly streaming through your mind. It is estimated that we have between 15,000 and 50,000 thoughts per day.[3] Ninety percent of them are spent regretting the past or anticipating anxiously the future. The vast majority of our thoughts are the same ones we had yesterday. Thoughts also quickly begin to coalesce into the creation of stories, like the discrete images on the film strip. They create the film – the drama and trauma —in our mind's eye. These are conditioned thoughts and stories learned from our cultural and social conditioning, from a life time of media, movies,

4: PEACE WITHIN YOUR MIND

and music – all conditioned but ultimately not who we really are.

THE FILM PROJECTOR OF THE MIND

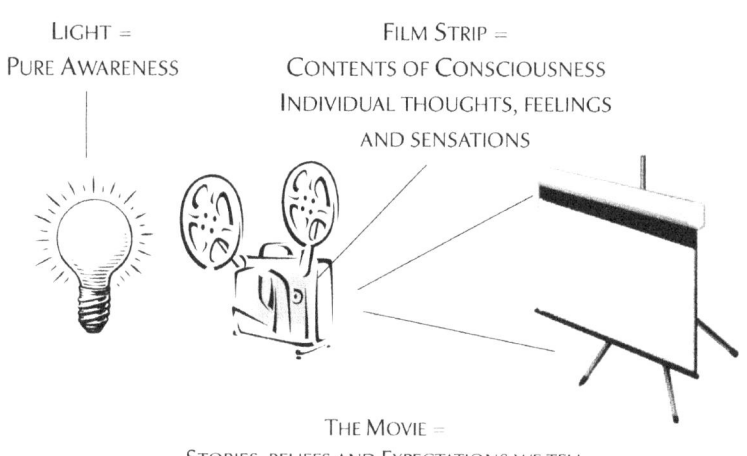

LIGHT = PURE AWARENESS

FILM STRIP = CONTENTS OF CONSCIOUSNESS INDIVIDUAL THOUGHTS, FEELINGS AND SENSATIONS

THE MOVIE = STORIES, BELIEFS AND EXPECTATIONS WE TELL OURSELVES ALL DAY LONG   MOSTLY CONDITIONED AND SUBCONSCIOUS

Everything passing through your consciousness (thoughts, feelings, and sensations) is like the small frames on a filmstrip passing through a film projector. These combine into the endless variations of stories you tell yourself all day long. Who are you if not your thoughts, feelings, sensations or stories? You are the light of consciousness—pure awareness without content.

DIAGRAM 8

THE PAST AND FUTURE

Thoughts are always about something. Thinking is an ongoing commentary on reality, not reality itself. Thoughts exert a magnetic force that pulls us into the past and future. Thoughts might replay regrets about the past: "Oh, my God! How could I have done that?"

Thoughts may also cause anxiety about the future: "Are we going to break up?" or, "Am I going to lose my job?" or, "Is my world coming to an end?"

 WHERE SENSES BRING US INTO THE HERE AND NOW, THOUGHTS TAKE US INTO THE PAST AND FUTURE.

By their very nature, thoughts are not present centered; they are an object of consciousness, but not consciousness itself. Does this mean we shouldn't think? Of course not! You couldn't stop thinking completely, even if you tried. However, in our egocentric, thinking society, most of us have grown sick from too much thinking. This is the "busy brain" epidemic we have today.

Because thoughts and emotions tend to reinforce each other, the problem is compounded. We think about the argument we had with our significant other yesterday. That thought leads to sadness, much like listening to a sad song or story. We develop the story further by recalling all the other relationships in which something similar happened, and we become more upset. Our sadness turns into depression. We tell ourselves, "I'm so bad at relationships. They'll never work out for me. There is something seriously wrong with me. I am a complete and total failure." This is exactly where I was before talking to my teacher Bill, caught in a negative thought loop of self-blame and self-pity. Tara Brach calls this the *trance of unworthiness.* We literally hypnotize ourselves into a negative story of our own creation. This trance is seductive, addictive, and dangerous to ourselves and our relationships.

This leads to deeper levels of emotion—namely, despair and even suicidal thoughts—created by a hyper-reflective loop of negative thoughts. This is similar to an eddy or whirlpool in the stream of consciousness. An eddy is created in a river when the naturally flowing downstream current hits an obstacle like a large rock. The eddy is the swirl of water on each edge of the obstacle, where the water actually begins to flow upstream in a circular motion, back toward the obstacle. Just like on a river, you can get stuck in these negative whirlpools of the mind.[1] I call this 'the chronic emotional pain cycle'. It can literally drive us crazy, as I personally experienced in 2004.

The following mantra can help you break out of this cycle. People who have repeated this phrase when they were lost in a negative whirlpool of the mind were granted relief and freedom. It truly has the power to transform your life and wake you up! This mantra is a wonderful accompaniment to your breathwork practice. I sincerely hope you master this powerful mantra.[5]

 I AM NOT MY THOUGHTS, BUT THE AWARENESS OF MY THOUGHTS FLOWING THROUGH MY MIND.

This mantra reminds us that we may not be able to stop our thoughts, but we don't have to entertain them, encourage them, or believe them. In fact, overcoming despair and becoming healthier does not mean we will never have dark thoughts again.

Getting in touch with our inner peace means we cease to believe and identify with our thoughts. Whatever we identify with has power over us. Refusing to identify with the thoughts that stream through our heads, gives us power over them.

The simple act of saying this phrase whenever you find yourself stuck in a negative thought eddy or whirlpool helps you step back from it. When you say the mantra while also doing deep belly breathing and smiling, you break the trance of thought identification with compassionate awareness – and before you know it, you're flowing down the river once again, with peace in your heart.

BOATS ON THE RIVER MEDITATION

I mentioned earlier that we have, on average, 15,000 to 50,000 thoughts a day. High level athletes and others who have developed their ability to concentrate, as well as those who are long term practitioners of meditation and mindfulness, have been estimated to have as few as 1,500 thoughts a day. Performance increases as thoughts decrease. Reflection is good, but hyper-reflection is not so good.

Studies show that those who perform best in life are not wasting precious energy and thoughts obsessing about the past or future. They have found a way to be exquisitely focused and present in the here and now, where thoughts don't get in their way.

A way to train yourself to be more mindful of thoughts is through the *boats on the river meditation*.

This meditation is a wonderful way to quiet your mind. It lets you observe your thoughts by imagining them as boats on the *river of awareness*. It helps you step back from the ongoing stream of thoughts pouring through your head, and it fosters compassion, consciousness, and curiosity toward yourself.

One of the first mistakes people make when they begin any kind of mindfulness or meditation practice is trying not to think about something. I liken this to a single person trying to keep a boat from floating down a river. It takes great effort and is seldom successful; you're working against the force of the water and expending an enormous amount of energy

The key is not to fight the thought but rather to notice it, label it, and allow it to float down the river of awareness. Don't pursue it; don't jump in the boat with it; don't try to swim after it. Simply allow it to arise and float by.

Some prefer to imagine their stray thoughts as clouds floating by. Perhaps you'll come up with your own image. One of my clients lets her thoughts disappear down an escalator. Use whatever image works for you.

This meditation also helps you concretely practice the first mantra—that you are not your thoughts, feelings, and sensations, but simply the awareness of these objects of consciousness (*See Diagram 8*).

Read the following exercise aloud, record it, and play it back as you practice. Many people find that music greatly enhances the experience of this meditation practice.[6]

Begin by making yourself comfortable, either lying down or sitting in a relaxed position. Close your eyes and take deep, cleansing breaths from the belly. Slowly bring your attention to your breathing. Notice the gradual, natural way you breathe from the abdomen. Breathe and relax: as each thought arises, notice it, label it as a thought, and imagine putting that thought or feeling into a boat. Watch it float down a river. The idea is not to resist any thought. Simply notice it, put it in the boat, and let it float away.

You will discover there are many boats constantly floating down your river. The beauty is that not one of them is final; rather, each gives way to yet another thought, all floating effortlessly away when you don't harbor, invite, or entertain any of them.

You will see how easy it is to become lost in these thoughts and weave elaborate stories about your past and future based on them: what you should be doing or saying, how you should be living, what you did wrong in the past.

When you notice yourself entertaining these thoughts, say "Thinking," then put them ALL in a boat. The longer you've been lost in thought and the bigger the story, the larger the boat you'll need to transport them away. Some people require cabin cruisers, cruise liners, or even aircraft carriers.

You can also use a short phrase when you notice yourself distracted this way, such as, "Lost in thought," or, "Thinking, thinking, thinking."

Breathe deeply from the belly, smile genuinely (mouth and eyes together), and repeat as often as you'd like: "I am not my thoughts. My thoughts are not reality."

If you find yourself stuck with an intractable, difficult emotion or feeling, use the first mantra's corollary: "I am not my emotions. My emotions are not reality."

Assistance with your meditation may also be found by paying attention to your senses throughout the meditation. Notice the sounds in the room, the points of contact between your body and whatever you are lying or sitting on, and the gentle sensations of your belly breathing in and out. Note any sensations of comfort or discomfort and how you automatically react to create stories that arise from these simple sensations.

CLOUDS IN THE SKY AND FISH IN THE SEA

Two alternatives to the boat on the river meditation are the 'clouds in the sky meditation' and 'fish in the sea meditation.' The principle is exactly the same, except that in the first, your thoughts are visualized as clouds; and in the other, fish represent your thoughts. For a variety of reasons, many people are drawn to one of these visualizations more than the other. Trust your natural inclination; you might even come up with your own visualizations to help you step back from intrusive thoughts. Whatever works for you is what you want to practice. The key is to gradually becoming more skillful at stepping back from your thoughts by being mindful of them – neither repressing (pushing them away) nor identifying with them (attaching to them). The river, sky, or ocean is then the awareness through which your thoughts pass.

As you become more practiced, you will find deep relaxation, peace, and contentment as you observe your conditioned mind at work while resting in your true nature; awareness itself. Like the vast, open sky, whatever passes through never affects it. Nothing can change or hurt the sky – the sky just is. Even as storm clouds gather, thunder and lightning appear, and rain pours down, the clouds eventually part to reveal a sky that is still blue. It's all just weather passing through the vast, open sky – resisting and grasping nothing – until we return once again to the cloudless sky of awareness.

In my mindfulness practice, I like to imagine that I'm on a plane. If storm clouds move in (a bad mood, for instance), I can explore them from a different vantage point by piercing through the clouds to always find the blue sky hiding above them. Some people enjoy the image of diving down to the calm waters under the rough seas of the ocean. You may find yourself moving back and forth between these images in your meditation and mindfulness practices, utilizing whichever feels most effective in the moment.

PEACE WITHIN YOUR MIND
JOURNALING EXERCISE

Take out your *Peace Within* journal and find a quiet time and place. Perhaps you'd like to light a candle. Take three deep, cleansing belly breaths, release into the now, and journal on the following questions:

1. *What thoughts do you find yourself returning to over and over again?*

2. *What do you enjoy thinking about? Notice how this feels in your body and how you respond physiologically and emotionally.*

3. *What thoughts give you energy?*

4. *What thoughts drain your energy?*

5. *What do you hate thinking about?*

6. *Does your mind spend more time in the past or future?*

7. *How much time do you spend in fantasy?*

8. *How much do you self-soothe by focusing on certain thoughts or beliefs?*

Next, place your journal aside and take a deep breath, tuning into your senses in the here and now, and allow yourself to finish with the mantra, "I am not my thoughts. My thoughts are not reality." Then, bring your awareness to your whole body as you begin three deep, slow full-bodied breaths, letting it all go.

MODULE 4 – MAIN POINTS

To summarize, the main points contained in Module 4: *Peace within the Mind* are:

1. *You are not your thoughts, but the awareness of your thoughts floating by.*

2. *Thoughts take you into the past and future – and out of the now.*

3. *The mind can be viewed as a film projector – where discrete images are individual thoughts. In this way, awareness (who you really are), is the light bulb, not the filmstrip.*

4. *Mindfulness of thinking (noticing thoughts) can be developed through meditations like the boats on the river, clouds in the sky, or fish in the sea meditations.*

5. *Stream of consciousness journaling is another way to observe our thoughts, getting them out of our heads and onto paper, which allows us to reflect on them instead of identifying with them.*

MODULE 4 - PEACE WITHIN PRACTICES

1. *Continue to practice mindful breathing with the addition of, "I am not my thoughts. My thoughts are not reality," mantra, particularly when you feel overwhelmed.*

2. *Work on noticing when you are 'lost' in thought, by simply saying silently to yourself, "Thinking," or, "Lost in thought."*

3. *Add daily micro-meditations of mindful thinking, where you practice awareness of thoughts passing through your consciousness.*

4. *Continue your seven-minutes of a daily sitting meditations, adding the 'boats on the river' technique. Add another thirty minute guided lying down meditation for a total now of twice a week. (You can always practice more if you like; these are the minimum as you begin the process.)*

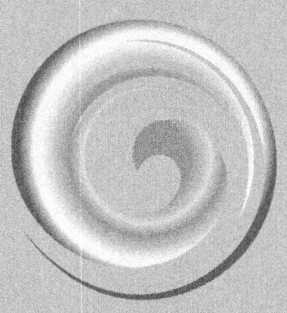

MODULE 5

We now move from breath, body and thought awareness practices to mindfulness of emotions. What makes the Peace Within Process so powerful and effective is the use of journaling meditation to work with your emotional life. Most Eastern practices, including yoga, give emotions little attention. This module gives you the tools to work with your emotions skillfully, creatively, and effectively.

5: PEACE WITHIN YOUR HEART

There are times when no amount of meditation will quiet our minds or heal our hearts, because the pain is too great or the inner chatter is too loud. Sometimes those who come to see me say in no uncertain terms, "I don't want to meditate! I just want to feel better."

I reply, "But meditation will help you feel better." Usually, they answer with some variation of: "First, I have to tell you what happened. Then you can show me how to meditate."

There are occasions when we need to express what is in our hearts before we can attempt to quiet our minds. Often, sharing what is in our hearts stills and settles the turbulence.

Madeline is an example of someone who desperately needed to share what was in her heart before she learned to meditate. She entered my office, sat down, and, before I even had a chance to say a word, the tears fell from her eyes like water pouring over a dam. She was in abject pain over the sudden death of her husband from a heart attack.

Before he'd left for work, the morning of his death, he and Madeline argued. She blamed herself for his death and was imprisoned in guilt and shame. She felt there was no way to make amends for the angry words she'd said to him that final morning. Not only did she feel guilty, but she was also horribly sad because she did not have the chance to say goodbye and tell him how much she loved him. She would forever hear her last words to him as cruel and heartless. Caught in a desperate grip of self-hate and self-contempt, Madeline's difficult grieving process was greatly complicated. She looked at me with desperation and pleaded, "What am I going to do?"

I experience the world primarily through feeling. I have to feel my way into a situation. When I listen to people, I don't hear their words as much as feel them deep within my heart. It is as though I listen with the ears of my heart. Before I answer a question, I often close my eyes, consult my heart, and peer deep inside for the words that need to be spoken. It is as if the words move through my heart before they come out of my mouth. I know this may sound odd, but I learned long ago to trust this process of speaking from the heart.[1]

Initially, I was self-conscious about this tendency to close my eyes before, or even while, answering a question. Not anymore. I now know it to be a gift. Now I think nothing of closing my eyes during therapy sessions or even television interviews, listening with the ears of my heart.

I had no words to comfort Madeline. I closed my eyes and nodded in agreement, feeling the depth of her pain deep within me. As I searched for what to say, my eyes welled up and when I opened them, I met her gaze. She burst into deeper tears again, her deep agony beginning to release.

I took a deep breath and said, "Breathe. Just let the feelings flow through you."

As her tears continued to fall, her body shook from the waves of grief crashing through her. I continued to breathe deeply in an effort to stay present to her feelings, imagining them moving through her like great waves, surfing them with the breath. As the waves of grief slowed, we sat in silence.

Much like Madeline's feelings that day, my own have always felt much deeper and vaster than words. I have struggled with how to put these feelings into language. Eventually, I found many different avenues to express them in ways that kept the river of feeling flowing clear and open, while avoiding log jams. Understanding emotions as patterns of energy, like the weather, helped immensely as I learned to surf these emotional waves instead of trying to conquer them, repress them, or allow them to take me over.

As I listened to Madeline, I knew her heart was in the process of being reformed, opening more fully to the great torrent of feeling that was pouring through her. Like water cresting over a dam, she needed to find a way to release her painful emotions in a more skillful way that would not destroy her or those around her.

Emotional pain is epidemic in our culture. Everywhere, there are emotions that breach the viaducts of our social personas, spilling over the dams and artificial levees we have created to keep them at bay. If emotions are like a river flowing through our hearts, to find peace, we must find ways to open our hearts wide enough to allow the river of feeling to flow freely. For Madeline, there was a lot of heart opening that needed to be done.

EMOTIONS FLOW LIKE A RIVER THROUGH OUR HEARTS. TO FIND PEACE WE MUST ALLOW OUR HEARTS TO OPEN MORE FULLY, SO THE RIVER CAN FLOW FREELY.

At the most fundamental level, emotions are simply energy moving, through us. Even the root word in Latin, *emovere*, means "to move." Because we live in an extroverted, thinking society, we are not taught how to experience, understand, and channel our emotions in healthy ways. Emotions are vital to discover what matters to us, what moves us, and what is important to us. It's critical that we learn to maneuver our emotional lives with skill and grace for the sake of our own inner peace, not to mention the *Peace Within* our families, our communities, and the world at large.

The epidemic of mass shootings, suicide, and many social ills is rooted in this shadow of our culture.

That's not to say thinking is unimportant. It most certainly is! Just as we need our egos to learn the language and function of the world, thinking is vital to our survival individually and as a species. In fact, thinking and feeling are two different, although complementary, ways of knowing the world. We have all encountered the painful conflict within us when our rational and emotional lives disagree.

THE HEART

We can only choose whether we will feel and not what we will feel.

~ Sam Keen

In the emotional circulatory system, sensations move through our body, thoughts move through our minds, and feelings move through our hearts. It is normal and natural for our rational and emotional sides to reveal to us different perspectives. However, we have not been taught in our culture that there needs to be communication. What we call emotional repression is when the brain (our thoughts) represses our emotions. It is as if the heart is gagged and bound before it even has its say. The *Peace Within* process is all about deeply listening to our emotions – not giving into them and acting out impulsively, but at least tuning into to them to find out what they are trying to say. So many people I have worked with have been repressing their feelings for so long that they don't even know what they feel, what they like, what matters to them, or who they are.

It is understandable that when our emotions start to feel like a torrential thunderstorm, a whirlpool of shame, or a waterfall of grief, we'd rather get out of the water entirely and avoid the whole messy situation. However, with the tools of deep breathing, journaling, and meditation we can learn to maneuver through these difficult passages on the river of life – even if it means navigating around them. In this way, we keep following the river, skillfully working with the obstacles and changing weather patterns we encounter on our life journey.

The best way to remain mindful of what is on our emotional radar screen is journaling.

FEELINGS JOURNAL EXERCISE

We often write with a great deal of editing and censoring, which stops the flow of feelings from being released. Your *Peace Within* journal is not a place to write facts about your life or day. It is more of a moving meditation using spontaneous writing. This is a journey of your heart.

Get a pen and a piece of paper or open a blank document on your computer. Find a quiet place where you won't be disturbed, take a few deep breaths, and center yourself. Now, give yourself permission to write what you feel without censoring or editing. Forget grammar, spelling, and sentence structure. The key is to focus on your first person experience of this moment and to write as spontaneously as you can. You are trying to get to the core of what it is that you feel in this moment.

Imagine you are listening to your heart and transcribing what it tells you. There are no wrong words, thoughts, or feelings. This exercise lets your feelings flow onto the paper. Notice the energy, how you open to it, how it tends to crest like waves, and then recede. Try to surf the waves of energy, breathing deeply as you do so and staying present to what you are writing. Keep writing until there is nothing more to say. This could be one line or ten pages. There are no requirements on length; this is about energy and quality, not quantity. If you have difficulty beginning, you can write, "I don't know what to write. I feel stupid. This doesn't make any sense." Simply stay with your honest flow of thoughts and feelings in the moment, and you'll be amazed at what happens. Once you find your emotional flow, you've tapped into your stream of consciousness, and you will be surprised to discover that you have written three, four, or more pages.

Sit back and take a deep breath, putting aside what you have written. Close the journal or turn off the computer, shut your eyes, and notice how you feel. This process is more about the current than the content or product. Notice how different you feel in your body. If you're still feeling stuck, sad, angry – whatever emotion you are struggling with— open the journal and keep writing. If you're exhausted or feel some sense of relief, take a walk outside, lie down, or do some sitting meditation practice and notice how much easier it is to quiet your mind now.

NOT RESISTING, NOT PUSHING

If our emotions are a river flowing through our hearts, then there are two key dangers we want to avoid: resisting them (often called repression or denial) or pushing them (often called acting out or being impulsive).

It is well known that repressed emotions, particularly anger, can lead to heart disease, strokes, and cancer. Often, a major factor in depression is repressed anger directed at ourselves. Denying emotions is the proverbial 'brushing of things under the rug,' until what you've been avoiding becomes so large you perpetually trip over it. Another metaphor is stuffing things in a closet until you can't open the closet without everything falling on top of you, so you stop opening it at all. Imagine resisting going down a river, or blocking the flow of water trying to move through you. What happens? You create internal pressure, often experienced as anxiety, which translates into stress that builds up until it explodes, which is the second problem.

Emotions themselves are neither good nor bad. They are merely energy moving through us. Emotions are created from complex feelings, beliefs, and expectations that develop over a lifetime. Distrust is founded on the second danger: acting unconsciously on our emotions. In psychological terms, this is known as acting out. This means impulsively acting on an emotion in a reckless, mindless way – literally becoming our emotions, as opposed to being with our emotions – as if our emotions had us under a spell. Think of young children who don't get their way and throw a tantrum. This is a form of acting out.

Think of an example when you acted out emotionally. Perhaps, like Madeline, you blew up at your spouse, parent, best friend, or child and were horrified with the words that came out of your mouth. Road rage is a common example. Someone cuts in front of you or pulls into the parking space you were headed toward. You erupt in a series of creative swearing that would give your mother a stroke. That's acting out.

Think of negative emotions—particularly anger, hate, and rage as hand grenades. You throw them (act out); they hurt others. If you swallow them (repress); they hurt you. So what is one to do?

Detonate them in a bunker where they don't hurt someone else (acting out) and they doesn't hurt you (repression/denial). Where's the bunker? Your *Peace Within* journal!

A psychological bunker is a safe place to talk or write out negative emotions. There is a reason they call psychotherapy 'the talking cure.' We know this works when we talk to a good friend or confidante and "blow off steam." Unfortunately, people are not always available, and some emotions and feelings are too personal.

Journaling can come in very handy in these situations. Writing out your feelings is a healthy way to process an emotion. It releases both the intense energy and gets to the root of the emotion. However, there are times, such as driving, when it is not possible or would be dangerous to pull out your journal. In these situations, practicing your deep breathing and focusing on the here and now are powerful ways to allow an emotion to move through you, until you have a chance to process it in your journal later.

In fact, many times, mindfulness breathing practices will be enough to allow the emotion to flow through you, and it will resolve with no need to journal. Journaling comes in when it is not just a momentary passing emotion but rather, when you find yourself with a chronic emotional state that is not dissipating through meditation, mindfulness, or breathwork. In those situations you need to get to the root of the emotion and process it with the feelings journal.

To help you understand how to process an emotion, I want to share my four-fold process of emotional healing, I've successfully used with clients for over thirty years. It's a straightforward way to avoid denying our negative emotions on one hand and not acting them out on the other.

My four-fold process goes to the root of the emotion, the belief, or expectation that gives rise to it. As your feelings journal unfolds, you will begin to maneuver your emotional world more skillfully and gracefully.

The heart has its reasons of which reason knows nothing.

~Blaise Pascal

As I mentioned previously, the word emotion comes from the Latin word *emovere*, meaning "to move." We all know our emotions move us. If I'm angry at you, I want to move against you; if I'm scared of you, I want to move away from you; and if I love you, I want to move toward you. Using our water metaphor again – imagine being in a canoe on a river, with your emotions as the current. Sometimes, the banks are wide and the river is peaceful and calm. Other times, the banks narrow and the rapids kick up, literally creating waves or eddies you must maneuver around and through.

Do you hide inside the canoe with your eyes shut, refusing to ride the river mindfully (repression/denial)? Do you fling yourself into the river with no protection and become drawn into the rapids and risk being injured or drowned (acting out)? Or do you take strong hold of the paddle, be mindfully present of each moment, and honor the power and direction of the river, maneuvering mindfully, even gracefully? The canoe is symbolic of the skills you are learning in the *Peace Within* process, including mindfulness, breathwork, compassion, and journaling. When it comes to particularly tough emotional rapids on the river of life, the feelings journal helps you process emotions, get to their root, and let them go. Here is how it works:

 PROCESSING AN EMOTION INVOLVES FOUR PARTS: 1) IDENTIFY, 2) EXPRESS, 3) EXPLORE, AND 4) RELEASE. THIS PRACTICE ALONG WITH MINDFULNESS, COMPASSION AND DEEP BREATHING LEADS TO HEART OPENING AND EMOTIONAL RESOLUTION AND

I will briefly introduce the concepts here and give you an opportunity to practice the process on your own through a very effective journaling exercise. I gave it to Madeline the first time we met.

FOUR STEPS TO PROCESS EMOTIONS

1. IDENTIFY

The first step in the process is to identify the emotion. Even after working as a psychologist for three decades, it never ceases to amaze me how few skills people have in identifying and differentiating what they feel.

Feelings are like colors. We learn to identify our primary colors in pre-school, but most of us never learn to identify more than the three primary emotions—mad, sad, and glad. Reading, writing, and arithmetic go on day in and out, while children suffer silently with emotions they can't identify, don't understand, and can't express or communicate effectively. Too many grow up to be violent on one hand (school shootings, bullying, murders, domestic violence) and/or depressed on the other (suicide). This inability to identify emotions affects their ability to develop a healthy relationship with themselves, much less with others.

For all our advances in science and technology, our culture continues to neglect and ignore the multifaceted world of emotions until it is too late, and a dangerous, explosive outburst occurs.

In our egocentric, thought-oriented culture, emotions are often viewed as messy and difficult. This is because they are wild, untamed aspects of our nature; as such, they are, the royal road back to our true, authentic selves. Herein lies the great paradox of emotions. On one hand, they are like the weather, hard to predict, and impossible to control – but they also bring the healing rains, the magnificent sunsets and cooling winds. They are life. They are us. No weather, no life.

Emotions don't behave or fit neatly into societal rules. To our rational minds they feel threatening. However, emotions are not irrational; they are trans-rational (beyond the rational). They are a legitimate, yet different way of knowing the world than through rational thought.

In fact, most emotions are full of meaning and have much to tell us about ourselves and our relationships, beyond what our thinking minds can grasp. Often, our emotions can actually clue us in as to what is true for us, what matters to us, and what has value more accurately than all the logical analysis in the world. Have you ever had a difficult decision to make and set up a pros-and-cons list? Then, when you ask your heart how you feel about it, your heart tells you to go with the one that doesn't make logical sense. You know deep inside it's the right decision, although you can't explain it. The heart, as Pascal says, has reasons the mind knows nothing of.

2. EXPRESS

The second step is to own the emotion by expressing it, saying, or writing it. For example: "I feel sad." As you write it, the key is to also be in touch with your feeling without judgment. It helps to practice mindful breathing.

WHEN WE PROCESS AN EMOTION WE LET IT FLOW — TURN IT FROM A NOUN (PARTICLE) INTO A VERB (A WAVE). IN THIS WAY, EMOTIONS CAN FLOW THROUGH US AND BECOME MANAGEABLE AND WORKABLE.

Practice this process by taking a few moments to write down what you are feeling, not what you think you should write, but what you are genuinely feeling, such as, curious, bored, silly, frustrated, fearful, or happy. What you often find as you identify and express emotions in this way is that they begin to shift and change much more readily. It is actually when we ignore and resist the world of feeling that a particular emotion becomes larger than life and overwhelming. In fact, when we lose touch with the feeling dimension (subjective felt sense) of an emotion, it can turn into an attitude – and attitudes don't flow, but are rigid ways of resisting the world. When we say, "That guy has an attitude," this is what we mean. We become stuck in a belief about ourselves, others, or the world and lose our flow, our natural rhythm with life. Often, we have emotions or feelings, particularly negative ones, that we keep at a distance, not recognizing them as part of us. We'd rather not own the fact that we feel jealous, hateful, angry, or even aroused by something or somebody. To own these emotions through speaking or writing them is a powerful step forward in moving beyond them and letting them go.

Identifying and expressing emotions is not acting on them. In fact, the whole point of identifying and owning your emotions is to paradoxically get some healthy distance and not over-identify with them, which may lead to denial and/or acting out.

Expressing the emotion is how you begin to enter the healing flow, a crucial stage in your healing process. This is the true therapeutic talking or writing stage of processing an emotion. Ironically, it is the very act of letting our emotions flow through us that allows healing to begin.

Imagine a faucet that has been turned off for a long time. When you first turn it back on, the water looks awful. How do you clear the water pipes? Let it run! You don't get fresh water by turning it off. Let the water flow, clearing the pipes.

When we journal in an uncensored, unedited way, bypassing the strategic, analytic, logical, yet rusty mind, we get a better sense of what it is we're feeling and learn to let it go.

This is a major counter-intuitive move when dealing with emotions. We don't get rid of them by repressing or denying them. In fact, acting out usually follows a period of repression and denial. It is true what Carl Jung said, that what you resist, persists. In psychology, we call this 'the return of the repressed.'

It's about the current, not the content, the process, not the product. Keep the flow going.

When we deny or repress an emotion, it is just a matter of time until we act it out in a distorted, twisted way. Of course, the other possibility is that the energy in the emotion goes underground and can turn into depression or even physical illness.

At this stage, it's counterproductive to go back and read what you've written in your journal. It's about the current, not the content, the process, not the product. Keep the flow going. Avoid blockages that back up your emotional life and leave you stuck.

When we refuse to identify, own, and express our emotional life, it is as if the water of life ceases to flow. We end up feeling dry as dust, emotionally constipated, and disconnected from our natural healing flow, which brings joy, renewal, and refreshment to our lives and souls.

3. EXPLORE

During this third stage, you bring consciousness and reflection to what you feel, and explore what is giving rise to it. This is the process of stepping back from your emotions and seeing them, along with your thoughts, as contents of consciousness and not who you are. This exploration stage allows you to discover (literally uncover) what lies beneath your emotions. What belief or expectation is giving rise to an emotion? For example, if you're angry that someone pulled into your parking space, it's because you're operating from the assumption and, therefore, the expectation that, the parking space belonged to you. Without that expectation and belief, you can't be angry, maybe frustrated, but not angry.

The vast majority of the emotional struggles we deal with on a day-to-day basis reveal the shifting shore between ourselves and the world, between the way things are and the way we wish them to be. In this way, many of our emotional struggles can be addressed with the healing wisdom and power of the serenity prayer: *"God grant me the serenity to accept the things I cannot change, the courage to change the things I can, and the wisdom to know the difference."* [2] The key element in the exploration phase is to find out what hidden beliefs we hold about ourselves, others, and reality.

Following up with the example, "I feel sad," we'll explore the emotion by journaling on the following questions:

1. *What led to this feeling?*

2. *How do you feel right now about this feeling?*

3. *What needs to change in you in order for this feeling to dissipate?*

Here is a real journaling exercise from one of my clients:

I feel sad. I started feeling sad the minute I found out my husband was not coming home for dinner. I had prepared a really nice meal and worked hard to have the kids bathed and the house clean so we could spend a nice evening alone, for a change. Initially, I was actually angry, but I know he has this big case he's working on. He's frustrated, and I could tell in his voice that he was also sad and disappointed.

I'm working on my deep breathing, and this journaling actually is already helping. Let's see...What's the question again? What would I need to change in myself for this feeling to dissipate? Well, I realize I had an expectation, and there was no guarantee it would happen. I became attached to the belief he was coming home at a particular time. So...as I sit here and try to let go of that expectation, I actually find myself smiling. It's really ok. He is coming home, just a few hours later. I told him I'll be happy to heat the dinner up when he gets home later, even though I'll probably eat earlier, and we can still have a nice evening and connect when he does get home. Wow, I can't believe how much better I feel.

As my client explored the emotion of sadness, looking in particular for her expectations and attachments, she began to let go of them, and they eventually dissipated and dissolved. Not all situations will be as easily resolved, but the more you undertake this kind of emotional archeology with your feelings journal, the more skillful you will become in dealing with and maneuvering the river of your emotional life.

EMOTIONS AND ATTACHMENT

Emotions move us and tell us what has value for us. A helpful way to simplify the vast array of emotions is to see how they stem from basic human motivations:

All positive emotions are a permutation of two states of being; either getting what we want or avoiding what we don't want. Similarly all negative emotions result from either not getting what we want or getting what we don't like.

When you begin to excavate your emotional life through your feelings journal, you will see five permutations of these two: *there is something you want that you don't have (desire), something you have that you're afraid of losing (fear), something you want that you have lost (sadness/ grief) something you don't want (avoidance/fear), or something you have that you want to get rid of (anger/hate/rage).*

Each of these emotional states arises because you are 'attached' to a certain way of being-in-the-world. Attachment blocks the emotional circulatory system, stops it from flowing freely and causes suffering, and it will eventually adversely affect your health. It stops the flow that you need to stay healthy, flexible, and creative.

The act of writing is often enough to 'expose' the attachment and help us release it.

4. RELEASE

Once emotions are identified and honored, most are easily released. Some are more persistent and require more exploration until they are also ready to be released. Releasing an emotion allows you to step back and allow it to unwind. Many cases dissolve and flow down the river of our consciousness or dissipate like a cloud after a rainstorm.

Emotions contain expectations of the world that are created as a result of certain beliefs we carry with us. Some common beliefs that give rise to a variety of emotions are:

People shouldn't treat me this way.

Life should be fair.

People who say they love me shouldn't leave me.

I deserve to get an A.

I will never lose money in the stock market.

Part of the release is to remind yourself that it is not the other person or the world hurting you, it is your unmet expectations of the other person, life, God, or reality that is causing the suffering. What is really being challenged are your beliefs and expectations of yourself, others, and the world and your attachment to them.

You may wonder, "Why can't I start with this stage?" Because it's easier to get to the root of our emotions (the hidden expectations of self, others, and the world) once we let go of the purely energetic aspect of it. I refer to this as siphoning off the toxic residue of the emotion.

Human emotions evolved over millions of years. We are the inheritors of these instinctual emotions that are filled with plenty of energy and very little consciousness. When we aren't mindful, these instinctive emotions erupt and can be acted out as murder, suicide, abuse, or disease.

Although emotions can be raw and dangerous when they're acted out, we also need to avoid throwing the baby (our rich feeling life) out with the bathwater (impulsively acting out).

Our feelings are as natural as a beautiful old growth forest. If clear cut, everything dies. This is where mindfulness and journaling can be effective, powerful tools. We cannot selectively numb ourselves. When we cut ourselves off from painful emotions, we also separate ourselves from joy. We begin to deny even normal healthy expressions of emotion and become cut off from the life flow emotions provide. Bringing consciousness to our emotional lives through this four-fold process, enables us to be with our emotions instead of becoming them.

In a traumatic situation, a great deal of the problem revolves around the person's feelings of helplessness. This is what occurred with me during my childhood surgeries, when I felt no control and had no preparation. Expressing our emotions in an uncensored, safe way (such as journaling or talking to a trusted friend or therapist) allows a release to occur, while also bringing compassionate awareness to the healing process. By honoring what we feel, we are able to maneuver the river of our emotional life more gracefully and skillfully.

THE RAPIDS OF GRIEF AND THE WHIRLPOOL OF SHAME

As the waves of grief subsided, Madeline's searching eyes and desperate question pierced my heart: "What am I going to do?"

I took a deep breath and said, "There's a way out of this hell you find yourself in."

"What is it?" she pleaded. "I'll do anything."

I began by describing to her what I call 'the river of grief.' "Imagine your life as a river, turning this way and that. Sometimes the river narrows and the rapids kick up, and sometimes the banks widen and the water calms. Right now, you are moving through a very tight canyon, where the river is particularly narrow and the rapids intense and dangerous. You must ride the rapids to get to calmer water. The great dangers are the whirlpools on this stretch of the river, whirling eddies of self-hate, guilt, and shame. Your grief is natural and normal, and your tears will take you to calmer waters if you travel down the rapids of grief in a healthy fashion. Don't allow the whirlpool of shame to suck you down and keep you from continuing to travel down the rapids."

She looked at me with tears in her eyes and a face full of expected failure, and said, "I don't think I understand."

I continued: "Guilt is feeling badly about something we have done. Shame is feeling badly about who we are at our core, the very center of our being and self. You need to find a way to make amends and heal the guilt without finding yourself sucked down into the whirlpool of shame and self-hate. That is what leads to depression and despair."

She asked me, "But how can I? I can't tell my husband I'm sorry. Therefore, he can't forgive me. Oh, my God! I'm cursed. I'm stuck. I'll never get out of this feeling. He's gone, and it's my fault. I'm such a bad, horrible person."

After sitting with her compassionately, and without judgment, waiting for her tears and feelings to once again crest and release, I went on, "There's a Native American saying, 'The soul would have no rainbow if the eyes had no tears.' What I have come to understand about what this means is this. When someone dies, we grieve and cry much like the rain preceding the creation of a rainbow. We miss the physical pattern of connecting with them. However, through our grief, we begin to build a rainbow bridge that connects our hearts in this world with the deceased in the other world. Native Americans believe we can create this bridge by talking to our lost loved ones. You must write your husband a letter from your heart to his heart, telling him everything you have ever wanted or needed to say, holding nothing back."

Madeline looked at me curiously. "You want me to write him a letter?"

"Yes, exactly. I want you to find a safe, quiet place, and I want you to gather some things that connect the two of you; pictures perhaps, or anything that helps you feel his presence. Then, I want you to sit down and write your heart out and keep writing until you can't write anymore. Start with the pain, hurt, and guilt, and keep writing, without censoring or editing, and slowly move toward forgiveness."

Although hesitant, Madeline's eyes shone with curiosity and a willingness to accept my invitation to write the letter. I also showed her some basic deep breathing, releasing into the now and centering exercises she could do before and after her journaling. She left as a woman on a mission, feeling calmer, more peaceful, and hopeful of being released from the emotional prison she had been living in.

NAMING YOUR FEELINGS MEDITATION

Find a place where you can be quiet and undisturbed, such as, your Peace Within space. Take a moment to center yourself by doing three deep, cleansing breaths, being in the moment, contacting your felt-center, and releasing into the now. You're going to work on simply labeling whatever feelings arise within you. This is a particularly powerful meditation to do when you are very emotional. Your feelings are neither right nor wrong; they simply are. This exercise is designed to help your emotional circulatory system flow freely. We are not trying to figure out emotions here, not explaining, thinking about them, or even understanding them. Instead, we are simply breathing, with curious compassion to whatever emotions arise, then labeling them. As you label them, notice how they shift and change.

For example, as you sit you might first notice anxiety. Simply say, "Anxiety," quietly to yourself, then breathe deeply. On the next exhale, settle in and notice what shifts if anything. You might notice a new calm. Then breathe deeply and let the breath settle and label the next feeling, "Sadness," …and so on. You will notice that, like thoughts, your feelings are always flowing and are never as permanent and continuous as you imagine them.

Notice that you are not saying, "I am anxious." You are simply labeling the particular feeling at this moment, then letting it pass. I imagine suggest saying, "Sadness is present." You are stepping back from the emotion versus 'being' the emotion. Unfortunately, our language betrays the simple fact that all emotions are in process, always moving and flowing. They are all verbs (energy), even though we treat them like nouns (things). This exercise helps you witness how the emotional circulatory system moves when we are not creating logjams with our thoughts, beliefs, and expectations.

THE THERAPEUTIC LETTER

My client Madeline wrote that letter to her husband, and it brought her tremendous healing. She read it aloud to me in a subsequent session, and she eventually buried it near her husband's grave. She has continued to write in her feelings journal and has, at times, felt the need to write an updated letter to him. She worked through her grief, and slowly found calm water on the river of her life again. She did this not by repressing her emotions, but by identifying, expressing, and releasing them in a safe, healthy, and meaningful way.

I call this process, "the therapeutic letter." Of course, it can be used for all manner of situations. It is especially effective with unresolved feelings or issues with someone who is deceased or a person you do not feel safe seeing or talking to in person, for whatever reason. A therapeutic letter is a powerful, transformative tool. Next to mindfulness, it is the most prescribed, most effective exercise I use in my practice.

There is no way to do away with our emotions. As we have seen, they are the very water that flows and energizes our lives. They provide us with motivation, meaning, passion, and purpose. However, they can also wreak havoc if we don't have the skills to deal with the emotional monsoons and hurricanes that visit us on occasion.

When the river is calm, with sunny skies, life moves along at a natural, enjoyable pace. When ominous emotional storm systems threaten to overwhelm us, however, journaling and the therapeutic letter are particularly powerful tools to increase our ability to skillfully and gracefully maneuver through the feelings flowing through our hearts.

A therapeutic letter is extremely helpful in any of the following scenarios:

- *You have unresolved feelings toward someone who has died.*

- *You have unresolved feelings toward someone who is alive, but you have no ability or desire to contact them in person.*

- *You have unresolved feelings toward someone who it is dangerous to contact.*

- *You have intense, unresolved feelings toward someone who you are reluctant to encounter in your present emotional state.*

- *You have intense feelings toward someone, but you fear losing a job or relationship if you express them directly.*

5: PEACE WITHIN YOUR HEART

There are other situations, but this covers the majority. As you can see, the therapeutic letter is a very helpful, important tool to have in your *Peace Within* tool box! Here is how it works.

Find a quiet place, preferably your Peace Within space you have created for yourself, where you can be quiet, undisturbed, and focused.

Do your peace within preparations, (deep breathing, contact your felt center, release into the now) and start the letter:

'Dear_____,'

It is crucial that you tell yourself that this is not a letter you will give or send to the person. Begin your stream of consciousness, unedited, uncensored writing. Let it all hang out. Keep writing until you can't write anymore. Allow the emotional circulatory system to flow. You are trying to get in touch with your heart, to allow it to have its say. This is not the time to judge your feelings as right or wrong, rational or irrational. This is putting the brain on hold and just allowing the heart to run freely and openly, with the full knowledge that you are not going to send this writing, that you are simply trying to get in touch with what your heart feels while not acting on anything in the letter. You're just getting it out to discover what you really do feel. Remember, at this stage, it's about the current, not the content.

After you've written the letter, don't go back and re-read it. I suggest writing at the top, "Therapeutic letter, for therapeutic purposes only," just to remind yourself you are honoring these feelings in order to let them go. Put it in a safe place after your done. Some people even delete, rip-up, or burn their therapeutic letters after they are done. That is fine too. I liken it to taking a bath; once you are clean, you don't keep the dirty water or climb back in! This is about the process, not the product.

After writing the letter, notice how you feel. In your feelings journal, describe how you felt prior to writing the letter, what it was like to write it, and how you feel afterward. One of two things will happen: Either the feelings will resolve and you will feel free of what you were struggling with, sensing a resolution and healing; or, you will find some relief for some duration of time (from hours to weeks), but then the old feelings return. In this case, continue to either add to the letter you wrote or write a new one. In some instances you might need a more structured approach to excavate the more difficult feelings. If that is the case try the more in depth Forgiveness Exercise in Module 9.

EMOTIONAL WEATHER PATTERNS

Another meditation is as powerful as it is useful in understanding the finer points of the emotional circulatory system. As your practice deepens and you become more aware of your body through mindful, compassionate attention, your awareness extends far beyond your body. Particularly in hearing and seeing, you are able to explore a vast space around you at all times. As you wake up to how vast you are and become more conscious of your breath and the ongoing exchange of energy you have with your ambient environment, you begin to truly realize what a mirror the world is – that outer nature truly is a mirror for our inner nature. We are a microcosm of the macrocosm.

The emotional circulatory system not only mirrors the cardio-pulmonary system, but also the water cycle of our planet. The water cycle of Earth is the ever-flowing circulation of life-giving waters on, above, and below the surface of the planet. Like our circulatory system, Earth's water cycle is essential to sustain life and nourish ecosystems. Like the blood in our bodies, the amount of water on the planet remains finite; however, it is constantly being cycled through three distinct phases of liquid, solid (ice), and gas (vapor/mist/clouds, etc). The water cycle is the Earth's natural water purification system, with evaporation and precipitation replenishing fresh water throughout the land masses of the world *(See Diagram 9)*.

DIAGRAM 9

The transfer of liquid water and ice literally transports minerals around the planet. The water cycle is also responsible for climatic changes. The entire circulation of water throughout the planet is an ongoing energy exchange – alternatingly cooling and heating the planet. As you can see, water truly is the life blood of our planet.

PEACE WITHIN YOUR HEART JOURNALING

Most of us know what type of weather conditions we prefer; sunny, cool, warm, or cloudy. The goal of this exercise is to also identify which emotions we're most at peace with and which are more difficult. For example, it's common for men to be more comfortable expressing anger than to identify, own, or express sadness or grief, particularly when it comes to shedding tears. Women are usually far more comfortable weeping but have more difficulty identifying, owning and expressing anger.

To keep the emotional circulatory system running well, we must allow the full spectrum of our emotional lives to be available.

Find a place that is quiet and undisturbed, preferably your Peace Within personal space you've created, so you can explore the terrain of your heart in more detail. This is a chance to discover which emotions you might avoid in your life versus the ones you are more skillful at maneuvering. Explore these questions in your Peace Within journal:

1. What emotions do you feel most often?

2. *What emotions are you least likely to allow yourself to feel?*

3. *What emotions do you fantasize about feeling?*

4. *What emotions are you most fearful of feeling and chronically avoid?*

5. *Are there any emotions you have never felt?*

6. *Which emotions are you most likely to get 'stuck' in?*

7. *What helps you maneuver through your emotional landscape more skillfully?*

8. *What beliefs do you hold about emotions? Do you see them as evil or bad? Do you believe you choose what you feel or that they simply happen to you?*

MODULE 5 – MAIN POINTS

To summarize the main points contained in Module 5: *Peace-Within the Heart:*

1. *I am not my feelings, but the awareness of my feelings flowing through me.*

2. *Feelings are like a river, flowing through our hearts. To keep the emotional circulatory system healthy, we must allow our feelings to flow through us, feeling them all the way through.*

3. *Health means not repressing our emotions, but also not acting them out. Through breathwork, mindfulness, and journaling, we can*

learn to process our emotions, maneuvering the waves and rapids more skillfully.

4. *By the four-step process of identifying, expressing, exploring, and releasing emotions we can practice being in touch with them without being overwhelmed or controlled.*

5. *Mindfulness of feelings can be practiced through the simple act of the labeling emotions meditation.*

6. *The therapeutic letter and Peace Within journaling are powerful ways to work through unresolved emotions in our relationships, bringing healing and resolution.*

MODULE 5 - PEACE WITHIN PRACTICES

1. *Continue to practice mindful breathing with the addition of the mantra, "I am not my feelings, but the awareness of my feelings flowing through me," particularly when you are overwhelmed by an emotional situation.*

2. *Work on noticing when you are 'lost' in a feeling, perhaps even acting out a feeling, and try to 'surf' the feeling through deep breathing instead of over identifying with the feeling.*

3. *Add daily micro-meditations of mindful feeling through labeling of emotions as they arise and dissipate.*

4. *Continue your seven daily minutes a day of sitting meditation, working up to ten minutes if you'd like, add the 'labeling emotions' technique. Continue at least two more thirty minute guided, lying down meditations a week; (You can always practice more—these are the minimum).*

6: PEACE WITHIN YOUR SELF

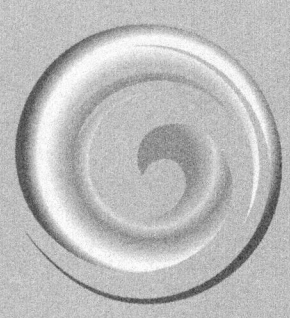

MODULE 6

After practicing breath, body, thought and feeling awareness with compassion we now move toward the powerful practice of self-compassion. As we do we notice thoughts and feelings about ourselves. Noticing our self-talk, we also notice our social roles and ego identities that are also not ultimately who we REALLY are. Learning how to be with ourselves in a more soulful, heartfelt way helps foster peace within ourselves.

I heard the words coming out of my mouth, but I could scarcely believe I was saying them. "You moron! You are such a f*#!&ing idiot. You stupid, stupid idiot!" Over and over, I cursed myself for falling on my crutches and re-injuring my knee and back. I spat my anger to the heavens: "God, I can't believe you! What is the matter with you?"

Looking back, I understand the utter fear, panic, and vulnerability I felt in that moment. After seven long months of working through the post-traumatic stress brought on by my surgery, I had fallen on my crutches as I went to the mailbox. Fearing I may have re-injured my knee and back, I was devastated.

At the very moment when I most needed compassion, nurturing, and understanding, I instead began flogging myself with the harshest, most critical self-talk I could muster. What was more embarrassing was that I was supposedly a successful psychologist known for my kind, loving manner, as well as a meditation teacher, ostensibly on a spiritual path.

"If only my clients, who trusted me, could see me now," I told myself, "What a winner," I thought, "I couldn't counsel a turtle to slow down." My panic intensified; "How can I be a good husband and father if I injured myself again and fell back into my emotional turmoil. How can I earn money, or run a business?" My mind knew this toxic self-talk wouldn't do me or anyone around me any good, but emotionally, I just couldn't help myself.

After my fall, I lay on the driveway, looking up at the sky, noticing storm clouds overhead. When it began to rain, my eyes welled with tears. Under my anger was grief and fear. It was yet another setback that I feared would take weeks or months to correct, and might have caused permanent physical damage. I had been rushing to avoid the impending thunderstorm, which caused my fall. I was not being mindful. Now, on my back, feeling defeated once again, the thunderstorm brewed over head as the rain grew steadier, and heavier. Not knowing what else to do, I finally allowed myself to sob along with the storm. A deluge of pain, grief, and hurt swept through me like a great torrent. In that grief, however, I was no longer in a whirlpool of self-hatred but in a river of grief that felt healing and, at the same time, began to open my heart so I could find compassion for myself again. Finally, after a few bolts of lightning and rolling thunder I began to laugh, finding humor and even a slight taste of joy in my lying in the driveway in the middle of a Florida lightning storm.

Be kind to everyone you meet because everyone is fighting a great battle within.

~Plato

We are so often cruel to ourselves. It is not simply that we don't allow self-compassion that promotes natural emotional healing; on top of that, we imagine the only route to self-improvement is to beat ourselves up. We truly are each the inheritors of hundreds, if not thousands, of years of a cultural belief that punishment is the way to motivate ourselves.[1]

Do you love yourself enough to listen with the ears of your heart to the other voices of yourself speaking.

~ Beno Kennedy

Child-rearing practices throughout most of history have been based on punishment, not compassion. As a result, we have been culturally trained and taught to inflict emotional wounds on ourselves: to crucify, divide, and abandon ourselves. This only leads us away from the inner peace we seek.

SELF-COMPASSION

I have always loved this quote attributed to Plato: "Be kind, for everyone you meet is fighting a great battle."

That battle is often with ourselves. The golden rule, "Love they neighbor as thyself,"[2] tells us that we will only be able to truly love others, the world, and life to the degree we are able to love ourselves. By self-love, I am not referring to loving an idealized version of yourself—an ego based love—rather, I speak of the ability to accept yourself as you are, warts and all. In his groundbreaking book *The Art of Loving*, Erich Fromm, the psychologist and social philosopher, describes a form of self-love that is the foundation for healthy, loving relationships with others. By self-love, he does not mean arrogance, conceit, or being egocentric, but rather, *loving oneself, caring for oneself, taking responsibility for oneself, respecting oneself, and knowing oneself.*[3]

Unfortunately, most people equate self-love not with Fromm's definition but with egocentric narcissism. As a result, I prefer the phrase, *self-compassion*. Just as we have been practicing compassionate awareness of sensations, thoughts, and feelings, we also need to learn to practice compassion toward ourselves.

Self-compassion is not the same as self-esteem. Self-esteem, although important, is based primarily on outward performance, academic and athletic achievement, social acceptance and approval, and so on. Self-esteem is tied to our perceived self-worth in the eyes of others and can often lead, ironically, to self-hatred when we don't measure up.

If you cannot find peace within yourself, you will never find it anywhere else.

~Marvin Gaye

Self-compassion means developing the ability to foster compassion toward ourselves when we are suffering. Often, when we fail, become injured, or view ourselves as inadequate in some way, we fall into negative, toxic self-talk and self-judgment. This is the origin of most psychological and emotional suffering. When we sit in judgment of ourselves, we are actually refusing to accept what is and who we are in the moment. The road toward accepting reality as it is and ourselves as we are is actually the prerequisite for change and healing. Self-compassion helps to move us toward this acceptance of self and life.

This involves learning to have a realistic evaluation of our strengths and weaknesses and accepting that, despite our imperfections and perceived failures, there is something valuable and unique about who we are. Self-acceptance is the ongoing practice of bringing compassionate awareness not only to our thoughts and feelings, but also to who we are and how life is, in this moment. It means being curious and not judgmental about what perceived weaknesses, inadequacies, wounds, and imperfections we have, without berating and criticizing ourselves. It is learning to have a sense of perspective and even a sense of humor when it comes to our many imperfections and shortcomings. It is about loving ourselves into health and well-being instead of beating ourselves into submission.[4]

Dr. Kristin Neff defines self-compassion as being made up of three main components—self-kindness, common humanity, and mindfulness.[5] Self-kindness refers to the capacity to be warm toward oneself when we are suffering or become aware of our personal shortcomings—as opposed to falling into either denial on the one hand (repression) or negative self-talk, what she calls self-judgment. Common humanity refers to the capacity to see and understand that suffering and failure are part of our shared human experience—instead of leading to isolation, our pain can actually lead to a sense of connection. She also states that practicing mindfulness towards our thoughts, feelings, and experience, instead of over-identifying with them naturally leads to cultivating self-compassion and an overall sense of wellbeing.

Ultimately, to experience an enduring inward, grounded peace requires loving ourselves, not as who we think we should be, but having compassion for our mistake-ridden, imperfect, broken selves.

SELF-COMPASSION MEANS HAVING COMPASSION FOR AND ACCEPTING OUR MISTAKE-RIDDEN, IMPERFECT, BROKEN SELVES AND IS ESSENTIAL FOR FINDING PEACE WITHIN.

Dr. Neff's initial research reveals that those who practice self-compassion have less depression and anxiety, and tend to be happier and more optimistic.[6] There are even indications that self-compassion can be more effective than will power when it comes to eating habits and losing weight.

Self-compassion is not about self-indulgence, nor is it self-pity. Self-indulgence is about 'acting out' our desires, and self-pity involves experiencing ourselves as victims and feeling incapable of dealing with life and adverse situations. Self-pity is about the loss of confidence, while self-compassion is about nurturing confidence in the face of adversity. It is about loving ourselves into health as opposed to beating ourselves into it.

Self-compassion has been shown to lead to higher levels of: psychological well-being, life-satisfaction, wisdom, happiness, optimism, curiosity, learning, social connectedness, personal responsibility, and emotional resilience.

On the other hand, low levels of self-compassion and high levels of self-judgment are associated with: self-criticism, depression, anxiety, rumination, thought suppression, perfectionism, and disordered eating atittudes (eating disorders).

SELF-TALK

One of the first ways we can practice self-compassion is to notice our self-talk.[7] Starting at a young age, we all talk to ourselves. If you pay attention to your ongoing, inner dialogue, you will notice its constant commentary on your life. The quality, tone, and character of your inner chatter has everything to do with how much or how little peace you experience. How do you talk to yourself? Is there a harsh inner critic who judges every decision you make and highlights every weakness and blemish you have? Or, is there a warm, loving, kind, generous voice that encourages and supports you when you feel down, lonely, or tired?[8]

When we first begin to pay attention to our inner dialogue, most of us are shocked by what we hear. Clients have told me they felt as if they were locked in a phone booth with a crazy person. Why? Because we have not learned to quiet our minds and simply witness the self-talk instead of identifying with it.

When you begin paying attention to your body (sensations), mind (thoughts), and heart (feelings), you can't help but notice how you treat yourself.

For the most part, discontent, depression, and even anxiety are the result of the quality, tone, and content of our incessant stream of self-talk and self-commentary. The scenario can unfold something like this:

Voice 1: "Wow, she's amazing! She's gorgeous! I wonder what it would be like to be in a relationship with her. I know she'd make me happy!"

Voice 2: "Get serious. A woman like that would never, ever go out with me. I'm a nobody, a loser. Besides, every relationship I've ever had has failed. I might as well face it. I'm going to be alone for the rest of my life. Why do I suck at relationships so much? There probably is really something seriously wrong with me; I might as well face it. I'm a hopeless, reject."

Perhaps this sounds painfully familiar or, perhaps not, but I'm sure you can recall some situation that really activated your negative self-talk, a civil war raging inside your head, a battle between the different sides of yourself.

To work toward stilling our minds, we first have to move from judgment to curiosity. Our experiences are never right or wrong; they simply are. Over my thirty years of practice, I've learned that if we judge ourselves, we will never understand ourselves. We become mired in regret, self-doubt, and self-aversion, missing the lessons our experiences can teach us. To move from judgment to curiosity requires listening deeply to whatever arises in each moment and witnessing it without judgment. It means bringing exquisite, sensitive, and compassionate curiosity to whatever arises.

CULTIVATING SELF-COMPASSION HAPPENS NATURALLY AS WE MOVE FROM JUDGMENT TO CURIOSITY ABOUT OUR MOMENT TO MOMENT EXPERIENCE OF LIFE.

Holding our experiences with compassion means doing so with gentleness and an open-ended curiosity that allow us to create—without judgment—spaciousness around what we are experiencing in the moment. It's difficult to be compassionate with ourselves, because we unfortunately rarely experience deep, abiding compassion in our culture. It's really one of the great challenges we face as a species.

It's not possible to be truly compassionate with others if we are unable to cultivate compassion toward ourselves. Paying attention to our own moment-to-moment experience with compassionate awareness is central to experiencing *Peace Within* the self.

SELF-COMPASSION EXERCISES

As we develop the capacity to be more self-compassionate, we learn to be 'with' our bodies, minds, and hearts in a healthier way. Because the entire *Peace Within* process is based on compassionate awareness, all the exercises up until now have an element of self-compassion. We will now look at more global care of ourselves. The next time you are struggling or feeling disconnected, isolated, or beating yourself up, the following exercise will help provide calmness and peace, especially if there's no one around to give you a hug.

EMBRACING THE UNIVERSE

In both Taoism and yoga, our bodies are seen as a microcosm of the macrocosm (the universe). This means that when we take care of ourselves, we are also taking care of the world at large. Although, this may sound far-fetched, who would argue that when we are happy, we help bring happiness into our families, communities, and the world at large.

This exercise is an old Taoist practice.[9] I do it at the end of every meditation and yoga class I teach. It's a wonderful way to end the day before sleep and a great way to start the day after you wake.

Lie on your back in a safe, relaxed place, perhaps on a yoga mat, bed, or even a carpeted floor. Close your eyes and take a few deep, relaxing breaths, as you imagine releasing into the now. Wrap your arms around your body, giving yourself a hug. Now, cross your ankles. Slowly, gently, and subtly rock from side to side as you imagine hugging yourself. Continue to breathe deeply and easily, until you are ready to unwrap your arms and ankles, then slowly put your hands at your sides, palms up or down, whichever is more comfortable. Notice how you feel in your body. This is a wonderful way to connect with your inner child, practicing self-soothing, self-nurturing, and opening your heart.

I recommend doing this for at least a minute, but three to five minutes is even better. Ideally, continue until it feels natural to stop. Notice your self-talk as you do this, the 'voices' you hear. Journal on the difference between the felt experience, (the sensations in your body and feeling of relaxation versus the self-judgments that arise such as, "I feel stupid."). Remember, this is not only a self-soothing and self-compassion exercise, but it will also reveal to you where you are still being judgmental of yourself and your experience.

VARIATIONS

Embracing the universe can be done seated or standing, though you should not cross your ankles if standing. Try this when you are emotionally upset. The physical contact with our own bodies in a nurturing method that has the same effect as a hug from someone else. Due to the release of oxytocin, the chemical hormone that induces a feeling of love, connection and bonding, self-soothing can provide a physical a way to keep our emotional circulatory system running smoothly by reducing stress.

COMPASSIONATE AWARENESS

Why do so many of us have such a difficult time being compassionate with ourselves? Because it's hard to give ourselves something we have never experienced directly.

Studies have shown that one of the main reasons psychotherapy works is that there is a listening, non-judgmental, benevolent, non-abusive human presence. This allows people to get in touch with their feelings in a safe environment. Those who are able to connect with another and share their feelings begin to be more accepting and compassionate toward themselves. Their increased self-knowledge gives them the opportunity to either develop the courage to change or to find the serenity within to accept themselves.

We seldom receive this kind of undivided, wholly compassionate attention anywhere else, so we are not aware of how it works to our advantage. This is exactly what the *Peace Within* process is all about, cultivating compassion towards not only toward our thoughts, feelings, and moment to-moment experience, but also to who we are at our core.

As we practice meditation and mindfulness, a fascinating process begins to occur. As our minds quiet and our hearts open we experience moments of deep, abiding peace. We begin to discover who we really are.

SELF, SOUL AND EGO

When you observe an infant, what do you see? Pure awareness! That tiny being is the living, breathing embodiment of the most true core qualities of being human: *wonder, awe, and mystery*. The infant does not know a language, has no yet identified with a name, and has no idea how to maneuver through the social landscape. Still, there is something powerful, miraculous, and amazing about being with an infant. Something that melts even the hardest of hearts. They are fully present, pure soul (natural awareness), without ego (social self-awareness).

An infant looks at the world with wonderment and awe. Think of a young child discovering her toes or fingers for the first time, or the power of a simple rattle that makes her squeal with delight. We each started this way, radically open, without judgment, infinitely curious. We were immersed in the small wonders of the world that were their own reward: a mother's smile, a kitten playing, the gentle rhythm of a sweetly sung lullaby. This childlike awe and wonder is the ground of consciousness. This essential awareness precedes and is more original than the ego we develop over time through our interactions with the social world around us *(See Diagram 10)*. I use the word *soul* to describe this state of being, not in a religious or spiritual sense, but as our innermost essence, our core, our essential self. The Latin for soul is *anima*, which is the root of the word animate. The soul is the animating principle of our bodies, our life flow. In this way, the soul is a child of nature, of life, and the cosmos.

As infants and small children, we are radically unselfconscious, living fully from the inside-out: all soul, and no ego. The infant doesn't have the capacity to step out of his own experience and look at himself through someone else's eyes.

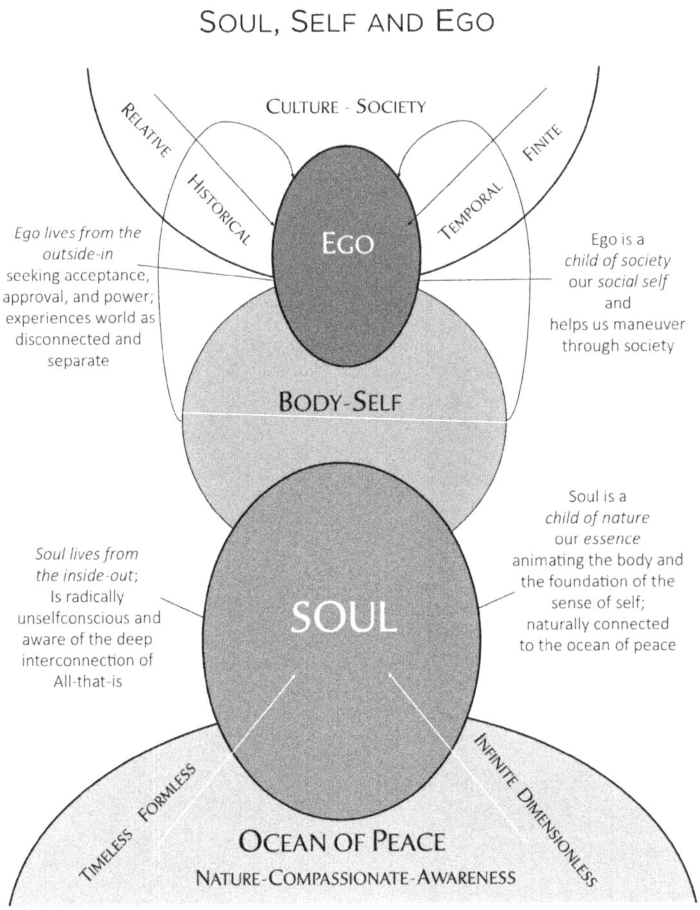

SOUL, SELF AND EGO

Culture - Society

Relative · Historical · Temporal · Finite

EGO

Ego lives from the outside-in seeking acceptance, approval, and power; experiences world as disconnected and separate

Ego is a *child of society* our *social self* and helps us maneuver through society

BODY-SELF

SOUL

Soul lives from the inside-out; Is radically unselfconscious and aware of the deep interconnection of All-that-is

Soul is a *child of nature* our *essence* animating the body and the foundation of the sense of self; naturally connected to the ocean of peace

Timeless · Formless · Infinite · Dimensionless

OCEAN OF PEACE
NATURE-COMPASSIONATE-AWARENESS

DIAGRAM 10

Infants and very young children look at the world with wide-eyed wonder, with few if any expectations.

They are radically centered in the present, with no regrets about the past or anticipation of the future. Infants live fully and completely in the now of the present moment. This is the fertile ground from which we grow our egos. Somewhere deep inside each of us, that sacred ground still exists. It is available to us if we know how to access it. The soul is the origin of presence. It is also heart-centered, and the source of our feeling dimension.

As we grow and mature, we begin to receive feedback from our social interactions (family and caretakers). We smile, and people smile back. When we scream and hit, people frown and shake their fingers at us. Later, we learn to say our names and to talk, and people applaud us; if we do something socially inappropriate, we may get punished or chastised. A few years later, we enter school. If we perform well on tests and receive an A, everybody cheers; if we get an F, we're grounded.

A few years later, we learn about sexual attraction, and the stakes become even higher. We're either considered attractive and noticed or perceived as unattractive and ignored.

Later, we may get the cool car, go to the 'right college', or find the high paying job, and family and society once again applauds; if we don't, we feel like losers.

PEACE WITHIN

The soul would have no rainbow if the eyes had no tears.

~Minquass Saying

Over all this time and through thousands of small and large social interactions, the second aspect of the self begins to develop and emerge: our ego, our social self. The ego is a child of society and grows through our interactions with family, society, and culture. The ego is not a bad guy; he's just a social guy. Without our egos, we wouldn't learn the rules and customs of a society, and how to fit in. Our egos help us learn not only a language but a particular accent and local customs that make us belong to a certain family and society. Our egos are constantly shifting and changing to adapt us to ever-changing social, historical, political, and cultural landscapes: When in Rome, do as the Romans do!

The ego develops over time and becomes our social mask, our personality (*persona*, literally Latin for "mask"). In fact, we actually develop multiple social 'masks' or identities. These are the many social roles we learn to enact, much as an actor learns different parts in a play. We first learn to play the 'child' in a family. Perhaps we play the oldest, middle, or youngest child and learn the roles of brother or sister. Then, we learn to play the teenager, the young adult. Finally, we settle into a career and learn to play the role of psychologist, banker, or police officer. If we marry, we learn to play the role of wife or husband, and if we have children, we take on yet another new role as father or mother.

Is it any wonder that our thoughts, feelings, and self-judgments can become so confusing and overwhelming!? Often, these many roles come into conflict with each other. Our inner landscape can become a mish-mash of competing ideas and feelings about who we are, what we should do, what we should be, how we should act, and who we really are. Many students and clients say to me, "I have no idea who I really am anymore!" Thank goodness there *is* a way to connect with our original nature—our soul.

The ego is our social self; the soul is our essential self.

The soul connects us to what is enduring, timeless, ageless, and eternal. A society that only fosters the ego and excludes or prevents people from connecting to their essence, which is their innermost nature, sets the stage for all kinds of emotional problems and struggles (depression, anxiety, etc.). In fact, many indigenous cultures use the term, *soul-loss*, to describe what we call depression.

The relationship between ego (our social roles and identities) and soul (our innermost nature and essential self) is the origin of most emotional struggles and difficulties at a psychological level. The word *heal* literally means "to make whole." Healing is about becoming whole, sound, and well.

When I speak of emotional healing, I am not talking about eradicating human pain, but rather, the possibility of rediscovering our natural wholeness, soul, and self. The reason the physical body can heal is that it is always working to establish homeostasis, that is, balance and equilibrium. The whole animating energy of the body is to promote and continue wholeness. Why would the emotional circulatory system be any different?

A great deal of my own pain during my breakdown was that my entire self-concept shattered. I wasn't able to practice as a psychologist because of my poor emotional state. I wasn't able to be much of a father or husband. I feared my days as a wilderness guide were over because of my knee and back injury. All those identities I had spent so many years developing and investing in felt like they were dissolving before my eyes.

There is nothing wrong with 'playing' our social roles; it's when we become nothing but our social roles that we get in trouble. A helpful image to understand this dynamic is to imagine our soul like the sun – radiating pure white light. Our body is like a diamond and each social role (or emotional state) is like the pure light being refracted into a particular color *(See Diagram 11)*. Often, we feel split into so many parts that, we are overwhelmed and forget our natural, innate wholeness. It's then that we need to reconnect with our true natures, the pure awareness that is the source of each role we play. In so doing, we discover an inner light that warms and nourishes us from the inside out.

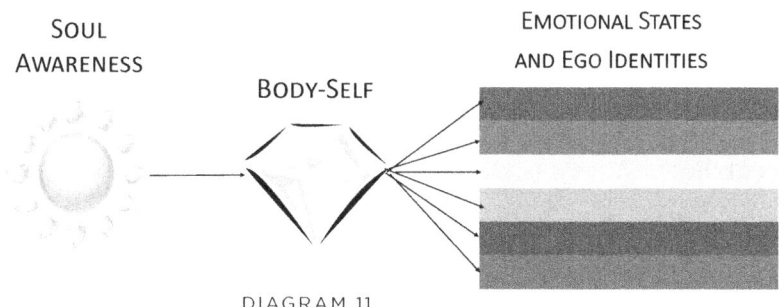

DIAGRAM 11

PEACE WITHIN THE SELF EXERCISE

It's time to find your center amidst your social identities. Locate a quiet place to do your journaling for this module. Take three breaths in order to de-stress and center yourself in the present moment. Release into the now and begin your stream of consciousness, journaling on the following questions:

1. *Write down the different roles you play in your life, such as wife, mother, husband, son, brother, doctor, etc.*

2. *Next to each, write what you love about each role and what you dislike about it.*

3. *When do you feel most in touch with yourself?*

4. *When do you feel most out of touch with yourself?*

5. *Do you feel connected to a higher or deeper self (soul/spirit)?*

6. *If so, when do you feel most connected to your essence or soul?*

7. *Who are you when you are not playing any role?*

8. *Are you at peace in emptiness?*

MODULE 6 – MAIN POINTS

To summarize, the main points contained in Module 6: *Peace Within the Self*:

1. *The Peace Within process is furthered when we learn to practice*

self-compassion and self-acceptance.

2. *Self-compassion leads to natural self-acceptance and fosters a healthy emotional circulatory system.*

3. *Self-esteem is related to the social self (the ego) and social roles that are an inevitable part of growing up and living in a family and society. Self-compassion, however, flows from the essential self—the soul, the true nature and the part of yourself that knows the ocean of peace that lies within.*

4. *One way back to our essential self is to connect with our inner child-like wonder, awe, and mystery—that part of us which is naturally awake, curious, and present.*

5. *The soul is like an acorn: No matter where you plant the acorn, it will turn into an oak tree. It is not socially conditioned, but has to do with what is most natural in our hearts, and is connected to our true and natural selves. It is unconditioned and wild, natural not cultural.*

MODULE 6 - PEACE WITHIN PRACTICES

1. *Continue to practice mindful breathing with the addition of saying, "I am not_____ (your social role or even your name)"*

2. *Pay attention to when you become 'lost' in a role. At the end of the day, imagine taking 'off' your social roles, the way you would your work clothes.*

3. *Take a mindful shower. While, you wash away the dirt and grime of the day, imagine also washing off your 'social roles' for a refreshing reconnection with your soul.*

4. *Notice during your daily micro-meditations how much of your thoughts are about your social roles—bolstering them, losing them, improving them, etc.*

5. *Increase your daily sitting meditation from seven to ten minutes. If you'd like, add mindfulness of social role stories. Notice when your thoughts become elaborate narratives about your social roles, how happy you will be when you 'get' what you want to achieve, and how fearful you are of 'losing' a particular social role. Each time, label all the stories as "Thinking," then return to breath awareness, body awareness, and full-bodied breathing. Work up to three thirty minute guided, lying down meditations a week. (You can always practice more—these are minimum.)*

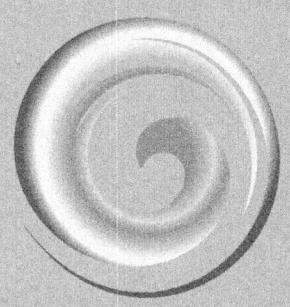

MODULE 7

As we have peered beneath the social and cultural conditioning into our true nature and become more aware of who it is we are, by practicing self-compassion – and feel more at peace with just being – it is now time to find out how our inner nature flows out into the world organically, naturally, instinctively and creatively – this is the realm of soul.

7: PEACE WITHIN YOUR SOUL

The irony of yelling profanity at myself and screaming at God was not lost on me. I was berating myself (quite well, I might add) with well-honed self-contempt and self-hate.[1] I routinely encouraged and supported my clients as they developed healthier ways to talk to themselves, yet there I was, doing the very thing I'd helped countless others to reverse, via my consulting room and speaking engagements. I had the fleeting thought that perhaps they would realize how normal they actually were if they could see me writhing on the ground, screaming curses at myself.

Picking myself up, soaked from the rainstorm after my fall in the driveway on my way to the mailbox on my crutches, I finally got up and hobbled back to my house. I knew what I needed to do. I went into the bedroom, opened a closet, and found an old photo album from my childhood. I dug out a photo of myself when I was a young boy, one I hadn't looked at in years.

The photo was one of my favorites, when I was about

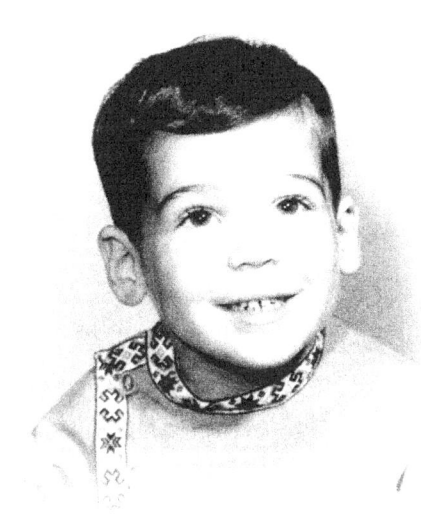

3 or 4 years old, wearing a festive little shirt and smiling up at the camera. I was called Michelino as a boy, "little Michael" in Italian. I loved when my mother called me that, as it was always laced with great affection. Staring at the photo, thinking of her lilting voice, I sensed and felt her love. It brought back times in my boyhood when I felt so safe, secure, and loved; although, right at that moment, I didn't feel any of those things. I sat back on the couch, with my knee and leg up trying to get comfortable as I studied the photo. Although I could not find any mercy or compassion for the 42 year old who had screwed up his life, I felt a flood of love for the little boy in the photo before me.

I mustered all the courage I could and spoke aloud to the black and white photo of my inner child, "Michelino, what do you need? What do you want to do today." Hearing no response, I closed my eyes, took a deep breath, and tried to focus on the sensations in my body. I then heard Michelino's voice, small and, hesitant, but very sincere:

"I want to color. I want to color with crayons." My eyes welled with tears, not of pity, but of joy at a kind of genius my inner child opened for me in that moment. There was no little boy physically in the room, but I distinctly felt his presence. For the first time, instead of becoming Michelino, I was with Michelino, a presence I could comfort.

The only meaningful outcome of a conflict is Creativity.

~William Blake

"Well, we're going to color then." I threw off the damnable ice packs I'd put on my knee and started looking for crayons and paper. It took me awhile, but I found an old box that hadn't been touched since my daughter left elementary school some seven years prior. I got comfortable, lay back down in the only position I could to avoid pain, and I started coloring.

I colored my first line on a blank white page in as long as I could remember. I felt exhilarated. I couldn't believe how much I enjoyed making scribbling marks on paper. Each stroke felt like freedom. No one told me what to color, what to draw, how to do it, or where to do it; I just colored. I couldn't magically go back in time, couldn't fix my knee, couldn't rebuild the house, and couldn't even get the contractor or insurance company to call me back, but, by God, I *could* color, and it felt great!

Page after page of white paper filled with the kind of doodling I remembered doing as a young boy. It was joyous, artless, and so meaningful. I was hanging out with Michelino, and he loved it. I realized I had been neglecting that part of myself, and he was the real key to my healing. If he wasn't on board with what I was doing, I would never recoup my energy, heal my heart, and recover my soul.

In the coming weeks and months, I asked Michelino what he wanted to do each day. Then, whatever it was, we did.

I began to imagine I was re-parenting Michelino. Not only healing my current wounding, but, more importantly, healing the times in my life I disconnected and silenced my inner child, that part of me that wanted nothing more than to simply be. I found renewed joy, not only in coloring, but also in following what gave me energy, like going to the park with my crutches and swinging on the swings or, laying on the grass and looking up at the sky to see what faces I could find in the clouds. Since I couldn't run, I bought a bike and began riding everywhere. I was a paperboy as a child and loved bicycling everywhere, another activity I hadn't done in years. It worked wonders not only for my knee, but for my psyche as well, and riding out in nature sure beat the recumbent bike at the physical therapist's office! I was outside again, breathing in fresh air and finding joy in looking at the trees, rocks, and sky. I imagined looking at the world the way Michelino looked at it, and as I did so, the world began to take on a magical quality again as I found myself living more fully in the now—hearing bird songs, feeling the wind, and smelling the scent of magnolias in the air, as if for the first time. It felt as if I'd died and come back to life. Everything was brighter, more vibrant and alive.

You must be your own lamp and refuge.

~Buddha

I made a commitment to myself: From that point on, I would do what aroused life within me and do my best to reduce or eliminate all that drained my life force.

 FIND WHAT GIVES YOU ENERGY AND BRINGS YOUR INNER CHILD TO LIFE, AND WHAT DRAINS YOUR ENERGY AND MAKES YOUR INNER CHILD RUN FOR COVER.

THE ROAD HOME

We see the world not as it is, but as we are.

~The Talmud

I started to realize my pain had much more to do with my state of mind and heart and less to do with my back and my knee. It was incredible to discover that when I practiced my lying down meditation, halfway through, all pain would disappear and just drop away. Also, when I found myself finding compassion for my body and allowed a caring attitude, instead of a harsh, critical one to develop in my mind, my pain also decreased. Most extraordinarily of all, the more my heart warmed and opened, the more peaceful my mind became.

The scientist in me became intrigued with tracking how my pain dissipated when I was more compassionate with myself. Part of this had to do with not obsessing about my pain and the burden of regret I carried for the actions that led to my injuries, which had occurred in a yoga class, of all places. The instructor had insisted I could go farther than I thought in the position I was in. Instead of listening to my own body, heart, and experience, I injured myself because of my ego. I actually heard the meniscus tear in my knee as the pain shot through my body. Of course, I then used that as an opportunity to crucify myself for being so stupid and not listening to my inner wisdom.[2]

I wish I could say that twelve years later, after practicing these techniques, skills, and strategies, I never say, "You idiot," to myself anymore, but that wouldn't be true. However, every time I do, I imagine my inner child, whom I have vowed not to treat harshly, and use it as a reminder—to practice saying, "I love you, Michelino. I know you're doing the best you can. Let's brush you off and try again. You can do this!"

This is what I mean by learning to develop self-compassion. *We don't see the world as it is; we see the world the way we are.*[3] If we are not feeling well physically or emotionally, the world is a dark, cold, uninviting place. Our mental and emotional states are the lens through which we view the world. If we feel well physically and emotionally—even in a crisis—we are capable, confident, and effective. Our ability to maneuver through life has a great deal to do with how we feel. The core of how we feel has everything to do with how we relate to ourselves.

Our first teacher is our own heart.

~Cheyenne

 WE DON'T SEE THE WORLD AS IT IS, WE SEE THE WORLD THROUGH THE LENS OF HOW WE ARE IN THE MOMENT.

I started realizing that my body didn't hurt nearly as much as my heart did. My heart had been broken, and I was trying to run from this truth through achievement and success out in the world. Even my spiritual quests and journeys were aimed at getting somewhere, finding something, and achieving something. Still, all the time, what I was looking for resided right in my own neglected heart. When I reconnected with Michelino—that inner part that was vulnerable, innocent, open, and deeply, unconditionally loving—it was the beginning not of seeking, but finding myself at home within my own heart. As the Cherokee say, "The longest journey you will ever take is from your head to your heart."

OUR FIRST TEACHER

When I returned to work after my experience with Michelino, I routinely began to ask students and clients to explore inner child work. It always, began with having finding a picture of themselves as children. When people embark on this exercise, something profound happens. Even just the journey to find the picture takes them on an inner journey of self-discovery. Although the different reactions are amazing, they all connect with the feeling and heart dimension in a powerful way.

All our relationships with others flow from our relationship with our own heart. As we age, we develop defenses around our hearts and abandon the natural openness we had as children. As Jesus said, "You must become as a child to enter the kingdom of heaven."[4] But what does that mean?

I am not recommending you become your inner child or childish in your interactions with others. Being with our inner child and rediscovering the childlike joy in our lives is a robust way to not only open our hearts but also create a warmth that naturally quiets the mind and allows a deeper, richer experience of being alive. It is also an evocative way to reach the ocean of *Peace Within* us.

In many ways, our heart is our inner child, our first teacher, and the road to the soul. Our inner child opens us to our first loves, our innermost vulnerability, and, at our deepest core — that radiant compassionate awareness we were born with. The road home, back to our hearts, can take time, or can occur suddenly (Think of Scrooge in *A Christmas Carol* who found his heart in one night!); either way, it can be fostered through a simple practice.

INNER CHILD EXERCISE

Find a photograph of yourself as a child, one you feel particularly fond of. If you don't have any of yourself, look for one of a child you identify with. The key is finding an image of a child, preferably between the ages of 4 to 6, though as young as an infant or up to 9 or 10 will do. Depending upon your childhood, this picture may elicit strong positive or negative feelings. The key is not to judge your feelings but simply be curious about them.

Study the photo and notice any reactions or feelings you experience. Now, place the photo down and begin a therapeutic letter to this inner child. Share the things you wish someone had said and communicated to you as a child.

This simple exercise begins to deepen an inner dialogue with the intimate and heartfelt core of yourself. What was said to you at that age was the beginning of the self-talk that grew into the adult you are now. Many times, we have to go to this more vulnerable, childlike source to begin to re-parent ourselves in a healthy way that frees and opens our hearts.

Next, I want you to write a letter from your inner child back to yourself. Let the child tell you what he or she needs from you and what you can do to help create a safer, more loving place for this inner child in your life.

Spend some time visualizing sending your inner child loving kindness, care, tenderness, and unconditional love. Once you're finished, take some nice, deep breaths, releasing into the now, then set this letter aside.

Commit to creating an inner-child date, when you can spend a few hours doing just what your inner child wants to do. Go to the park, to the beach, or on a hike on a nature trail. Perhaps you can retrieve an instrument you've stored in the attic, or even color in a coloring book. You may feel silly, but remember that it's about retrieving part of your soul and bringing that childlike awareness and joy into your present life. There are now a whole host of adult coloring books created for this very purpose.

CAUTION: It is important as you do inner child work that you are working at being 'with' the inner child and not 'becoming' the inner child. Part of my trauma made me regress to being my inner child, which actually caused me to act childishly, as opposed to being childlike. This exercise is not about letting go of our responsibilities as adults or regressing to an earlier stage of development. Rather, it is a skillful, conscious meditation on our hearts, meant to recover the 'baby' (our childlike wonder, joy and natural, compassionate awareness of the world), while letting go of the 'bathwater' (our childish, self-centered, attachment to certain desires, needs or wishes that someone else will take care of us.) This also helps us let go of blaming others for our past, or expecting others to make up for our childhood woundings, or seeking someone else to 'care' for our inner child. It also opens the way toward taking 100% responsibility for our health, healing, and wholeness.

FIRST LOVE

Although my inner child exercises helped me heal my body and mind, my heart and soul still often felt aimless, lost in a great sea with no fixed star to steer by.

I continued to struggle with fear and anxiety. I knew I had to get back to work. I had clients who needed to be seen and new referrals coming in, but I was fearful of taking on the crazy and intense schedule I'd always kept. I continued to see Bill Mikulas, who helped me stay connected to my meditation practice. I had stopped physical therapy and started individual yoga sessions with

PEACE WITHIN

When you do things from your soul, you feel a river moving in your, a joy.

~Rumi

a kind and compassionate teacher,[5] who helped me create a custom practice that suited my body, age, and injuries. I also began weekly massage therapy appointments with a gifted therapist[6] who taught me a great deal about self-care for body, mind, and spirit. I worked with a number of energy workers who helped me experience my body energetically and work with the pain, both emotional and physical.[7] However, I was still in search of my north star to steer by.

Earlier in my life, I'd undergone a life changing experience, a wilderness vision fast that had been guided by a dear, wise and gifted Native American teacher. It changed my life in 1993 as I experienced for the first time a genuine soul initiation and rite of passage. It was also the first time I ever heard the Native American flute, which remains one of the most powerful moments of my life. The bittersweet, strangely familiar sound brought tears to my eyes and felt like finding an ageless friend.[8] In fact, the Native American flute accompanied me on my journey over the following decade and was the central spiritual practice of my life until the catastrophic year of 2004.

It had led to my training with Dr. Bill Plotkin to become a vision fast guide myself with his wonderful organization, the Animas Valley Institute.[9] I guided people into the wilderness so that they could connect with their souls, and experience their full membership in the natural world, Earth, sea, and sky, in a profound, rich way. Several times a year, I guided quests to throughout the Southeast and Colorado. These experiences were some of the most powerful, joyful and challenging of my life.

I actually had to cancel a vision fast I was to guide in the spring of 2004 and was sure I wouldn't be guiding any in the foreseeable future. I felt it was an important part of my life's work, and a great deal of my depression was the perceived loss of it in my life. It wasn't that I couldn't have done it if I really wanted to, but it held no energy for me anymore. I felt aimless.

I'd spent a decade of my life training, learning, and practicing to be a wilderness vision fast guide, and now I felt physically unable, and what was worse, it held no energy for me. Worse yet, I had no idea what held energy for me anymore. Although I was enjoying coloring—and had graduated to acrylic paint and canvas, I was also sure there was something more waiting for me.

Feeling lost and uncertain, I reached out to Bill Plotkin. We had actually been talking during the year prior about me working for or with AVI, and I needed to update him on my circumstances. When I heard his voice on the other line, my eyes welled up. We had shared a great deal over the years, and he had seen me at my worst in the past. Amazing things happen when you are fasting alone in the wilderness, and you experience your primitive vulnerability with the elements.

I struggled to speak and share all of what I was going through.

Wisdom comes only when you stop looking for it and start living the life the Creator intended for you.

~Hopi Saying

Bill listened intently, as always, and he politely waited until I was through. He then said, with his characteristic depth and love, "Michael, you have created a beautiful world through your guiding, your practice, and your work. However, it seems that all this is now dissolving, so something much more wonderful, amazing, and closer to your truest calling on the planet is trying to be born through you."

"I know all of this, Bill," I said to him, "but I don't feel the energy for anything. I feel dead inside. Although I'm not in debilitating physical pain anymore, I have no energy to go forward. I don't know what to do."

Bill allowed silence to fill the space between us, separated by a thousand miles on the phone. I was actually talking to him while standing in the water; I had graduated to rehabbing my knee in a therapeutic pool.

Then Bill spoke, "Michael, what is most effortless, instinctual, and natural for you?"

Without blinking an eye, the words formed in my mouth, and I responded without even thinking about it, "Music." *Music was my first love.* As I spoke the word my eyes welled up again as I felt a deep recognition of this truth in every cell of my body, "It's music!"

"Then let music be your path." With those few words, Bill helped me see the fixed star that was already there, the one I'd been unable to discern during my dark night of the soul.

Growing up, my music teacher, even in kindergarten and first grade, said I had a rare gift for music, but my parents were petrified I would strive and struggle to make a living as a musician and discouraged me.

My first memory of the healing power of music was as I was recovering from abdominal surgery at the age of 7. Home from the hospital, I'd go into our living room, stand at the family piano, take a deep breath, hit one note at a time, close my eyes, and simply listen to the notes as they dissipated into silence. I loved the feeling I received listening to the silence that would follow. I then lifted a finger up and and struck another note and another, one at a time, and just enjoyed the sound of it. I did this for long periods of time, as if I was coloring in empty space with sound.

My parents thought I was autistic, and years later people made fun of me, saying I was a new age musician before there was a new age. Looking back on it as a psychologist, I realize now that I was self-soothing, putting myself into a trance, of sorts, that was healing for me. The sound literally took me to another world – or perhaps reminded me of the true, real world of silence and vibration infusing all we see.

I had kept a thread of music alive in my life, but I had never devoted myself to it. Up to that point, I'd lived off scraps of creativity,

Peace is not merely a distant goal that we seek, but a means by which we arrive at that goal.

~Martin Luther King, Jr.

never enjoying three square meals of it a day. It was something I had once dreamt of doing, but my practice sessions had fallen to the wayside. After talking to Bill, I became energized and started feeling hopeful again.

ACORN THEORY OF THE SOUL

Our essential self, the soul, at the deepest level, carries instructions for health and wholeness. Much like an acorn, we each have a soul-print as an individual and unique as our thumb print. The soul is our inner nature, who we are beyond simple genetics and environment.[10] No matter where you plant an acorn, given the right environmental conditions, it will follow its natural course to grow and become an oak tree. In this way, the soul is nature, not culture. The oak tree will vary tremendously, based upon where you plant it, what the weather is, and the quality of the soil, but its inner essence is always to become an oak tree – and no two oak trees are ever alike. Your soul is the same way. So how do we get back to our souls?

The heart is the natural doorway to our soul, and the doorway to our heart is our inner child we have always carried with us, since we took our very first breaths on this planet. Take a moment to remember the depth of love you were capable of as a child when your heart was fully open and your world was filled with enchantment and the joy of simply being.

For me, the essence of emotional healing is to reclaim the natural way of being that lies at the core of each of our souls, the very root of our consciousness: pure, spontaneous, open awareness of the miracle of just being. Is this possible? I assure you it is as easy as waking up in the morning and realizing that you were sleeping only moments before. When you wake up to this extraordinary quality of consciousness, healing simply happens, as a form of grace.

 THIS NATURAL RADIANCE, WHICH IS THE NATURAL STATE OF PURE AWARENESS, IS OUR BIRTHRIGHT AND THE ESSENCE OF FINDING PEACE WITHIN.

In some ways, this process is very easy. In others, it is quite difficult. To be innocent is to leave our hearts open. When our hearts are open, the river of feeling that connects us to each other, to nature, and to the cosmos becomes as natural as when we were young children. In this state, there is no effort required in loving our lives, or ourselves, we simply do.

Children have natural wisdom. Their tender hearts are open, more soul than ego; however, as the necessary socialization process begins and, as our egos grow, our connection to our souls, nature, and life begins to diminish, and we become socialized.

In the process of living our lives, we have all developed different sides of ourselves: the child, adult, teacher, mother, wife, etc.

> *Remember that self-doubt is as self-centered as self-inflation. Your obligation is to reach as deeply as you can and offer your unique and authentic gifts as bravely and beautifully as you're able.*
>
> *~Bill Plotkin*

These are the result of learning and adopting different social roles (ego identities) as we develop and maneuver through our families, communities, and society. From our gender, to our race, sexual preference, birth order, ethnicity, and religious affiliation, our simple, pure awareness and presence takes on different shapes and textures, depending on the social role we are playing (or forced to play) in the moment.

We learn to function, perform, and develop in a particular family, community, and culture. This is inevitable, healthy, and good. We learn a language, and what is right and wrong in a particular society; however, this comes at a price. At the same time when we are learning important skills for survival, we also begin to disconnect from our feeling life – our souls. We lose our simple, uncomplicated connection to pure being. So, how do we gain experience while learning to survive and maneuver in a harsh world? How do we stay connected in an open and innocent way to our hearts, the true core of emotional healing, while also maneuvering through society and playing our social roles without being trapped or duplicitous?

WHAT KIND OF TREE ARE YOU?

As you begin to discover your 'acorn,' your passion and calling, you move from having a sense of self created by others' expectations (family, friends and society), and instead look within yourself for what moves you, gives you energy, and brings you alive. This is listening to your soul. In so doing, you will find yourself belonging to life and to the world in a way that will transform you and all those you encounter. As Rumi says so accurately, "When you do things from your soul, you will feel a river moving in you, a joy!" In my own experience, it is also helps you discover who you really are, and what and who truly matters to you. In a phrase, what you are willing to die for.

The soul is all about finding our authentic work and self-expression in the world. If you are an acorn and designed become an oak tree (e.g., a pilot), but your family expects you to be an apple tree (e.g., dentist) you won't be very happy or effective. Because our society is ego-centric and not soul-centric, this is an epidemic problem.

Some people's childhood helped them discover their path early on. As a result of the tragedy of losing his mother, who was a single parent, when he was 18, my good friend and fellow musician, composer, and eleven-time Grammy® nominee, Peter Kater, realized he could do and be whatever he wanted. This set him on the path early toward sharing his heart through his music, finding his soul work at a much younger age than most.[11]

SOUL WORK AND SURVIVAL WORK

While our soul work is what brings us alive and is our greatest joy, our survival work is what puts a roof over our heads and food on the table. It is my ardent hope that once our culture becomes increasingly soul-centric, more people will be able to merge their soul work and survival work into one and the same thing. In the meantime, however, you can weave your soul work into your survival work. In fact, your soul work can often be done regardless of your survival work. There are times when you'll realize that it is not what you are doing, but how you are doing it. When you work from the soul level, everything is done with more care and purpose.

As we explore and discover our social roles, this often includes our survival work. However, when you know your survival work is simply a stepping stone to discovering your soul work, your whole life can light up. To paraphrase Nietzsche, if you know the why, you can endure any how, meaning we can endure suffering when it has a purpose and meaning.

What we cannot endure is meaningless suffering. Most people come to me in this state. They feel stuck, as if they are at a dead end. Discovering that there is something out there that will make you alive, something that you are willing to suffer to achieve, makes all the difference, particularly when it's tied to helping others.

There are a number of ways to discover what you were born to do, what your soul work is. Although, many cultures explore this in what is called *soul initiation*, such as a vision quest, there are a number of other ways you can get started right now.

WRITING YOURSELF TO TEARS

This exercise, which I have used with many people, is simple and straightforward.[12]

Set aside thirty minutes to an hour for this exercise. As always, prepare yourself by doing the centering breath exercise and releasing into the now. Take out your Peace Within journal and follow these steps:

1. *Write at the top, "What is my true soul's purpose in life?"*

2. *Write every answer that pops into your head. It doesn't have to be a complete sentence. A short phrase is fine.*

3. *Repeat until you write the answer that makes you cry. This is your purpose.*

Although seemingly simple, tears are the key here. A saying of the Minquass, a Native American Tribe, is, "The soul would have no rainbow if the eyes had no tears." In our culture, we try to be too rational about our life direction. Remember, the heart is the doorway to the soul. Finding what opens your heart will lead you to your calling. In fact, the Lakota word for vision quest is *henblacheypai*, which literally means *to lament*. The Lakota believe a person must weep for a vision of his life, that it has to come from a place of great sincerity, genuineness, and depth for the Creator to have mercy on the seeker's soul to grant a vision.

For some, this way of approaching soul work will feel strange, while it appeals to others immediately and is very effective for them. Regardless, give it a try. Usually, your first set of answers will come from your mind or ego. That's fine, since this is a stream of consciousness practice, it is designed to help you free up your creativity. Keep the flow going, and after a while, you will find the answers coming from a deeper source in your body and heart. You might even start to feel like it's coming from a different source altogether. You may get the urge to give up, but stay with it. After a while you will find yourself circling particular themes. As in other journaling exercises, let yourself be completely unedited and uncensored. Write ridiculous and outrageous things. Really rev up your creativity and connect to your own innate wisdom. Nietzsche also said, "If you don't have chaos in you, you can't give birth to a dancing star." Your dancing star is your soul work and your soul's path, so let yourself explore some of the chaos within. As you give it room and space to breathe, you will find it coalescing and converging into a powerful statement. Steve Pavlina, from whom this exercise is adapted, came up with his answer on his 106th try: "To live consciously and courageously, to resonate with love and compassion, to awaken the great spirits within others, and to leave this world in peace."

If you find yourself getting tired, take a break, close your eyes, do some deep breathing, and release into the now. Often, clarity and the circling of your calling will begin to become clearer after brief breaks like this. Some resistant people may need multiple sessions to hit on an answer. In this exercise, although the 'product' is important the process will tell you a great deal about yourself.

CHILD WISDOM EXERCISE

Another way to discover our soul work is to consult the inner child. By exploring childhood dreams, we move close to what our earliest awakenings were about, before culture and family moved in to mold us. As self-help writer, Jess Lair says, "Children are not things to be molded, but people to be unfolded." One of the reasons I love the spiral Koru is that it symbolizes in Māori culture the unfolding of their beloved silver fern. We are all part of nature, and have something we are here to unfold from within us and offer to the world.

Take out your Peace Within journal. Find a time and place (such as your Peace Within space) to be alone and quiet. Take out your inner child photo and ask that part of you the questions below. Journal unedited and uncensored. It is important to avoid focusing on dreams that pleased your parents, or that would profit you with ego satisfactions like fame and fortune; rather, think of what literally makes your heart sing:

What did you want to be when you were a child?

What were your childhood dreams for your life?

What did you want to be when you grew up?

After journaling on these questions, look once again for patterns, connections, and what emerges as your core elemental dream. Compare it to the previous writing exercise and see what themes keep arising. How can you weave them into your life? Take a deep breath, set the journal aside, and realize that this is an unfolding process. Great satisfaction and joy can come from simply feeling like you are beginning to move in the direction of your soul once again.

DREAM LIVES EXERCISE

> It's never too late to be who you might have been.
>
> ~George Eliot

Julia Cameron's *The Artist's Way* contains a wonderful exercise she calls "Imaginary Lives."[13] The journaling exercise involves imagining five other lives to lead and what you would be doing in each of them. She encourages people to have fun with them. I'd like you to at least pick three. Mine would be: filmmaker, world explorer, and astrophysicist. Then each week, look over your list and do at least one thing that will help you connect with this 'unlived life'. For me, it could be going to the bookstore and purchasing a magazine or book on filmmaking or watching a documentary on astrophysics. Take your time, have fun, and remember that part of what you are doing is trying to find out what is most natural, instinctual, and effortless for you. *What makes you feel alive and gives you joy? What helps the water of life, that is, your life energy flow?*

TUNING INTO THE SOUL

A variation of this can be journaling on those people, living or dead, who inspire you and mirror to you who you really are. We often 'tune' ourselves to the song of our souls through other people. Those we are drawn to often reveal to us (mirroring) what it is that is already in us, albeit, latent, buried, or hidden. In this way, we can come to know ourselves through others. *Write down who your heroes are, along with a list of their attributes and qualities that attract you to them, those things you most admire. Then ask yourself how you can manifest those qualities in yourself, in your own life.*

THE EMOTIONAL CIRCULATORY SYSTEM 2.0

When we understand the soul as part of nature, we begin to realize it is also part of the emotional circulatory system. At this point in the *Peace Within* process, I like to share a second metaphor regarding the emotional circulatory system[14] (*See Diagram 12*). If the soul is a tree, then imagine your mind as the sky, Earth as your body, the sun as awareness itself, and the ocean and all water that circulates throughout the Earth as the heart and feeling dimension of your life.

EMOTIONAL CIRCULATORY SYSTEM 2.0

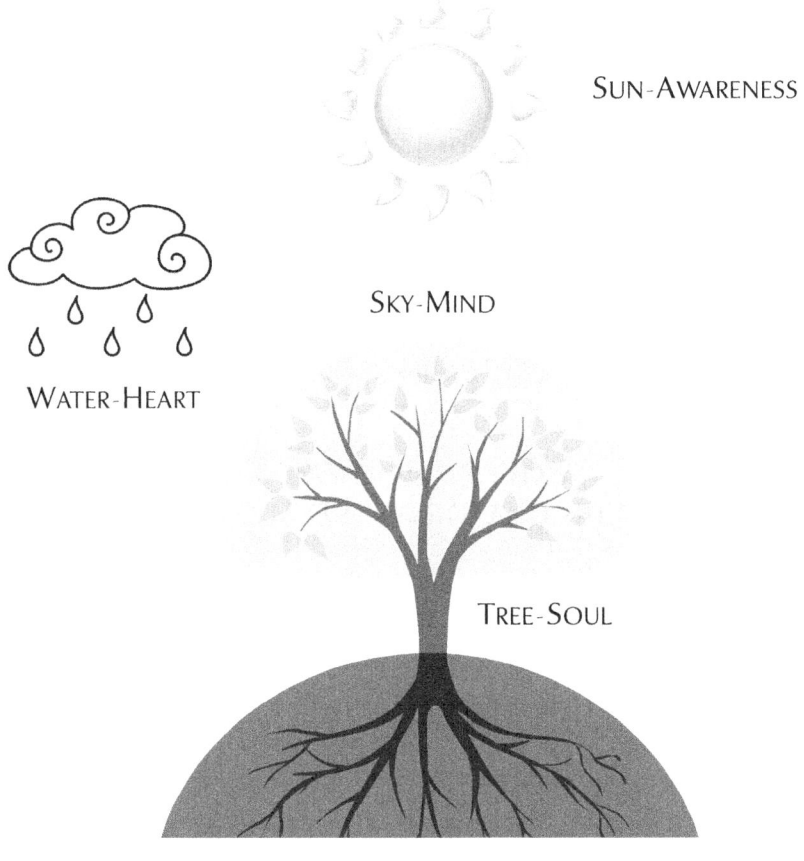

DIAGRAM 12

This diagram is a metaphor that helps us connect with the natural world, while we also begin to explore the vast universe within us.

This image makes it easy to see that awareness is not synonymous with the mind (thinking), but super-ordinate to it, for we can be aware of thinking and even explore being aware of awareness. Like the film projector of the mind metaphor of consciousness, this metaphor is another way to further your mindfulness practice and help you step back from the thoughts streaming through the mind.[15]

There is no doubt that all the practices up until now can help us manifest our soul work in the world while trying to play our social roles honorably and well, without being over identified with them. Bringing mindfulness and compassionate awareness to each moment, while properly caring for our bodies, minds and hearts are all part of helping the acorn (soul) within grow into the tree we are to be, and it will help us bear the fruit we came here to bear. When we bring care and compassion to the curiosity about what is emerging within us, amazing things can happen.

EARTH, SEA, SKY MEDITATION

Drawing on this new metaphor for the emotional circulatory system from Diagram 12 (you can also imagine the water cycle diagram from Module 5), find a place to lie down where you can be comfortable and undisturbed, such as your Peace Within space. Before lying down, do your centering breath and releasing into the now exercises (See Diagram 13). As you lie down, imagine and feel not only your body, but your soul on the Earth. Experience the points of contact between your body and the ground, feeling grounded and connected to the Earth below you, while also being aware of the top of your body and the air above you. Breathe in, imagining water being drawn up into the sky above you, then breathe out, experiencing all the sensory channels back down to the Earth while rain falls down and back to the Earth and oceans.

Breathe in, imagining water through evaporation being drawn up by the power of the warming sun of awareness from the Earth (body) and ocean (heart) up to the sky (mind). Now, breathing out, imagine this water falling down to the Earth and into the oceans again through condensation and healing rain.

What is wonderful about this practice is that it helps us begin to understand emotions to be like weather patterns, energy moving through us, instead of something to be controlled. Who can control the weather?

Just as we don't say, "I am rain" when rain is present, we can also learn to say, "Sadness is present and moving through me," instead of, "I am sad." As we learn to be present to our emotional states without either denying them or identifying with them, we can simply honor that they are part of a necessary circulation of our emotional circulatory system. In this way, waking up doesn't mean our emotions disappear; rather, emotional energy becomes manageable and workable, an essential part of being whole and human.

7: PEACE WITHIN YOUR SOUL

DIAGRAM 13

EARTH AND SKY
FULL-BODIED MEDITATION

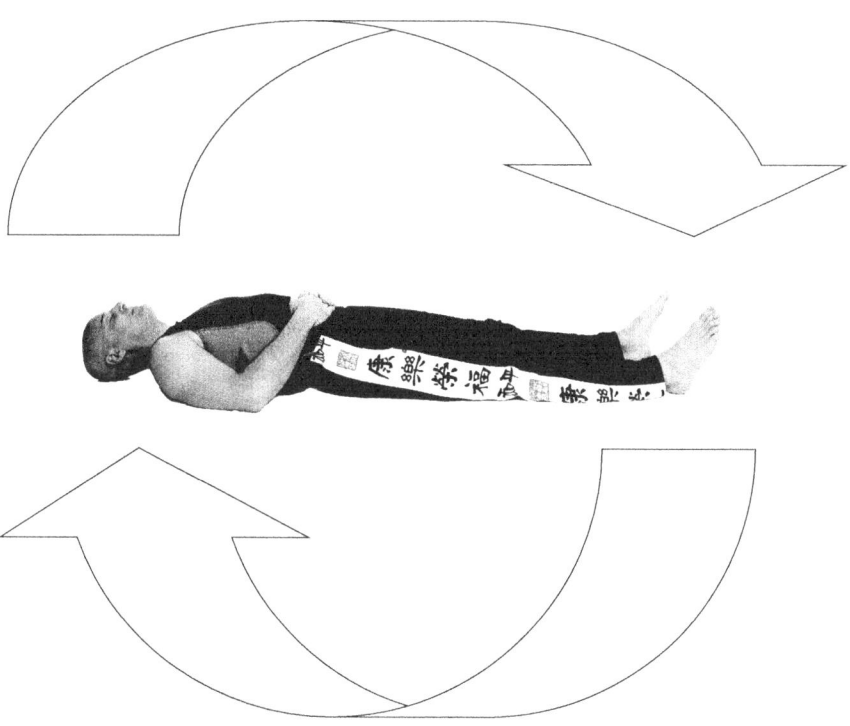

As you breathe in imagine and say 'breathing up to the sky and space' and breathing out imagine and say, 'breathing down into the earth and sea'

THE CAPTAIN (SOUL) AND FIRST MATE (EGO)

It's not a matter of doing away with the ego, we couldn't if we wanted to. Instead, it's about finding a proper relationship to it. All of our social roles (ego identities) are part of us and important to honor. The problem occurs when we reduce ourselves to nothing but the ego. The ego makes a wonderful first mate, but a terrible captain of the ship of the self. The ego can tell us 'how' to do something, such as how to maneuver through a social situation, but it can't tell us what has deep meaning to us. It can't tell us where we are going or what it is we must do. When we let the ego take control of the ship of the self, we turn into egomaniacs and end up on the rocks. The ego, always out for acceptance and approval is interested in fame and fortune for its own sake, power and control. The soul, on the other hand, seeks above all for deep and authentic connection to self, others and the world at large; genuine love, compassion, and purpose. The soul helps set our course in life, and then the ego can be a wonderful first mate to help us get there!

People fear that if they follow their souls they will hurt others by discarding their social roles altogether, like Gauguin, who left his family to paint in the South Pacific. I can't guarantee that as you become more connected to your soul there won't be changes in the roles you play, but these changes should be organic and take time.

Let's say you realize that in your heart of hearts you are meant to paint, but you have young children and a wife to support. You feel like your soul is telling you to quit your job, but you would then have no way to support your family, much less pay for art lessons. I actually found myself in a similar position.

When I realized I needed to compose music and write the stories that were in my soul, I knew I couldn't go back to life as usual. Seeing twenty-five to thirty clients a week was actually killing me, and as much as I loved the wilderness guiding I was doing, I realized that what I was actually doing was helping other people realize their soul work, but had not embraced my own: being an artist, musician and poet - not a guide. Only then did I begin to see my knee and back injuries as gifts that forced me to pause and listen to what was missing deep in my heart, what soul-loss I was suffering from.

I realized I needed to completely revamp my life. Although, I could not financially quit my work as a psychologist, I figured out exactly how much income I needed to cover my expenses and overhead. Then I decided how much I needed to work to cover that; for me, that meant seeing fifteen clients a week. However, there was another necessary adjustment. I had always wanted to stop taking insurance. It cost $25,000-30,000 a year to pay someone to collect insurance for me. I saw that if I stopped taking insurance and moved to a cash fee for service practice, I could practice without a secretary, office manager or insurance person.

I was nervous, but excited because I knew if I could cut back on my survival work, I could spend more time on my soul work (being a healer/artist, creating healing/meditation music, poetry and writing the plays I always said I would write some day). I changed my office to reflect the changes, including my office hours, building in time to workout, practice yoga, journal, and meditate every day. My Mondays and Fridays also became my composing/writing days. I was edging my life in the direction of my soul work, and when I checked in with Michelino, he was ecstatic. At the same time, I honored my social role commitments as father, husband, and psychologist. It was amazing how much energy I had for those other roles when I was making sure I was feeding my soul as well. Because I had a why (being a healer/artist), I could endure any how (my therapy practice). My suffering became meaningful, something I could endure.

During those years following the injury and storm and living at my office, I rode my bike everywhere. Sometimes, I went ten days without getting into my car. Fortunately, my office, where we continued to live, was downtown, so I could bike to the bank, post office, grocery store, and yoga studio. What had started off as the worst time of my life eventually turned into a decade of unimaginable personal/spiritual growth, inner satisfaction, and joy.

MODULE 7 – MAIN POINTS

To summarize, the main points contained in Module 7: *Peace-Within the Soul*:

1. *The soul is a child of nature, while the ego is a child of society. Learning to connect with the soul helps us put our social roles in perspective.*

2. *Since breath, heart, and soul are intimately connected, we are connecting to our soul whenever we practice deep belly breathing and compassionate awareness.*

3. *Inner child work is also a very helpful practice on the road to reawakening and reconnecting to the soul.*

4. *The soul is about connection (connected breath, connecting to nature, connecting to what brings us energy), while the ego primarily seeks social acceptance and approval.*

5. *The soul is like an acorn. No matter where it's planted, the acorn will turn into an oak tree, obeying an inner calling to become fully what it was designed to be. In the same way, our souls are related to what is most natural, instinctual and effortless for us. Souls are unconditioned and wild, nature not culture.*

6. *The soul is natural and expressive of our inner nature, nourished by the sun of awareness, the sky of the mind, the body of the Earth, and the river of feeling coursing through us. The soul is the point where all these forces are brought into relationship and harmony – balancing sky*

and Earth, masculine and feminine, life and death, joy and sorrow.

MODULE 7 – PEACE WITHIN PRACTICES

1. *The soul is present when we find a quickening of energy in our lives. Be aware of what energizes you and what drains you.*

2. *Notice and be aware of what is most natural, effortless, and instinctual for you – journal on your discoveries and reflections on this question.*

3. *Take notice of what you gravitate toward when you are left alone with nothing you have to do. This can be another soul clue!*

4. *Explore and journal on the 'discovering your soul' exercises and write down your current understanding of your 'soul work' or 'soul's purpose.'*

5. *Continue your seven-minute daily sitting meditation, working up to ten minutes if you'd like, now adding mindfulness of social roles. Notice when your thoughts become elaborate narratives about your social roles. How much time and energy is tied up with needing acceptance and approval or fearing the loss of acceptance and approval? Label these stories as, 'Thinking,' or, 'Lost in thought,' and return to breath awareness, body awareness, and full-bodied breathing. Continue doing three thirty minute guided lying down meditations a week. (You can always practice more – these are a minimum).*

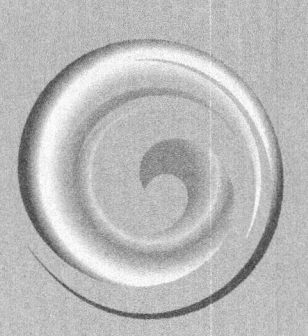

MODULE 8

This module introduces us to how to be ourselves and hold our center, while being in relationship which requires honoring the others center and truth, while not abandoning our own. These exercises remind us to be 100% responsible for our own health and wellbeing while being compassionate and accepting of others truth and needs. These practices are an antidote to our culture of co-dependency.

8: PEACE WITHIN RELATIONSHIP

The morning of my 2004 surgery, my painfully familiar anxiety and dread consumed me. Intellectually, I knew the operation was the right choice., but deep within my psyche, I had reverted to the petrified 6 year-old boy on a gurney outside the operating room, feeling abandoned and certain he would never see his family again. Yes, it was irrational from a logical standpoint, but my feelings were all too real.

I announced to my wife, whom I had put through hell with my whining and self-pity for months, that I wasn't going to the hospital. In that moment, I wasn't thinking about anyone but myself. I wasn't thinking about the doctors, nurses, and hospital staff who were prepared and had set aside time for me, nor my wife who had taken time off work to be with me. Instead, I was fully immersed in and deeply attached to the ongoing inner drama in my mind, body and heart. Once again, I was being drawn into the past, into a particular set of thoughts, beliefs, ideas, and feelings that were not only causing me to suffer, but also everyone else around me. It was not a pretty picture.

8: PEACE WITHIN RELATIONSHIP

Fortunately, my wife is a sensible, grounded, practical woman. She said firmly, in no uncertain terms, "Get in the car."

I did.

 WHILE WE ARE AT THE CENTER OF OUR UNIVERSE, SO EVERYONE ELSE IS AT THE CENTER OF THEIRS.

The greatest challenge we face as a species is the amazing truth that we are each the center of the universe, literally and symbolically. Of course, this means no one has priority over anyone else, but at the same time, no one has less priority. No one is better or worse than you. It is the ultimate democratic truth: None of us lie above or below another. Understanding and living fully in that knowledge has the ability to change and heal not only our individual relationships, but also our families, communities, nations, and even the world.

Be at peace with your inner self and you will be at peace with everybody.

~Nisargidatta

For a moment, ponder how different the world would be and how differently we would move through it if we could live this truth daily. To live from from a place in our hearts where we know we matter, and so does everyone else.

Of course, this is easier said than done. Unfortunately, human nature, which is rooted in the need for survival, often compels individuals to seek safety and protection at all costs. The ordinary

Love consists in this, that two solitudes protect and touch and greet each other.

~Rainer Maria Rilke

person tries to achieve peace of mind in a relationship by insisting their partner look, think, and behave in a certain way so he or she can feel safe and secure. Is it any wonder that things don't turn out well, and that close to 50 percent of marriages end in divorce?

Working with couples as a psychotherapist, I've identified two primary factors that torpedo relationships, often leading to divorce:

1. *Having unrealistic expectations of a relationship and partner.*
2. *Expecting a partner to be responsible for your emotional wellbeing and happiness.*

SELF AND OTHER

Love is the greatest mystery and, perhaps, the most profound miracle we know of on Earth. In Western culture, we have a poverty of language when it comes to describing the vast spectrum of loving. We use the same word to describe the love of a child, parent, friend, flower, or lover. Unfortunately, this is one of the reasons we often make a terrible mess of it.

Romantic love is sung about on the radio, written about in novels, and filmed for the big screen. The theme is well known: "I am alone in the world. I find you, my missing piece. You are the part of me I have searched for all my life. You are the one who will make everything right, who will make all my dreams come true. You're the one who will make me feel all right, the one who will make me happy and will finally bring me my long sought wholeness and inner peace."

Unfortunately, 90 percent of what people call romantic love is actually the attraction people initially feel for each other, a great deal of which can be attributed to physiology and biochemistry, basic physical attraction. This is not wrong, but it's only one stage and dimension of love in the vast world of loving.

"If you wish to experience peace, provide peace for another."

- Dalai Lama

What often creeps into the relationship is a growing lack of compassion. It is inevitable that a flesh-and-blood person, being imperfect, will ultimately fail us in one way or another. Miraculously, that is exactly when love becomes a real possibility, as well as most interesting.

We are not just bodies with omputer-like brains and skin encapsulated egos. Rather, we are each a world, with tremendous complexity, vulnerabilities, and inner and outer struggles. As Rilke, the German poet, says, *"For one human being to love another; that is perhaps the most difficult of all our tasks, the ultimate, the last test and proof, the work for which all other work is but preparation."*[1] With this great task of loving, which is so much deeper and vaster than romance, how do we develop realistic expectations of our relationships, and learn to be truly compassionate and empathic? After all, if we are two worlds, two centers, how can we meet, relate, and love without colliding?

WHEN TWO CENTERS MEET

Growing up, I loved the writings of Kahlil Gibran. My mother kept a beautiful copy of *The Prophet* in the living room by the piano; those were two of my favorite things in the world. I continue to find new meaning in his words as the years go by. When I began practicing psychotherapy, I printed a copy of his powerful words on marriage to read and give to struggling couples I counseled. I continue to believe it is the best Marriage 101 course. I'd be hard pressed to find a better description of a healthy relationship. It cuts to the core of the issue of what to do when two centers meet.

I have shared his beautiful words at weddings and on a regular basis when working with couples who are confronting the inevitable disillusionment of long-term relationships. I also regularly read it myself, to be reminded of the simple truths and challenges of all genuine and authentic relationship. I also credit it with helping me stay married to the same beautiful, thoughtful and talented woman for over thirty-four years.

Kahlil, like so many wise teachers before him, employs the power of metaphor to communicate the deep truths of healthy relationships. He first likens love to a moving sea between two shores, then to two strings of a lute, separate but playing the same music. He ends with the two most vivid and powerful images:

"Stand together, yet not too near together: For the pillars of the temple stand

apart. And the oak tree and the cypress grow not in each other's shadow."[2]

Gibran's words are poetic, but more than that, they are true. I even developed a diagram based on the wisdom of his imagery *(See Diagram 14)*. It helps couples, families, parents and children, lovers and friends find a way to meet and encounter each other with respect, love, wisdom, and compassion. I developed this while struggling with a particularly difficult marriage therapy session. I had read the passage, but it didn't resonate with the couple. As they say, a picture is worth a thousand words, so I pulled out pen and paper and created an unpretentious diagram of the final part of the poem, regarding the pillars of the temple. The picture opened the idea for the couple, and they began to heal and find a healthier way to relate to each other.

WHEN TWO CENTERS MEET

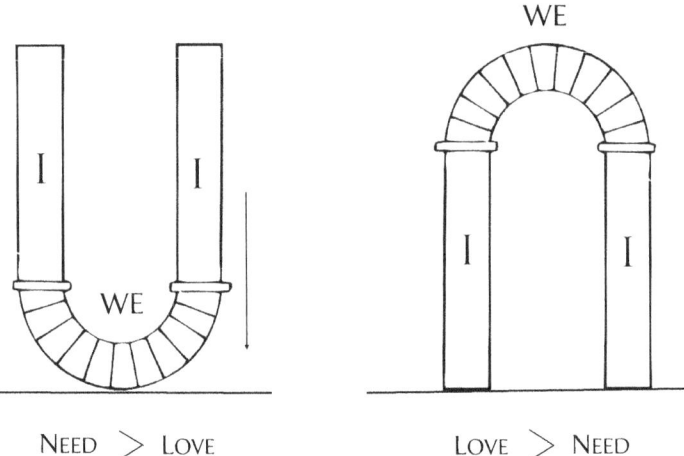

NEED > LOVE

LOVE > NEED

In a co-dependent relationship the need for the other person is greater than the love. The sense of self rests on the 'we', instead of the individuality of the 'I'. This puts great pressure on the relationship making it volatile, unstable and overly dramatic, something people often mistake for passion and love.

In a healthy relationship, the love is greater than the need. The sense of self rests on firm ground. Each person knows who they are with or without the relationship. In this way, the "we" becomes a bridge between two worlds, while not pressuring the 'we' with supporting their identities—a sense of space within togetherness—time for solitude as well as communion.

DIAGRAM 14

On the left side of the diagram is what we call a codependent relationship, where the need for the other person is greater than the love. The two I's (sense of self) in the relationship rest on the we. The relationship defines the person: "I am only who I am if I am in a relationship with this person." Focusing so intensely on the relationship puts far too much pressure on it; (the arch is holding the pillars up, instead of the pillars holding the arch up). Out of fear and dependence, the relationship becomes a place of suffocation. Two worlds become one (in an unhealthy way), thus limiting both. When you feel fused in this dependent way, you fear losing yourself if you lose the relationship. If the we falls, so does the I.

Clearly this is an ego, needs-based relationship, basically piggybacking one's sense of self onto the other person. This puts tremendous stress on the relationship and the other person to be who we need them to be. Relationships like this are extremely 'rocky' (the arch is rocking), volatile, unstable, and overly dramatic—something people often mistake for passion and love.

This is what happens when our need for the other person is greater than our love for them. The other person often has a need to be needed, another definition of codependency. Ultimately, love is not the same as need. Love should free the other person to be who they ultimately are, as opposed to imprisoning them in our expectations and dependency needs. Love is an open hand, not a grasping one. Likewise, if the other person becomes our center, we begin to live in fear of losing them and become the needy, dependent one, instead of realizing that our center always resides within us and not in another person. As Buddha says, we must strive to be our own "lamp and refuge."

On the right side of the diagram, we see a healthy relationship, where the love is greater than the need. The I's are on firm ground. Each person has a sense of self, with or without the relationship. In this way, the we becomes a bridge between two worlds, and the I's do not pressure the we with supporting their identities. Therefore, the we stands without effort or pressure. This is a healthy sense of spaciousness within togetherness, leaving time for solitude as well as communion.

The relationship becomes a bridge between two worlds instead of their base.

Here our love for the other person is greater than our need. We are then able to act unselfishly, without fear of losing the other person. It doesn't mean one will not suffer a deep sense of loss if the other leaves, but one's sense of self and existence won't be rendered meaningless and they won't feel as if they have been plunged into a pit of suicidal despair.

I find the diagram to be a very helpful way to conceptualize the difficulty we experience when our sense of self becomes dependent on a relationship. This almost inevitably happens if we don't know fully who we are. As Sam Keen says in his book, *Fire in the Belly*, there are two questions we all must ask ourselves:

1. *Where am I going?*

2. *Who will go with me?*

This is why the modules on *Peace Within the Self* and *Peace Within the Soul* come before *Peace Within a Relationship.* True *Peace Within* a relationship is predicated on you discovering your own life's calling or purpose. This helps greatly in your ability to hold your ground in a compassionate way in a relationship, to say, "Here is where I stand," while also respecting the other person's need and ability to stand his or her ground.

Conversely, the ultimate codependent phrase is: "I will die without you." This isn't love, but need based on fear from someone who does not know who he or she is without the other. Because we live in a codependent culture, almost all relationships harbor some degree of this. For our own health, and the health of our relationships, families, communities, and world, it is important that we make sure our hearts are on their own firm ground.

In our emotional development and maturity as individuals and a species, a deep intimacy within ourselves is necessary to build stronger relationships. This may be based on spirituality, religion, or a deep connection to nature or service to others.

Whatever it is you feel connected to, it will be deeper, more meaningful, and sustainable if it grows out of your own felt center. Then you actually have something real to offer a relationship. If you are merely being what the other person wants you to be out of fear of rejection, any love they show you will never reach deeply into your soul. The other person is not loving you, but an image that you project. If the soul is a tree, we must plant our souls far enough apart in a relationship so as not to crowd or impede the growth of the other. In a healthy relationship, two worlds find relationship. This is a far cry from our codependent culture, which gives us the false impression that love means simply merging or surrendering all of who you are to the other person. It is a hard lesson to learn, but this simple diagram has saved marriages by helping each partner see clearly what we call in psychology know as differentiation and individuation.

Studies show that the most successful relationships and marriages are highly differentiated. This means simply that two separate individuals have found a way to relate, despite their differences and that both are able to stay grounded in who they are while also relating to the other person and giving them the freedom to be who they are. Love, in this way, is an open hand, not handcuffs.

A codependent relationship is one in which our emotional circulatory system is so entangled with another's that we have difficulty differentiating our two worlds. We can no longer maintain a sense of peace when the other person is off balance. (Is it any wonder relationships can drive people insane?) *Diagram 14* provides a wonderful way to understand how to maintain your center while also honoring the other person's.

KEEPING YOUR WALLET

A process that can be helpful is visualizing your sense of self as a wallet. In our culture, wallets symbolize freedom, identity and power. They contain our personal identification, which is also a license to be free to drive, credit cards and money that empower us to purchase food, clothes, and things that are important to us. Wallets are a great symbol of individuality and our sense of empowerment to do and be who we are.

An intimate relationship develops when we truly share ourselves and our world with another person. This means our past wounds, and our stories as well as our dreams. Imagine, for just a moment, that each credit card and photo in your wallet represents parts of your personal story: memories, childhood, painful struggles, hopes, and dreams.

You are not in this world to live up to other people's expectations, nor should you feel the world must live up to yours.

~ Fritz Perls

In the early stages of a relationship, we get to know each other's stories and often respond to their newness and freshness with great compassion and understanding. We see beauty and courage in the other. It's a beautiful time in a relationship, but also tricky, because soon, something else begins to happen. One or both individuals may say, "Wow, you love my wallet (my memories, wounds, struggles, hopes, and dreams) so much. It seems you appreciate and understand it better than I do. Will you hold it? Will you keep it for me and take care of it for ever and ever?"

Because we are so flattered, we agree to hold their wallet and, likewise, give them our wallet as well. This is often the time when we become exclusive in a relationship, which is scary because we feel as if we are putting our hearts in another's hands. Then the trouble starts.

This type of scenario is quite common:

I arrive home after a great day at work and say to my partner, "Hi, honey. I'm home!" Unfortunately, she's in a terrible mood, as she hasn't had a good day herself. She scowls at me and barely speaks.

All of a sudden, I completely forget my own terrific day. I focus instead wondering and worrying why she's feeling down, withdrawn and angry. She may think this is because I care about her so much, but it's really because I know she's got my wallet. If she's too upset and angry, she might just trash my wallet (my sense of self), tear it into pieces, or tell me what a lousy, unlovable wallet it is, or perhaps even toss it away forever.

Suddenly, I become desperate and pushy, trying to figure out why she's upset. I no longer come from a place of compassion, but from a place of fear.[4]

Before arriving home, I was looking forward to taking a bike ride, an activity I love, but now I've lost interest. My anxiety is too great. I can't be okay if she's not okay.

Do you see the dilemma? The trap? By giving the other person your 'wallet' (your self-esteem), you have put someone else in control of your life. Your sense of self is literally in their hands!

On the other hand, if I love my partner, but I have full possession of my own wallet and she is firmly in possession of hers, the scenario unfolds quite differently:

"Hi honey. I'm home! What a great day!"

"Not for me," my partner grumbles in reply and won't even turn my way.

"I'm sorry," I say. "Do you want to talk about it?"

"No, I don't." she answers sarcastically, trying to egg me on.

"Okay, well, if you change your mind, let me know. I'm going for a bike ride. I'm exhausted, and it'll wake me up. You want to come?"

She shakes her head and leaves the room.

I respond clearly from a grounded place, from my felt center while also being compassionate, "No worries. See you when I get back. I'd be happy to talk then if you want. In fact, I'll be in a much better frame of mind to be able to give you my complete, undivided attention after I've had a chance to chill out and relax."

See the difference? This is a wonderful example of keeping your wallet, holding your felt center, while being in a healthy relationship. Being too affected by the other person's ups and downs is not healthy and makes you reactive in a negative way. Remember, emotions are like the weather, so when dealing with another person's difficult emotions it's best to take cover and wait till it passes. Put another way, don't play outside in the thunder and lightning!

TAKING BACK YOUR WALLET EXERCISE

Take some time in your Peace Within space to journal about a relationship in which you feel you need to take back your wallet. What are some ways you feel too responsible for the other person's feelings. Perhaps, you perceive that your partner is responsible for how you feel. Consider what may have led to this situation?

Can you come up with when this codependency first occurred? Review past relationships. How has this dynamic played out in the past? Is this a common tendency for you? Are you someone who tends to give other people your wallet, or do others tend to give you theirs?

The good news is these patterns develop over time. You can often backtrack and explore exactly when this shift occurred.

What are some ways you can take back your wallet in your current relationship? Is your partner someone with whom you could explain this concept? If so, pick a time when neither of you are sad, angry, hungry or tired and have a discussion about what it would mean to give your wallets back to each other; for each of you to have your 'pillar' (sense of self) on firm ground. Try using the reflective listening exercise (described below) for this purpose. Perhaps you can create a ceremony to symbolize this process. If you do, journal on the changes you feel and how it shifts your feelings about yourself and the relationship.

REFLECTIVE LISTENING EXERCISE

Reflective listening is a wonderful practice to help create healthy communication in a relationship. It simply means that when you are having a conversation with someone, before you respond, take a moment to reflect back what you heard them say. Start with the phrase, "So, what I'm hearing you say is_____." Then allow the person to validate whether or not you heard them correctly. One of my professors used to say 80 percent of communication is miscommunication. This practice helps reduce the amount of miscommunication that occurs in a relationship and maximizes understanding between partners. I do this often with couples and families, and it is always a powerful way for people to slow down the conversation and practice mindful listening.

EMOTIONAL QUICKSAND

I often hear clients say, "Okay, Dr. D., I get it, but what if someone I love is really in a bad place, like cutting himself, suicidal, or strung out on drugs? Don't I have a responsibility to jump in and rescue him? What if he will truly dies without me, and it's not just a momentary bad weather pattern? What if it's a hurricane that kills him?"

Ah, the trump card: death. It is scary when someone you love is teetering on the edge of life and death, whether through suicidal ideation, drug addiction, or some other self-destructive behavior.

In this situation, visualize the person you love in quicksand. If you try to pull him out with your own hands, you will probably get sucked in and stuck too. Has this ever occured for you? It's likely, because it's all too common. What would you do if someone was literally sinking in quicksand? You wouldn't go to the edge and stick out your hand, because the other person's weight, strength and the power of the quicksand has all the leverage. You wouldn't be strong enough to pull them out on your own.

Instead, find a rope, anchor it to something stable, fixed, and strong, like a large rock or tree. Then you throw them the rope after it is secured to something other than you.

This scenario shows several important concepts that you may have experienced. Often, people in a self-destructive cycle don't really want to be rescued. By throwing a rope attached to something stable, instead of trying to drag them out yourself, a critical piece of information will become clear.

You will be able to tell whether they are willing to help themselves. If they grab the rope, you can give them encouragement, maybe even help pull the rope. But do this only if the rope is anchored to someone else, such as a professional psychologist, or therapist.

You might notice that they refuse the rope and only want to grab your hand. Unfortunately, some people have grown accustomed to drama in their lives (quicksand). As the old saying goes, misery loves company. They may be less interested in getting out, than they are in pulling you in with them so you can wallow together in the quicksand. If a relationship is making you feel powerless, you might be unwittingly playing a role that is enabling the other person to act out an abusive, self-destructive cycle.

Alternatively, if you find yourself becoming compulsive in your efforts to save everyone in your life who is in quicksand, it could be that you are addicted to being needed. Having your own dependency needs met by being dependent on people in quicksand may be satisfying your personal addiction. Do you see the circle of chaos this can create? Often, we need to seek help for ourselves when someone we love is in such quicksand, and this is a healthy, valuable step in your own healing. It will help you develop healthy boundaries, and possibly work on healing some unresolved wounds within yourself.

No matter how much compassion we have for others, we do them no good by betraying ourselves in the process of trying to help them. Ultimately, there is only one life you can save: your own.

HEAL THYSELF

During those months of 2004, I was stuck in quicksand that, at times, threatened to do me in. I hate to admit it, but I even tried to start fights with my wife, just so I could discharge my own pain that I was unable to manage on my own. Thank God that during that time, my wife held her center simply and clearly. One day, she said, "You know, there is only one person who can help you."

I'm not sure if I was just being a smartass, or genuinely obtuse in my cycle of emotional pain and chaos when I retorted,

"Really? Who? You'll have to tell me, because I'm desperate…"

She shook her head not appreciating my dark humor at the moment. "You! It's all up to you. There is nothing else the rest of us can do."

She was right, and I knew it. I had said the same thing to my clients and students regularly. I understood it at the core of my being, yet like the diabetic, who eats the cake anyway, I had to relearn it.

I had to take full responsibility for my own health and happiness. No therapist, doctor, surgeon, family member, or friend could do it for me. Although I was greatly helped by my therapists, friends and guides – fundamentally, the deep care and healing my soul cried out for was a task only I could accomplish.

Ultimately, we each must feel the full weight of our existence on our own shoulders. Parents and spouses have a particularly difficult time with this. Too often, we believe that saving people from the consequences of their actions means we are helping them. It's often the exact opposite: It can cripple them.

We see this today in our culture, in cases of so-called affluenza. Children are indulged and aren't taught the value of hard work, which results in grandiose feelings of entitlement. A certain amount of struggle is critical to growing a sense of self. This truth is wonderfully illustrated in the story of the man who saw a butterfly struggling to release itself from its cocoon and decided to help it by cutting it free with a small pocket knife. The butterfly emerged with crippled wings, because the man did not realize that struggle was critical for releasing fluid in the butterfly's wings to help it stretch out and strengthen them. Often, in rescuing others from their pain, we are also keeping them from learning to fly.

Love isn't finding a perfect person. It's seeing an imperfect person perfectly.

~Sam Keen

Even worse, this sense of entitlement thwarts the experience of a genuine sense of self. This sense only occurs from bumping up against the world to find out where we end and others begin. In psychological terms, this necessary life stage is called separation and individuation. It is our truest journey toward our own felt center and wholeness.

THE SEARCH FOR THE MAGICAL OTHER

IT'S NOT ABOUT FINDING THE RIGHT PERSON. IT'S ABOUT BECOMING THE RIGHT PERSON.

The central theme of the *Peace Within* process is discovering and practicing a form of inner peace that is not dependent on external circumstances. This includes people. Although, fundamentally we are social creatures who require and need each other to create and make a life together, that doesn't mean there is a 'magical other' out there who will save us from ourselves, who will make us eternally happy, and complete us.[5] This fantasy is not only dangerous but also, leads to great disappointment and suffering. We do this in love, politics, and even in our search for religious and spiritual teachers.

When we stop searching for the magical other whether, a lovers, political leader, or guru we return to our own first person experience of the world. In the practice of self-compassion through awareness of self, we learn to breathe and release not only any place we are holding in our body, but also where we are holding in a relationship. Consider what expectations you're holding onto regarding the other person. What expectations of yourself are you holding onto in the relationship? Often, it is the fear of letting go of our expectations and beliefs, not only of ourselves but other people, that causes so much pain.

TWO EMPTY GLASSES

When I work with couples, I often use the metaphor that we are each born as an empty glass. When someone pays us a compliment, gives us a hug, or is affectionate or loving toward us, it is like pouring water into our glass.

On the other hand, when someone does something invalidating, mean, or hurtful, water is removed. As we grow older, the way we fill our glass is based more on achievement and accomplishment, and the way water disappears becomes more varied and numerous. Daily life stress depletes the water in our glass, as does the endless stream of tragic news stories, arguments in the workplace, your favorite sports team losing, or the stock market plummeting.

When we first meet a romantic partner, it's as if there is an endless supply of water to fill both glasses. The novelty is wonderful, heady, even addictive. However, over time, most people settle down. They may marry, buy a house, and have children. Then, all of a sudden, the person we went to for filling our glass is running on empty. Between work, raising kids, and the daily struggles in our culture, both husband and wife arrive home at the end of the day and look to the other to fill their glass. It is as if we are saying to each other, "Fill my glass! I'm thirsty!" and the wife says, "I don't have any water! You, fill mine!"

Both end up feeling frustrated, used up, and emotionally empty.

Each of us must learn a way to fill our glass that is independent of another person. This is why knowing what your soul needs is so crucial. And it's what practicing the self-care practices throughout the peace within process is all about.

A great place to start filling our own glass is through proper nutrition, exercise, and adequate sleep. However, this is just the beginning. We also need to take stress breaks, do centering

Once the realization is accepted that even between the closest human beings infinite distances continue, a wonderful living side by side can grow, if they succeed in loving the distance between them which makes it possible for each to see the other whole against the sky.

~Rainer Maria Rilke

breaths, release into the now, and practice mindfulness and meditation. These activities fill our glass and are part of caring for our souls.

Studies show that self-actualized people actually have what is called the selfish/selfless paradox. They take time to make sure their needs met, so they can then meet others' needs without resentment, frustration, or becoming depleted. This is the key to healthy, happy, and fulfilling relationships.

The paradox is that once we learn to be more at peace with our own frailty, vulnerability, and imperfections, the more we can be merciful, tolerant, and compassionate of others. Milton Erickson, the great psychologist, used to tell those he married that if they wanted a successful union, they needed to do one thing: *"Remember your failings, so you can see your partner's failings through the eyes of compassion."*[6] This also means we let go of our unrealistic, idealized expectations of ourselves, others, and the relationships and start learning to accept our humanness and that of those with whom we share our lives.

I have come to realize the root of my own suffering in 2004 was this: Like most people on a spiritual path, I was always willing to give things up for my spiritual growth, such as, food, creature comforts, and status. I'd fasted for weeks, having nothing but water. However, in 2004 I was finally forced to give up the one thing I had never contemplated giving up, my spiritual ideas and ideals. In my mind, I could not reconcile that someone who had done as much spiritual work as I had, could fall so low and fail so miserably. In that falling, it was as if God and the Universe were laughing at me. I imagined that all I had been was meaningless, little more than a cosmic joke.

I started to realize that peace wasn't something to achieve or a destination to reach; it had been there all along. I only had to give up my ideas about it to experience it. It had been my ideas about it, that kept me from it. Once I let all ideas go, I felt a vast ocean bathing me.

In the following weeks, while biking, on the elliptical at the gym, or just walking I would find my self laughing hysterically as I experienced this truth over and over again. With no ideas to keep me from it, the ocean of peace was ever available for a refreshing swim! My mind became as still as glass, my heart began to open like the sky…and my breath the sweetest part of my day. I came to understand Rumi's words in a whole new way, *"I have lived on the lip of insanity, wanting to know reasons, knocking on a door. It opens. I've been knocking from the inside."*

MODULE 8 – MAIN POINTS

To summarize, the main points contained in Module 8: *Peace within Relationships*:

1. *Although you are the center of your universe, remember that everyone else is also. Honoring your truth and the truth of others, through tolerance and compassion, is the starting point for Peace Within relationships.*

2. *Being the center of gravity of your world also means knowing who you are, speaking your truth, while deeply listening to and respecting the truth of others.*

3. *Some friction in relationships is normal and healthy; it helps you know where you end and the other begins.*

4. *An antidote to codependency and the illusion of fusion are the practices/visualizations of 'keeping your wallet' and 'the two pillars' exercises.*

5. *There is only one life you can save: yours!*

6. *Having a healthy self-interest allows you to get your needs met, so you can genuinely help others without burning out or suffering from compassion fatigue.*

MODULE 8 - PEACE WITHIN PRACTICES

1. *Practice therapeutic letter writing to deal with unresolved emotional issues in relationships.*

2. *Practice reflective listening with a partner or friend to learn how 80 percent of communication can be miscommunication – and how best to find a 'bridge' between your worlds.*

3. *Practice learning to agree to disagree with at least one person, noticing how both of you can voice your perspectives. Practice accepting that neither of your views contains the complete, whole truth.*

4. *Work on at least one relationship where you need to 'take back your wallet' and create a ceremony to do so.*

5. *Write down a list of activities that fill your glass and help you care for your soul without expecting others to make you happy.*

6. *Continue your ten-minute daily of sitting meditation, now adding mindfulness of relationship stories. Notice when your thoughts become elaborate narratives about relationship issues and struggles. Journal on what beliefs, ideas, and expectations you are attached to with your relationships and how you might feel if you could work on letting them go. Continue with at least three thirty minute guided lying down meditations a week. For one of these, begin using the lying down meditation for 'emotional healing.' (You can always practice more; these are a minimum.)*

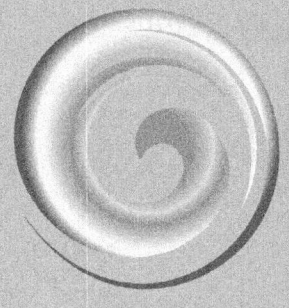

MODULE 9

This module explores our relationship with life itself. We put expectations on life as we do on a relationship. We either trust or don't trust life and often fantasize another life, or afterlife. Fundamentally, most believe peace is found not within life, but divorced from life. This module explores and challenges us to find Peace Within Life itself and how necessary it is to forgive life and find peace within the lives we are living.

9: PEACE WITHIN LIFE

John looked at me with deep, haunting eyes. "I hate my life," he said. He lowered his head in his hands and began to cry. John had just come through the most difficult four years of his life. At mid-life, he had faced a true dark night of the soul. His gut-wrenching divorce cost him his business, life savings, kids, and a dear friend. It was his second divorce, and he felt like an absolute failure: empty, with a deep sense of dread that he would never recover. He'd lost energy to go forward in his life and felt no passion for anything.

After his tears subsided he stared at the floor as if gazing inward. The room was cast in shadows, lit by a solitary candle. With the full gravity of the present moment upon him, he spoke. "I now know what it is that haunts me."

I leaned forward and listened intently, not wanting to miss a word.

"The dark cloud that hangs over me is my refusal to accept who I am and where I am right now. I've known that, but what I didn't realize until this moment is that

I don't know how to love myself, much less my life, without all the things that used to define me. I'm no longer a husband, father, or business owner. I could only love myself as a result of those things. How do I love myself now? I don't even know who I am anymore."

My religion is very simple. My religion is kindness.

~Dalai Lama

I nodded in understanding, knowing all too well how difficult it is to accept, much less love your life when it's in shambles. It's a tall order that, at times, feels completely out of reach, yet, it is often the moment that brings energy back into a shattered soul.

As his words sunk in and his eyes grew moist with feeling, he continued with a noticeable cracking in his voice, the kind that reveals that someone is in profound contact with the truth at the core of his heart, "I vow, from this day forward, to love my life with all my heart and all my strength, no matter what." The whole room shifted with those noble words.

There was a palpable presence. John's breathing slowed, and I felt the depths of the words he spoke into the night. I bore witness to a seismic shift in his ability to become healthy and whole. His words touched me personally, for they gave voice, suddenly and unexpectedly, to the riddle of my own life.

Unknown to John, I was suffering from a similar dilemma myself.

In my case, I could project my unhappiness on a thousand things: my knee, my back, Hurricane Ivan, my wife's busy work schedule as an attorney, and my daughter leaving for college. I could go even further back and project it onto my parents moving me to Florida in my teens, or my surgeries as a child that caused my chronic PTSD. I could project my unhappiness on some of my fallback favorites: society, the dismal state of the human condition, and the seemingly hopeless, dysfunctional relationship we humans have created by poisoning the eco-systems that sustain us. Yet, none of those touched the core of the problem.

Life is an adventure in forgiveness.

~Norman Cousins

All my bitter resentment, frustration, and dissatisfaction ultimately hid a deeper truth from which I was running. I had found the limits of what I had believed and had so often spoken of—the ability and even the call to love life in all of its chaos and uncertainty. Not just any life, but to love *my life*.

Loving one's life is not easy. You must learn to tend, cherish, and honor the extraordinary network of relationships that make us all of who we are. We do not exist as separate beings, but as an amazing interdependent web of endless connections that nourish us – like so many creeks, streams and rivers that eventually flow into the ocean.

Confusion often arises when we attempt to love ourselves by indulging ourselves. This is the primary reason I prefer to use the words mercy and compassion to describe what is required for a heart-centered life.

Mercy is an instructive word. It means to "refrain from harming or punishing those within one's power; kindness in excess of what may be expected or demanded by fairness." Mercy calls us to forgive and be kind. We know this in our relationship to others – but seldom practice mercy towards ourselves.

Kindness can be the root of a grounded life worth living. What does it take to truly love our lives? We need to learn and practice loving all people, all places, and ultimately, even death. It is to follow what Jesus called us to when he was asked what the greatest commandment was: *"To love thy God with all thy heart, all thy soul and all thy strength. And this is to be followed by loving your neighbor as yourself."*[1]

"If you wish to experience peace, provide peace for another."

~ Dalai Lama

Unfortunately, we often miss the inmost truth of this call: how best to love God means at the most fundamental level, completely loving the greatest gift of all, our own lives. The only way to do this properly is to *love the mysterious being living in your shoes and looking out of your eyes,: the blood coursing through your veins; the bones providing your frame; your precious organs, eyes, and ears; and even your broken, mistake-ridden life.*

Loving life is not an intellectual affair. The idea of love is not the felt experience, nor the activity of loving. The intellectual idea of love does not heal anything. This is a serious problem in a world where words are cheap. We use the word love so much, it fails to mean anything.

> *Within you there is a stillness and a sanctuary to which you can retreat at any time and be yourself.*
>
> *-Hermann Hesse*

Loving our lives is a daily, moment-to-moment practice of being heart-centered as we move through the world. It is not in spite of our struggles but, through them that our hearts are opened and we begin to embrace the compassion that has been trying to break open within us our whole lives. It is to become a *heart warrior*.[2] It requires the heart of a warrior to embrace and love our own lives and the ones of those around us.

We have spent a great deal of time practicing stepping back from our thoughts and feelings, not denying them or controlling them, but actually stepping back from them in a kind of listening. We have worked on dis-identifying from the inauthentic (conditioned) stories we tell ourselves. Borrowed stories about who we are, which are really nothing more than cultural, social, and familial filters on reality. When we move from ego to soul, we are begin to listen and learn about the authentic story living within us.

This is being a heart warrior: learning to trust and listen to the deepest part of our unique story, to the true grief we can call our own. We practice mindfulness and meditation not to detach from our lives, but to find the authentic story lying at the core of each of our hearts. This is the soul, the existential corrective to so much of the misinterpretation of well-meaning new age and Eastern and Western teachers. If our meditation practice has no heart and, does not help us become better husbands, wives, fathers, and brothers, it isn't authentic and is only being used as an escape from life, instead of helping us enter the stream of living more fully and completely.

Carl Rogers, the influential psychologist, once said, "When a person realizes he has been deeply heard, his eyes moisten. I think, in some real sense, he is weeping for joy. It is as though he were saying, 'Thank God, somebody heard me. Someone knows what it's like to be me.'"[3] I like to call this 'deep listening.'

DEEP LISTENING

Everything we have been practicing up until now could be considered a form of deep listening. We have learned to listen to our bodies, thoughts, and feelings. As you practice this form of deep listening, it will help you be more skillful in listening to others, particularly those you love and, ultimately, to life itself.

What is most personal is most universal.

~ Carl R. Rogers

Seeing is our dominant sense for us humans. Perhaps, that is why we are always looking for something, seeking something. Listening, on the other hand, is deeply receptive and open. Listening slows the world. Sound waves travel very slowly, while light travels extremely fast. For me, deep listening helps slow my brain while opening the beautifully receptive organ of the heart. Listening provides access to the ocean of peace much more readily. I learned this at a very very young.

As I have mentioned previously, after my childhood abdominal surgery, when feeling disconnected and emotionally overwhelmed,

I soothed myself by sitting at the family piano, deeply listening to how a single note arose and dissolved back into silence. I use to believe it was the sound that was healing. I have come to know the real healing came from the silence following the sound. The silence simply became more present through toning one note at a time on the piano. I adored how the sound deepened the quality of the silence.

In my explorations as a psychologist and sound healer over the last three decades, I have found this was not unique to me but true for many others. Hearing begins in the womb and is the last sense to depart as we are dying. There is a great deal we can learn about quieting the mind and opening the heart through deep listening. As we have seen, when we allow the flow of sensations, thoughts, and feelings to move through us (like sound waves flowing through air), the emotional circulatory system flows in a healthy way, establishing a natural balance (emotional homeostasis). Tuning into the sense of hearing automatically puts us in touch with sound waves; this is flow. Noticing sounds in a room immediately begins to bring you into the here and now. It reminds you of the fluidity of experience and can relax and quiet the mind.

Can we listen deeply enough to find our own inner music? Often it starts out as a terrible cacophony of competing thoughts, feelings, and sensations. Slowly, through the practice of compassionate awareness and deep breathing, these can unite into alignment and harmony, as if they all begin to play the same song in the same key.

I often imagine each of my clients and students having an inner music all of their own, the song of their soul that is seeking expression, when I practice listening to them in a deep way. Often, through cultural conditioning and negative self-talk, the natural inner beauty of their souls has become tangled in a mess of competing inner thoughts, judgments, and negative self-talk. However, simply by letting all of these thoughts, feelings, and sensations flow, a natural arrangement and order begins to emerge out of the chaos.

IN THE FLOW

To this day, particularly when playing the flute, I have chills travel up and down my spine when I finish a note and hear it dissipate into silence. This is a major reason why music remains such a central part of my life. Music not only moves in waves like water, but also has the ability to cleanse and heal like water. Healing music has a powerful effect on the emotional circulatory system, by allowing feelings, thoughts, and sensations to flow more freely, even having the capacity to quiet the mind and open the heart.

I have always loved how water possesses its own sound and is musical at its core. The sound of rivers, waterfalls, or the gentle surf at the beach have a unique ability to soothe the human heart.

Emotions, water, and music all move in waves. They all shift and change, having the unique capacity to express the subtle qualities and exquisite ever changing landscape of human life. Oceans can appear angry, serene, or playful. Music and emotions each possess a feeling tone, and they are ever fluid, changing, and always flowing. This is also one of the reasons so much of my own music is inspired by and expressive of water (for example, my albums, *The River, Ocean, In The Flow*).

Music is the ultimate fluid art. Like the dimension of feelings, it is unseen, yet reveals to us the invisible relationships that lie within our hearts. Music, water, and feelings flow, and when we drop into the flow, healing happens. In this way, music can be a powerful accompaniment to fostering *Peace Within*. Music helps us remember and reconnect to our innate wholeness, soundness, and wellness.

After music brought me back to life during my low point in 2004, I made a commitment to myself to create time to really focus on it and my writing. Even the simple act of making that commitment made me feel better. Although I had lost several of my favorite flutes in the storm, I was able to salvage some of my recording equipment. I also knew a few flute makers who were kind enough to give me a special price on a number of flutes to try to help me rebuild my collection.[4] I asked Geoffrey Ellis, one of my favorite flute makers from northern California, to make a special flute for me.

9: PEACE WITHIN LIFE

 HEALING MUSIC FOSTERS 1) EXPERIENCING FLOW 2) BEING PRESENT IN THE NOW 3) QUIETING THE MIND AND OPENING THE HEART AND 4) ENERGY FLOW THROUGHOUT THE EMOTIONAL CIRCULATORY SYSTEM.

During this period of exploring the ocean of peace, and trying to heal my relationship with the Gulf of Mexico, I began having dreams of swimming with dolphins and whales. In one dream, in particular, I heard the most amazing music. Upon awakening I knew, more than anything, I wanted to find a way to create those sounds and gift this healing music to others. Geoffrey made me a beautiful low-E flute that became the centerpiece of my album *Ocean*, which I spent the next four years composing.

One particular evening, I took the flute out on the pure white beach that had been devastated by Hurricane Ivan. The full moon was out, shimmering over the water. The ocean, which I loved, until it had turned into a raging torrent that devastated my life in one short night, had now become so peaceful, quiet, inviting, and alluring. It was like two lovers making up after a terrible fight. I began playing my flute, and my "Moonlit Sea" was born. It continues to be a personal favorite healing song of mine.

I did not have the best recording equipment set up in the back of my therapy office, where my family was also living, but I poured my heart and soul into the album. I listened to it over and over, for my own healing and in an attempt to accurately capture and express all I had gone through. Throughout the album, I tried to impart that feeling of floating in the ocean of peace that I had grown to experience, an ocean as deep as it was vast, comforting, and endless.

The title track, "Ocean," was eventually included on Eckhart Tolle's album, *Music for Inner Stillness*.[5] I had worried that the music might be too personal, ambient, or perhaps even too dark for wide commercial appeal. To my surprise, it struck a chord with many others. It not only debuted at number one on the New Age Music Chart, but it also stayed there for three months and went on to be nominated for a Grammy® award later that year. It remains my bestselling album to this day. Since *Ocean* became my own ode to healing from Hurricane Ivan, I was overjoyed that it spoke to and provided similar healing to others.

DEEP LISTENING EXERCISE

This exercise expands the notion of listening to encompass all of your experience. Deep listening refers to listening to experience itself with compassionate awareness: hearing the unfolding of all thoughts, feelings, sensations, images, self-talk, and beliefs. To do this, you should allow yourself to be attentive, receptive, to what arises in your awareness without judgment. Listening, in this way, can be seen as a metaphor for mindfulness itself, as we cultivate compassionate awareness in all we do.

Read through the following exercise first before you try it for yourself. Even better, read it aloud and record it, then listen again as you do the exercise. You may be surprised at the immediate and profound effect it has on you.

1. *Find a comfortable place to lie or sit. Begin once again with three cleansing belly breaths as you bring yourself into the here and now. Then close your eyes and simply listen to the sounds in the room you are in. What do you hear? Do you hear thunder in the distance, the steady humming of the air conditioning, or the barely, imperceptible sound of the refrigerator in the other room, maybe even the steady trickling of a water fountain? Simply listen.*

2. *Notice how there is nothing you have to do in order to listen; it is the most natural and delicious of senses, because it demands so little. Simply closing your eyes immediately reduces stress on your bodily systems and reduces brain activity by one to two thirds, as if downshifting the mind to a slower pace and more peaceful rhythm.*

3. *Notice how some sounds come and go and others remain constant. Without judging any sounds, simply allow them to arise and dissolve or continue. Try to hear the furthest sound, perhaps a car or plane in the distance. Now, try to hear the closest sound. Can you hear any sounds inside your body? As you listen more deeply, can you hear the sound of silence? What is the sound below the sounds in the room? This takes some practice. Be patient with yourself.*

4. *Next, allow your attention to be free to experience all the sounds simultaneously without trying to focus on any single one. Enjoy*

the effortlessness of hearing. If your mind wanders, gently bring it back to listening. You may also bring awareness to the sense of touch; notice the points of contact between your body and the chair you're sitting on, or the couch or bed you're lying on. Really notice the feeling of pressure – the sensations that move, flow, and swirl through your body.

Now bring your attention back to simple hearing for a while, then back to touch, then hearing and back again. Take a deep, cleansing breath as you slowly open your eyes, feeling more serene, relaxed, and peaceful.

THE HARDENED HEART

My client John came to realize that a hardened heart was what preventing him from loving his life. We talk a great deal about hardening of the arteries, but we seldom talk about hardening of the heart, which comes from our slow withdrawal from life, coupled with avoiding feeling deeply. A hardened heart comes from a loss of the water of life (our emotions and feelings). Our lives become dry as dust, an emotional desert.

A hardened heart occurs when the emotional circulatory system ceases to flow. When we opt not to feel pain, we also shut down the entire emotional circulatory system and are unable to experience joy or empathy. This also prevents us from being able to connect to others and life itself. Empathy not only allows us to connect with the feelings of other people, but also to be one with the natural world. It helps us realize we are part of life and that it is constantly moving through our veins, arteries, and nervous system. In fact, the branching of our own circulatory system is a beautiful fractal of the branching phenomena of trees and rivers. This is one of the powers of nature-based meditation and mindfulness practices contained in these modules. They help you experience yourself as a full member of the natural world, which is essential to belonging to your body, to the Earth, and to your life. We are all native Earthlings!

Let us forgive each other only then will we live in peace.

~ Leo Tolstoy

The feeling dimension is the language of the heart. To stay connected to this dimension, we need to stay present in the moment and stay open, which means being vulnerable. It means not defending ourselves against the world's inevitable failure and disappointment, but opening ourselves to whatever arises in each moment.

The heart is the organ of connection, what genuinely connects us to others and to life in general. When we cut ourselves off at the heart level, the meaning in our lives suffers. We are shut out of the vital center of our lives that confers meaning, value, presence, and purpose to our existence.

Carl Rogers once said, "When I have been listened to and when I have been heard, I am able to re-perceive my world in a new way and to go on."[6]

FORGIVENESS

The curious paradox is that when I accept myself just as I am, then I can change.

~Carl Rogers

The difficult work John had to face was forgiveness: first toward himself, second toward his ex-wife, then toward the many others he felt had wounded and wronged him.

The healing power of forgiveness is at the heart of the *Peace Within* process. Forgiveness is literally the act of making *Peace Within* and without. It does not mean condoning, excusing, minimizing, forgetting, or even reconciliation, which is rebuilding a relationship. Forgiveness is, most purely, making peace with the past so we can rest in the present.

Virtually everyone intuitively understands the importance and power of forgiveness. In 1988 the Gallup Organization conducted a large scale poll. A whopping 94 percent of those polled said it is important to forgive; however, just as startling, 85 percent of those people said they need some form of outside help to help them forgive.[7] I find this just as true in my thirty-year practice. Most everyone who comes to see me is struggling with forgiveness, either with themselves, with someone else, or with life.

Research has also revealed that people who forgive are happier, healthier, and more optimistic, with improved functioning in their cardiovascular and nervous systems. They also suffer fewer illnesses overall.[8]

Studies have also shown that forgiveness can be learned. Those who forgive experience less anger and hurt, as well as higher levels of compassion, self-confidence, and optimism. In addition, those who master the art of forgiving, suffer less stress and gain increased vitality.[9]

So, how do we learn to forgive?

Remember Madeline in Module 5? Her only way out of her private hell was through a therapeutic letter. The emotional circulatory system teaches us this essential truth: to let go of feelings, we must first acknowledge them. This is the great paradox of emotion. It's the reason we struggle so deeply with our feelings.

Forgiveness is the final form of love.

~Reinhold Niebuhr

To paraphrase psychologist Alice Miller, forgiveness is like the sun. No one needs to tell it to shine, it just does. Yet, it's a mistake to say it's shining when it's not. To be authentic, is to honor the clouds, thunderstorms, and hurricanes of our emotional lives so we can allow the sun to break through of its own accord and in its own time.

Many of us repress our feelings because of shame and the guilt that often lurks in the depths of our emotional pain: the anger, hate, murderous rage, frustration, resentment, fear, and terror we feel. We forget that these emotions are woven into the human condition, the result of millions of years of evolutionary survival and development. We cannot erase them, but we can learn to maneuver through them more effectively, gracefully, and skillfully.

As we saw in Module 5 with Madeline, it is important that we honor feelings and express them in order to let them go. I did a similar exercise with John. I told him to write a therapeutic letter to his ex-wife. It was an uncensored, unedited letter he wouldn't actually send to her, one in which he could 'let it all hang out,' without fear. It was tremendously liberating for him, particularly when he brought it in and read it to me.

Once he siphoned off much of his toxic anger, hate, and rage, John wrote a second letter to her. It helped him move toward forgiveness. I encouraged John to continue writing letters until the sun shone for him again. His initial attempts were like thunderstorms moving through his heart. The more he wrote about the clouds, acknowledging his anger, hate, and rage, the more they began to dissipate, and the light of forgiveness began to break through.

The remarkable and beautiful thing about our emotional life is that as soon as we acknowledge our emotions, they begin to shift and change. When we don't acknowledge them or, even more damaging, when we deny and repress them, they have the power to destroy us from the inside-out through disease, emotional pain, constriction, and silent suffering. I find yet another helpful metaphor in nature for this: Repression is like turning the water of emotion into ice, and it can give us emotional frost bite. Frostbite occurs when the blood in our veins literally freezes and begins bursting and destroying our fragile cells and body tissue. This happens to us emotionally, when we deny and repress our feelings.

If we imagine compassionate awareness being like the sun, just giving emotions loving, non-judgmental attention, allows them to flow through us and keep circulating. As soon as this happens, they are released and can begin to move, change, and transform, just as a river does as it moves through different terrain.

FORGIVENESS EXERCISE

This exercise is adapted from Jack Canfield's *Total Truth Process*.[10] It has been my favorite exercise to work through particularly difficult emotional entanglements that prevent people from forgiving and moving on. If you have difficulty with the therapeutic letter, you may want to try this more comprehensive forgiveness exercise.

To fully process an emotion, we have to get at what is blocking our emotional circulatory system. This is usually the result of repressed feelings that have turned into hardened attitudes, beliefs that are not only self-limiting, but also life-limiting. They literally get in the way of our being open and receptive to the natural flow of feeling (life energy) moving through us, others, and the world around us. This is another way to help move us from ego to soul.

The reason this practice is so powerful is that it moves us through five stages of emotional processing that can sometimes take months of therapy. The five stages are: *1) Anger, 2) Hurt and Fear,*

3) Remorse and Regret, 4) Clarification, and 5) Forgiveness.

As you can see, we need to honor the rain, thunder, lightning and stormy weather first; otherwise, it will be what I call 'cheap forgiveness' and won't have any lasting effects in freeing up energy and healing past wounds. However, when we honor these emotions, we can actually experience the cathartic effects of doing so, while welcoming renewed energy, healing, and light into our lives and relationships.

Get a piece of paper and start with just one person you feel a need to forgive. As in previous exercises, find a quiet spot where you won't be disturbed, like your Peace Within space. Relax, doing the centering breath and releasing into the now exercises. Begin simply with filling in the name of the person next to "Dear_____,"

In the stream-of-consciousness way I have encouraged, respond to each question as unedited and uncensored as possible. Start by identifying, owning, and expressing everything you feel. This is a stage when you let feelings flow. Keep writing until you can't write any more. Then set aside the writing for at least a day before looking at it again.

If you get stuck on particular sections or need more room, take a break, get some extra paper and keep going. Try not to go onto the next section until you're finished with the first one. The sections are like excavating our emotional life. Under anger is hurt and fear. Once we acknowledge that, we can get to the grief that can help us clarify what we really want or need and move forward. If you get stuck or something doesn't come to you, don't worry; not all relationships will involve all these particular feelings. Also, moving toward reparation and reconciliation is not possible for some people, for example, if the person has died or is dangerous. In these cases, just leave anything blank that doesn't apply, but make sure it doesn't apply for a solid reason and not just that you are avoiding an emotion that is difficult for you.

When you're done, take some time to journal about how you felt prior to doing this forgiveness exercise and how you feel afterward. Notice how your feelings may have begun to shift and change. Often, I ask people to perform a ceremony of some sort to honor the letting go process and the act of forgiveness that can come from this exercise:

Dear_____,

1. Anger

Write, in a free-form way, about anything you are feeling angry, fed up, or resentful about, even if you are feeling hate or rage. Anger is what we call a third-order emotion and is usually a defense against underlying fear or hurt. However, we have to start with anger to reach what is underneath it. You might begin with, "I'm so angry with you because…" The key here is not to censor, but to get at the heart of what makes you angry about this person or situation.

2. Hurt and Fear

Do a free-writing exercise concerning what you are hurting about regarding this person or situation. You might start off with, "I really feel hurt that…", or, "I really feel pain when…." Hurt also involves a sense of sadness or disappointment. If you feel hurt is too strong a word, explore what has led to you feeling sadness or disappointment in the relationship or situation.

An equally powerful, difficult emotion that can stand in the way of forgiveness is fear. As I've mentioned, fear also lurks beneath anger, which is often an attempt to regain a sense of power and control in the face of feeling vulnerable and scared. A couple trigger sentences that might help you get going are, "I feel vulnerable when…", or, "My greatest fear with you is…" Keep writing until you have nothing left to say.

3. Remorse and Regret

Another obstacle that can stand in the way of forgiveness is our own remorse and regret. We might be projecting our anger on the other person, when we are actually feeling bad about something we have done ourselves. I often see parents who take their anger out on their children when they feel powerless and ineffective. Identifying what we feel, whether it is regret, remorse, guilt, or even shame, can often defuse our anger toward the other person, and pave the way to a deeper understanding and forgiveness for the other and, ultimately, ourselves. Some sentences may begin with, "I am sorry that…", "I apologize for…", "I regret…", etc.

4. Clarification

Sometimes we are simply unclear about what we do or don't want in a relationship, and not knowing can keep us distant and result in avoiding dealing with some of the stickier aspects of that relationship. Clarifying our desires in a relationship can help us find healing by letting go of unrealistic expectations of ourselves and others. A helpful writing prompt might be, "All I ever wanted was…" This may also be a place where you come to realize what you may need from them or yourself as part of reparation to move toward forgiveness. In the twelve-step model, this is known as making amends.

*I'm not perfect…
But I'm enough.*

~Carl Rogers

5. Forgiveness

Finally, we move to the goal of the entire writing exercise: the healing power of forgiveness. Forgiveness opens the way to compassion, appreciation, and, in some cases, even love. Fundamentally, it is a deep way of making peace with ourselves, the situations we find ourselves in, and those we share our lives with. Try beginning with, "I forgive you for…" or, "I forgive myself for…"

FORGIVING ONESELF

Forgiving oneself can be challenging. There are those who believe self-hate is at the root of all mental and emotional disorders.

I sometimes ask people to write a stream of consciousness, uncensored letter, berating themselves so they can see how unmerciful and even hateful they are toward themselves. When they are able to do this, they often catch a glimpse of the tyranny of shoulds, oughts, and musts under which they live. Then I have them personify their inner critic into an image that they can work with and make peace with. It is a powerful practice!

However, for others, there is a simpler way to gain forgiveness from someone, especially when you are unable to connect with that person for a variety of reasons. First, you write a letter of apology to this person, explaining yourself and the reason you acted as you did. Then, you write a letter from that person, reversing the process and offering yourself forgiveness.

If you are unable to contact the person, and it will not cause further harm to you or them, you can make amends in person. This is one of the cornerstones of the twelve-step program (Steps 4 and 5), in which people create a "fearless moral inventory" of their lives, then seek to make amends whenever it is wise and safe to do so. This is a powerful practice that I highly recommend, one that lightens the heavy emotional burden so many of us carry on their shoulders.

FROM SHAME TO REGRET

As we explore the beliefs and stories that keep us from experiencing *Peace Within* through our meditation, mindfulness, and journaling practice, many people encounter that most dreaded of inward emotions: shame.

We feel guilty when we have *done* something regrettable. We feel shame when we feel bad about who we are as a person.[11] We feel something is fundamentally wrong, bad, or evil about us. Shame is toxic because it links us with our behavior so completely that we feel diminished.

When I work with someone who is experiencing shame, I give them the mantra: *"No mistakes, only lessons."* This is very therapeutic. To know you can make a mistake without *being* a mistake can help begin the process. When we look at our past experiences as opportunities for growth and learning, we can even see the most shattering experiences as lessons, painful and difficult, but lessons nonetheless.

I find people are able to forgive themselves and others when they can phrase it in terms of being skillful or unskillful. For example: "I am so sorry. I handled that very unskillfully." In this way, we acknowledge our error without descending into shame. In fact, the original meaning of the word *sin* in both Hebrew and Greek is to *miss the mark*,[12] a reminder that we are all practicing to become better versions of ourselves. We would all be better served to replace the outdated and inaccurate word bad with unskillful. Many clients and students have told me over the years that making that one substitution in their vocabulary has made profound changes in their lives and families.

FROM HARD HEART TO WHOLE HEART

Brene' Brown, the gifted research professor and author of the number one bestsellers *The Gifts of Imperfection* and *Daring Greatly*, has hit a strong chord in our national psyche with her research on shame and wholeheartedness.[13]

To forgive is the highest, most beautiful form of love. In return, you will receive untold peace and happiness.

~Robert Muller

According to Brown, shame is the painful feeling tied to feelings and beliefs that we are fundamentally flawed and, therefore, unworthy of love and belonging. Research shows that shame and blame are connected, because blame is actually a way to discharge pain and discomfort.

Shame is a trance of unworthiness in which we become trapped. It leads to isolation that thrives on secrecy and not sharing how we really feel, what Brown calls, 'shame stories.' The paradox is that the very thing that shame is keeping us from, genuine, authentic connection, is what heals it, allowing us to be really seen. What does being seen mean? Being vulnerable and, sharing all of who we are, not our ideal selves, but our mistake-ridden, imperfect, broken selves. This is the practice of moving from ego to soul, from ideal self to real/authentic self.

Brown calls this being 'wholehearted' – feeling worthy of love, connection, and belonging. The way we get there is through courage, which derives from the Latin *cor*, meaning "heart." In its original meaning, Brown shares in her popular TEDTalk, it meant, "to tell the story of who you are with your whole heart."[14]

 THE GREATEST GIFT YOU CAN GIVE YOURSELF, YOUR CHILDREN, LOVED ONE'S AND THE WORLD, IS THE COURAGE TO BE IMPERFECT

VULNERABILITY AND SHAME

By sharing our brokenness and imperfection, our wounds and warts, we experience vulnerability, but it is that very vulnerability that leads to connection. For me, this is becoming heart-centered which is the opening and doorway to the soul. It is the ability to cultivate compassion and kindness toward self and other. Acceptance and approval based on pretending to be anything other than we are does not nourish the heart and soul; it only flatters the ego. Since it is based on a social status definition of belonging and is primarily cognitive, it leads to an inauthentic belonging based on social roles alone, not on heartfelt experience. Conversely, being loved for who we are in our rawness and vulnerability leads the way toward genuine compassion and love for the imperfect real self, our common humanity.

Basically, perfection isn't human. We can all relate to imperfection.

For Brown, vulnerability is at the core of shame and fear, and the struggle for worthiness, but it is also the birthplace of joy, creativity, genuine belonging, and love. Imperfection is also tied to the ability to tolerate uncertainty. As she says, to allow ourselves to be deeply seen in our essential naked vulnerability, is to learn to love and be loved with our whole hearts. It also wakes us to being alive. Finally, as she beautifully points out, until we feel deeply enough, it is hard for us to truly stop and listen to others with our hearts. It is then that we learn to be kinder and gentler to ourselves and those around us, with whom we share our lives.

PLEASE BE PATIENT WITH ME; GOD ISN'T FINISHED WITH ME YET

My client, John, had made great progress over the months I'd been seeing him, and had begun to learn to love his life.

On one of our visits, I said to him, "I'm really proud of you. I know this has been so difficult, but there is much to love about you. You are a generous man and a kind soul. You've been dealt some difficult cards these last few years, but you know what? You're getting there. You are so much more genuine, real, aware, and awake than when you first came here two years ago."

"Yes," he said, "Still, I should have…." Before he finished, I interrupted him by handing him a plaque my mother kept in our house when I was a child. I loved the plaque, and it had helped me be more merciful with my parents, brothers, and myself when one of us let another down. It read: *"Please be patient with me. God isn't finished with me yet."*

"Here. I want you to hang out with this for awhile. I want you to eventually make a copy of the words and place them on your refrigerator, by your bed, and by your computer, and recite them whenever you see it."

He broke into a big smile, which I hadn't seen in a long time, and nodded. "Ok, I think I can do that."

FORGIVING LIFE

Among other advances, John had made amends with many people in his life, including his ex-wife. He began arriving at my office for his sessions without the world weighing so heavily on his shoulders. He smiled more, and the amount of anger toward himself and others diminished considerably. His eyes and skin glowed.

"John, you know, you really have a terrific smile," I told him. "When you smile, other people feel good. It's a gift you can give them."

"I've been noticing that when I smile, more people do smile back," he said. "It's a nice feeling and doesn't cost a thing."

John was now ready for a ritual or ceremony of loving life. We discussed something he could do to honor his life and express his gratitude for the gift of it. Often, when we begin to forgive others and ourselves, a form of grace descends upon us, and we begin to feel more grateful for the many gifts we receive each day. Many of these, as John noted, are free.

John's ritual was straightforward and simple, yet it spawned powerful, positive effects in his life. He took a few moments every morning upon waking to get on his knees by his bed, something he remembered doing as a child. With his head down and hands together in prayer, he said the following, "Thank you for eyes to see, ears to hear, air to breathe, and a day to grow into."

He followed that with specifics of his own life, naming at least three other things he was grateful for every morning. Some days, it was as simple as being grateful for having food in the fridge, clean water to drink, and a roof over his head. He said that daily ritual was the best natural antidepressant he had tried, and he didn't suffer any negative side effects from it!

It is not unusual for people to forgive others and themselves while still holding a grudge against God or, for the less spiritually minded, life itself. Just as we saw how letting go of unrealistic expectations of a partner can help us find *Peace Within* a relationship, letting go of unrealistic expectations of life, can help us find *Peace Within* life. In this way, forgiveness is no longer merely an occasional act; rather, it is a ongoing stance we continually cultivate toward life.[15]

EXPECT NOTHING, BE READY FOR ANYTHING

John's ceremony acknowledged his peace and gratitude without diminishing the reality of anyone else or their suffering. Because it came from his felt center, the results were positive and long lasting.

My happiness grows in direct proportions to my acceptance, and in inverse proportion to my expectations.

~Michael J. Fox

Finding our *felt center* is an experiential truth and reality; however, it does not mean the world revolves around our needs and concerns. Our perspective is as important as the perspective of others, but it doesn't make it more important. The school of life is all about letting go of unrealistic expectations so we can be with life in an open, compassionate, and even playful way. It is about realizing that all expectations are created out of beliefs, which emerged out of thoughts; none have any ultimate reality. As our minds quiet, our hearts have a chance to open.

Richard Lazarus was one of the early pioneers who explored the rich world of human emotions. His key insight, born out of studies, was how our expectations (and what he called *appraisal*) of a situation greatly affects our emotional state afterward.[16] In particular, he found that you cannot predict a person's happiness based on their external circumstances. This is what we have been discussing all along, that peace itself can't be dependent on external circumstances. A powerful example is Robin Williams' tragic suicide. Most believed he had it all: fame, fortune, and love from all the world. Still, for whatever reason, Robin was tortured within, and was unable to access his own inner ocean of peace.

Lazarus's work suggests that people who live with a great deal of hardship and deprivation make positive assessments of their well-being, while those who are objectively well off often make a negative assessment of their wellbeing. He found this paradox over and over again, and I'm sure you can think of plenty of examples in your own life, among your family and friends. Lazarus made sense of this paradox by realizing that people's assessment of their level of wellbeing always relates to their expectations of what their life should be.[17]

Marketing research has also indicated that people who have lower expectations of a product report being happier with their purchase. This has often been cited to reveal how our expectations and happiness are *inversely* related, as in the equation below, where happiness is determined by reality divided by (or minus) expectations.

Given this understanding, the more expectations of life you have, the more unhappy you will be (less *Peace Within*). Conversely, the fewer expectations of life you have, the happier you will be (more *Peace Within*).

> *To forgive is to set a prisoner free and discover that the prisoner was you.*
>
> ~Louis B. Smedes

$$\textit{Happiness = Reality - Expectations}$$

Does this mean you shouldn't have dreams, visions, and goals? Not at all! In fact, if you get this next subtle point, you will see that letting go of expectations can help you reach your dreams, visions, and goals more effectively than ever before.

Expectation is tied to belief in outcome. It's a mindset, a filter through which we are perceive what is about to happen, or will happen at some point in the future, based on past experience. Expectation has developed to help us deal with the radical uncertainty of human life. It actually becomes a subconscious process, developed over years of interacting with the world. Like the ego, it helps us maneuver our social landscape.

I act without expectation of success or fear of failure.

~Gandhi

However, this also reinforces that we should shy away and avoid many new experiences or challenges because we expect (fear) failure. It keeps us doing the same old things (habits) because doing them feels comfortable and familiar, and we expect them to lead to feelings of being okay. In fact, this is also what creates addiction. We repeatedly return to the drug, alcohol, video game, or sugar because we expect it to make us feel good. Addictions lose their hold on us when we stop believing their false promises. Mindfulness is a powerful tool for seeing through the false promises of expectation, seeing it as nothing more than a insidious behavior of the mind, with no fundamental reality of its own.

When we are acting out of being fully in the moment, realizing life is an ever-flowing stream of new possibilities, challenges, and beauty, then we can allow ourselves to be more comfortable with uncertainty. Expectation is based on helping us feel secure and certain, which has its place, but more often than not, robs us of the ability to remain awake and aware, being present as opposed to simply being on autopilot.

Visualizing a positive outcome is wonderful. However, you must relinquish your attachment to the outcome. If it happens, great; if not, accept it as a valuable learning experience and try again. Henry Ford said, "Failure is simply the opportunity to begin again, this time more intelligently."

Expectations keep us focused on trying to control, predict, and anticipate the future, which ultimately keeps us from being centered in the present moment. By leading us to focus on future, expectations can lead to a loss of our felt center, and present moment awareness.

Many years ago, I first heard, *"Expect nothing, be ready for anything,"* and it gave me the chills. I intuitively felt the power of the phrase. I have never found a direct reference of who said it first, although it is most commonly attributed to the Bushido code of the Samurai of Japan. Blending elements of being in the present moment, and knowing that you could be attacked at any time, allows you to feel very present.

The ancient Samurai practiced their mindful art with death over

9: PEACE WITHIN LIFE

their shoulders. As a result of my brush with death as a child, this phrase has touched me in the deepest part of my heart. I imagine almost all warriors throughout the history of the world have had similar sayings. In fact, our ancient hunter-gatherer ancestors, literally not knowing where their next meal was coming from, or what danger lurked around the corner, truly lived the phrase. They expected nothing, but had to be ready for anything, just to survive. This is the way we were wired to live. Furthermore, I don't recall Jesus ever saying, "Blessed are the comfortable and certain." Comfort and certainty are often the enemy of being fully awake, in the moment, and grateful to be alive. As Lazarus's work illustrates, those who live with the least are often most grateful and experience a greater level of happiness than those with the most creature comforts.

The weak can never forgive. Forgiveness is the attribute of the strong.

-Gandhi

As a vision quest guide, I often took my questers out into the wilderness and gave them a piece of paper bearing that quote: "Expect nothing, be ready for anything," as a reminder of this truth and the importance of being present in each moment, and breath. I continue to have that reminder in a number of key places in my own life. If life truly is a river, one we have not yet been down before, this is a wise way to journey, knowing that each and every moment is ever new, filled with great challenge and beauty. This is to live what I call *The Way of the Heart Warrior.*

PEACE WITHIN

THE HEART WARRIOR

Your heart is the size of the ocean.

~Rumi

I heard the term heart warrior from my teacher and friend Bill Plotkin on our first meeting. Although Bill has some very specific ways he understands and discusses being a heart warrior, I have my own interpretation of the phrase. For me, the first motto of the heart warrior is to be present, with death over your shoulder, meaning that you honor the preciousness of today as a gift. In addition to letting go of expectation, you also cultivate gratitude toward for what is. Gratitude is a deep quality of the heart. Even the universal act of bowing is an act of gratitude, appreciation, and humility.

On my first vision quest, when I went without food or water in the Canadian wilderness, I came face to face with my vulnerability and nakedness. Days without water can put you on death's door, and I felt it. I found the tears flowing, even though I had lost a tremendous amount of water weight. I was camping alone on the banks of the Belly River, feeling the full weight of my existence on my shoulders. So many failures, so many mistakes, and so many wounds unhealed.

Somewhere between waking and dreaming, I lay by the river feeling as close to death as I could remember since my surgeries as a child. As I closed my eyes, I heard an old woman's voice rising from the river. She whispered in a subtle chant, "Ever flowing on, ever flowing on, ever flowing on..." I opened my eyes, and the chanting stopped. I closed my eyes, and again it began. I could scarcely believe it, the river was calling my soul name. With my spirit renewed from this otherworldly experience, I felt a surge of energy as I stood up and began to dance as if in a trance, obeying what felt like an ancient shuffling movement in the symbol of infinity (a figure-eight) over and over again. As I did, the words to a song arose out of me complete with a melody, "River, call my name. Call me, ever flowing on. Call me ever flowing, ever flowing, ever flowing on..."

Tears flowed as I felt the lament turn to joy. I experienced the melody as it joined the sound of the river. I felt an infinite spring of love pouring through my heart, as if I was one with everything around me; the rocks, trees, river were all singing with me, through me - until there was no more me.

I looked up at the sky – and there were two eagles flying above me, making figure-eights that mirrored my dance. I fell down, as if struck by lightning. I felt the earth spinning below me, and I felt a sense of exquisite emptiness. I lost sense of my body, as the space around me stretched out in all directions to infinity. I heard the whispered chanting once again this time as if from all directions, "Ever flowing on, ever flowing on, ever flowing on..." On my knees I could only keep saying, "Thank you, thank you, thank you..."

From that day on, every morning, I take a drink of water and say a simple prayer to each of the directions: "Thank you for some air to breathe and earth to be."

A heart warrior not only expects nothing, but practices being grateful for everything. This leads to a new equation of happiness:

Expect Nothing + Be Grateful for Everything = Peace

The entire *Peace Within* process can also be considered training in the way of the heart warrior. Over the years, I have put together my list of the qualities that make up a heart warrior. These include someone who:

1. *Lives in the now.*

2. *Lives with an open heart (able to be vulnerable) by identifying and expressing true feelings skillfully.*

3. *Practices letting go of unrealistic expectations and is able to tolerate uncertainty.*

4. *Understands and honors the interconnectedness of the web of life.*

5. *Is able to play their social roles honorably and well, without becoming lost in them or over-identifying; knowing who they are always transcends any particular role.*

6. *Practices genuine forgiveness for self and others, through learning from every experience and practicing compassion for self and others.*

7. *Tries not to confuse thoughts with awareness (practices quieting the mind).*

8. *Reduces attachments (and addictions).*

9. *Honors the river flowing through the heart, working with life's natural flow instead of against it.*

10. *Living like this gives you the ability to love your life, no matter what comes your way.*

MODULE 9 – MAIN POINTS

To summarize, the main points contained in Module 9, *Peace Within Life*:

1. *Just as we practiced finding a healthy relationship with others, we are actually in relationship with life as well and possess expectations, ideas, and beliefs about how life should be. Finding Peace Within life means letting go of our unrealistic expectations, beliefs, and ideas about life – so we can meet it on its own terms.*

2. *Life is a river flowing through us. Understanding life in this way allows us to learn to flow, maneuver, and navigate skillfully.*

3. *It can be difficult to let go of expectations and beliefs. We need to be*

able to forgive life as much as to forgive another person, and ourselves.

4. *Practicing love of life – as a form of compassion for self, others, and reality.*

5. *The heart warrior is a way of putting the Peace Within process into action in the world. It takes courage (heart of a warrior) to practice being present, vulnerable, while letting go of attachments, quieting our minds, and opening our hearts to ourselves, others, and life – all while we release unrealistic expectations of self and others.*

MODULE 9 - PEACE WITHIN PRACTICES

1. *As you become aware of all life around you, continue your mindfulness practice. Extend your awareness beyond your body to the space within the room, around the landscape where you live and eventually the space around the Earth and the Universe.*

2. *Journal on your relationship with life. Write life a therapeutic letter, expressing any frustration, anger, and resentments—as you also move toward compassion, forgiveness, and understanding for your life as it is.*

3. *Continue to work on the forgiveness practices with yourself and others, working on letting go of any old resentments, anger, hate or rage you may still be carrying and holding on to.*

4. *Consider what elements of the heart warrior you currently possess – and which ones are weaknesses. Write those down and note at least*

one way you can begin to work on strengthening those skills.

5. *Work up to fifteen minutes a day of sitting meditation, adding mindfulness of life. Notice if your thoughts become elaborate narratives about your life story. Journal on the beliefs, ideas, and expectations you are attached to regarding your life up until now. Consider how you might feel if you let go of those beliefs, ideas and expectations. What if you could trust the twisting, turning river of your life fully and be at peace with it? What beliefs would you have to let go of to allow yourself to be at peace with your life just as it is? Work up to four thirty minute guided, lying down meditation a week. (You can always practice more – these are a minimum.)*

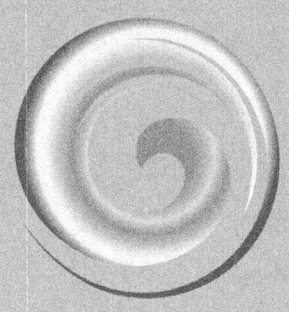

10: PEACE WITHIN DEATH

MODULE 10

The practices within the book have culminated in this final module where we explore how to find peace in the most challenging place of all - in the death of those we love and when facing our own mortality. We discover through these practices that death itself, like sleep, is not the enemy, but an intimate ally in the process of waking up to who we really are and has been with us all along – in every out breath – in every silent, still, and empty moment of our lives.

I lay on the Earth, staring up at the starlit sky and wept. Hurricane Ivan had brought so much devastation and loss to me, my family, and community. My immediate family was safe, at least physically, but our neighborhood was unrecognizable. Although months had now passed, the destruction was still ever present. The place where I had taught my daughter to ride her bike, turn her first cartwheel, and jump rope were gone. My beautiful rose garden and the soil I had cultivated for my vegetable garden for over a decade were gone. Twelve live oak trees gone; gorgeous magnolia tree gone. Our entire lawn had been ripped away by a fifteen-foot wall of water, that left nothing but dirt in its wake. Our swimming pool was now a cesspool of debris.

Yet, despite the physical destruction, there was a stillness and silence. In the middle of the devastation, there were no electric lights, so no light pollution drowned out the sparkling of the stars in the night sky. No air-conditioning units or pool pumps obscured the sounds and smells of the ocean. It was so quiet, so still, I could hear my heartbeat.

THE STARS WITHIN MY HEART

That night, the new moon and countless stars illuminated the black velvet of the sky. My wife was working late, and my daughter was out with friends, trying to salvage her senior year of high school with some moments of normalcy, but I continued to avoid social situations. I was still healing and enjoyed going out under the stars alone to play my flute.

Just like when I was a boy, my music again, became my solace and best friend. I carried my flute with me everywhere, and my favorite time to play was at night like this, alone, under the canopy of twinkling stars. Playing helped me grieve and express the feelings that were too large for words.

I played that night with eyes closed, exhaling completely, savoring the disappearance of the last note into silence, as I did as a boy on the piano decades earlier. I took a deep breath, slowly opened my eyes, and looked out at the still water and vast night sky. I stared at the stars and took another deep, cleansing breath. The Milky Way shimmered across the night sky, because of the pitch blackness undisturbed by electrical light. Just moments before, I'd been consumed with grief, but now I felt my chest and heart open. A strange mixture of sorrow and joy came over me. Alongside my sadness for all that had been lost, there was also something else, alive and growing in me.

Everything is changeable, everything appears and disappears; There is no blissful peace until one passes beyond the agony of life and death.

~ Buddha

PEACE WITHIN

Your heart is the size of the ocean.

~Rumi

There, in the still silence, I felt the deep shift in my consciousness that I had begun to grow familiar with in my lying down meditation practice. I closed my eyes again as I became aware of sensations throughout my body, particularly my hands, feet, and the surface of my skin. I experienced body breathing from the tips of my toes up to the top of my head, and back down again – tracing the points of contact between my body and the Earth, the surface of my skin and the air caressing me from head to toe.

Then, with another deep breath, I felt the Earth under me move, waves cascading through my body, coming from around me and moving through me – like an electromagnetic current.

The sensation was deeply peaceful, even blissful, as if my entire body was floating in vastness.

After what felt like moments, but may have actually been hours, I opened my eyes. Suddenly, I felt as if the stars in the sky were now in my heart, the Universe as much in me as outside me. I experienced a deep sense of expansiveness. As I breathed now, the stars and Earth breathed with me. I was part of everything, and everything was part of me. I felt reborn. My small, tight, confined ideas about myself and reality dissolved. I experienced a profound connection to everything around me, stretching out infinitely in all directions. I no longer was simply floating in the ocean, I became one with it….a great cosmic, quantum ocean…of peace…flowing…endlessly.

Tears flowed again, but this time they were tears of awe. There was no longer any inside or outside, no self or other, no separation between me and the world around me. The veil had dropped; I had awoken, and the river that had been flowing through my heart merged with the cosmic, quantum ocean of emptiness.

I'm not sure how long I lay there, but I remember thinking, "If this is what deep grief brings you, I'll never try to save someone from it again. Instead, I'll encourage them to trust their tears, to follow them and their breath. If they traverse the full length of the river of their grief, and cry all of their tears, it will take them home to the sea, the cosmic, quantum ocean of peace that bathes everyone and everything."

My struggles dissolved in that moment: Nothing had any sway in that blissful, timeless space. There was no more struggle, conflict, or separation. From that point on, whenever I was lost, alone, struggling, or fearful, I found I simply needed to be present to what was, to be fully and compassionately aware of what was flowing in my heart and remember to lie down and breathe. When I did that, I knew the ocean of peace was never far away.[1]

DEEP STILLNESS

As painful as tragedy is, it also stops us in our tracks and forces us to be still. In 2004, God captured my full attention. I kept fighting against the mounting rapids and circumstances I couldn't control.

Then, finally, I let go, into my breath, and chose to be still and listen. Instead of trying to influence the course of the river of my life, I decided to really listen and see where the river was flowing and wanted to take me. It was then that I began to experience the river flow into the ocean of peace lying in the depths of my heart and all around me.

If we listen to the flow and current of the river of life running through our hearts, it takes us exactly where we need to be. When most people talk about stillness, they are referring to the surface, like the calm of a pool of water or leaves on a windless day.

Deep stillness, though, is far more than that. It is dynamic, pervasive, and unthinkably powerful. To quote Bruce Lee, "The stillness in stillness is not the real stillness; only when there is stillness in movement does the universal rhythm manifest."[2]

You might like to think of it as:

~Subtle movements in the ocean depths.

~Barely perceptible swaying of a 3000 year old great sequoia tree.

~The sun exploding with cosmic energy, yet perfectly still, creating the gravitational center of our solar system.

~Earth as it spins at just over 1,000 miles per hour, careening through space at 67,000 miles per hour around the sun, while we experience a solid, stable stillness under our feet.

This dynamic stillness—perhaps most deeply and mysteriously expressed in the black hole at the center of our galaxy—is the ultimate emptiness that provides centering and movement in its vast, fathomless depths.

Deep stillness lies within and can only be contacted by letting go. As in sleep, when we recline into the deeper recesses of ourselves, true, deep relaxation can occur, not only relaxation of the body but of the mind as well. One client of mine refers to it as having her 'toes uncurl."

Our bodies, minds, and hearts require dropping into deep stillness and silence every day. Even if you don't meditate, your body and mind won't survive long without the silence and stillness that come every night in sleep. In a way, sleep is an eight hour meditation you practice every night!

The Greeks knew about the intimate relationship between sleep and death. In Greek mythology, *Hypnos*, the god of sleep, is the son of *Thanatos*, the god of death, they even referred to sleep as 'the little death.' They knew they could learn a great deal about death and dying, but studying the world of sleep and dreaming. In fact, exploring sleep is one of the ways we can learn in a very personal way what it is like to let go into death.

Each night during sleep, you have to 'let go' of your ego consciousness, as well as your complete sense of your body and self.

We must each completely dissolve our sense of self to drop into the ocean of sleep. From the viewpoint of the sleep-wake cycle, you could say we are more like a strobe than a fixed light. We truly are blinking in and out of existence, (our conscious awareness) every day for a full eight hours. In fact, if you live to be 75, you have spent roughly 25 years of your life on Earth in dream time!

Even the amount of time we spend dreaming isn't the whole story, because in deep, dreamless, slow delta wave sleep, we truly are in a kind of suspended animation. During this period, our brain waves move into their most smoothest, most relaxed, most synchronized rhythm, more than at any other time. Delta waves look like beautiful sound waves compared to the chaotic brain waves that dominate during our waking hours. This is also when our bodies and minds receive the greatest benefit of rejuvenation and healing. Who is to say that during this respite we are not like our smart phones, being recharged and receiving the latest downloads from a non-local place outside our bodies? Perhaps, from the 'soul-cloud' of being. There is no way we can 'prove' that we are not in some way going back to the 'source' from which we arrived, just as we recharge a computer by plugging it into a power source. The real question is: What power source are we plugging into when we meditate and drop into deep dreamless sleep?

It is odd that the mind panics at the prospect of death, yet welcomes sleep. Leonardo da Vinci's evocative words speak to this:

"As a well spent day brings happy sleep, so life well used brings happy death."

We are greatly served when we begin to see sleep as a powerful teacher that can show us how to cultivate deep stillness in our lives. We can't force ourselves to sleep any more than we can force ourselves to quiet the mind and open the heart. We can, however, create the conditions in which sleep is more likely, and the same is true for stilling the mind and opening the heart. A wonderful way to begin is to unplug from the ubiquitous electronic world. We can create an atmosphere of less outside stimulation, by turning off televisions, radios, computers, and telephones. Lighting some candles, or turning on an amber light from a Himalayan Salt Lamp, turning on peaceful music, deep breathing, journaling, and perhaps reading some calming, inspiring poetry.

THE OCEAN OF PEACE

After my 'stars in my heart' experience, my lying down meditation practice shifted dramatically. I noticed, in the days that followed, my thoughts had less ability to Velcro to my consciousness as I began experiencing my entire being floating in a vast field of awareness. Something was happening, something I couldn't fully describe. Although I had tastes of it in deep, extended sitting meditation, this was more pervasive, vaster, and lasted longer. My mind, like my head and body, was resting against the Earth. My awareness expanded in all directions. I became aware of the space above and around me, stretching out infinitely. I felt the Earth under me, not as something solid, but as fluid. I sensed everything flowing...a sensation not unlike floating in water. There was a subtle, wave-like motion moving through my body and radiating in all directions; I felt cradled, rocked, and even loved.

You are not a drop in the ocean, you are the entire ocean in the drop.

~Rumi

Reflecting on this shift in my meditation practice I recalled stories I had read about the Neolithic goddess of old Europe, Mari. It was said that she was the great cosmic ocean and that we are all being cradled in her arms. She forgives everything because she had experienced everything. This was how I felt, as if I was being cradled in an infinite ocean of peace. To this day, it has been my daily practice. At times, I practice for five to ten minutes between transitioning from one activity to another. Usually, I spend every evening and morning in a 30 to 60 minute version of this lying down meditation, sometimes I do so for as long as 90-120 minutes. The lying down meditation I have shared with you in this book is a distilled version of this practice.

I also spend time before sleep and upon awakening to realign myself with the ocean of peace. I lie down with a thin pillow under my head, with my body in alignment left to right, anchoring myself in the sensations in my hands (particularly palms and fingers) and feet (toes and tips of the toes), and top of the head. Then I do a body scan to make sure my soul is centered and fully present in the body.

This is not only a form of rejuvenation and cleansing, but it also actually feels as if I'm recalibrating my brain and body for the day, just as one would adjust the timing belt on a car. It feels as if there is another energy taking over, scanning my body, mind and heart for holes to be filled, cracks to be sealed, and wounds to be healed.

The ocean of peace is the ground upon which everything else in my life is built. In many ways, it is the most real thing in my life. Everything else consists of waves and patterns that occur through this ocean of awareness. It is a groundless ground, because it is dynamic, integrative, and all pervasive – like space itself but experienced in subtle, flowing waves.

The mind and body are so deeply connected that just the act of stilling the body begins to still the mind. Paradoxically, when we are fully present in the now and drop into the nourishing waters that live in deep stillness, we are transported to the ocean of peace.

Releasing our beliefs and opinions about ourselves, others, and reality aids this process. These are activities of the mind that create a wall between us and the ocean of peace. Each belief, opinion, or expectation is a brick in the wall between us and the creative flow, what in Asia is called the *Tao*.

I began this book bu discussing the ocean of peace that lies within each of us. It is always with us, but we become so preoccupied with the busyness of life, that we often ignore or forget about it. The most effective way to readily contact that ocean is to be still and tune into the present moment.

How often are you still during the day? The week? The month? The year? We all avoid stillness and deep listening because it brings us face to face with emptiness.

In the West, emptiness is something to be avoided; whereas within spiritually mature wisdom traditions of the world, it has always been viewed as sacred, the place where all things arise and return. Emptiness brings peace. True healing and awakening can only occur when we begin to empty ourselves – which is to touch and taste that bitter medicine that is also our greatest teacher – death.

REST IN PEACE

Beneath every fear, worry, and anxiety lies an unacknowledged and undealt with fear of death.

Death is the ultimate ending to this physical existence. How we deal with all endings in our lives (including the ending of each moment) will reflect our attitude (conscious or unconscious) about death. At the root, is the fear of ceasing to exist one day in the future. What happens to us? What part of us dies? At the same time, when death does confront us, either via illness or the death of a loved one, it is almost as if time stands still and everything is put on hold.

There have been many songs, poems, and movies to remind us of the wisdom that can come when we or a loved one faces death. It truly puts everything in perspective, showing us what matters, and what doesn't. It helps us understand the truth of the phrase, "Don't sweat the small stuff, and it is all small stuff."[3]

WHEN WE PUT OUR LIVES IN PERSPECTIVE FROM THE STANDPOINT THAT EACH DAY, EACH MOMENT COULD BE OUR LAST, IT REVEALS STARKLY WHAT REALLY MATTERS.

Traditions across the world may disagree about what happens when we die, but they all agree that how we live during our lifetimes will have a great deal to do with our psychological and emotional state at the moment of death, as well as what may happen after. In fact, some traditions don't see heaven or hell as places, but as the emotional space people find themselves in on their deathbeds. Many traditions also give a special place to how open or closed the heart is at the time of death. To the Egyptians, your heart at the time of death was measured against a feather. If your heart was heavier than a feather, it would be devoured, but if your heart was as light as a feather your soul was released into heaven.[4]

Over the years, this image of keeping one's heart light as a feather has informed my life and those I work with and teach. Everyone seems to have an immediate understanding of the word, light-heartedness. I love the double-meaning of the word light in this usage; it can refer to luminous light and the weight of lightness.

A photon of light is itself dimensionless, weightless, occupying no space at all, while it moves in waves through complete and utter emptiness. The materialistic, reductionist, scientism of the twentieth century went so far as to declare that the soul doesn't exist because when you weighed a person just before death and just after, there was no difference in weight! The pseudo-scientific assumption and conjecture was that since the soul could not be be observed, weighed, and measured it did not exist.[5] Of course, if the soul is something like a photon, but even more complex and subtle – a dimensionless, weightless, timeless and deathless wave flowing through emptiness - of course it could not be detected by gross measures of the rational mind after physical death.

DYING WITH PEACE

Over the years, hospice workers have identified five critical pieces of unfinished business that greatly determine whether a person who a dying person experiences deep peace during their dying process or struggles greatly at the end:

- *Asking for forgiveness from those we have offended.*

- *Forgiving those we need to forgive.*

- *Expressing gratitude toward those who have made a difference in our lives, whether this impact brought happiness or pain at the time.*

- *Expressing affection.*

- *Saying goodbye.*[6]

As you can see, forgiveness is front and center. It's no coincidence that this list is similar to part of the fourth step in the familiar twelve-step program. So much of our pain is centered on unfinished emotional business, which can be healed through the process of *forgiving and being forgiven; and expressing and receiving gratitude, affection and love.*

This is as simple as it is difficult, but it does help to lighten the heart. It lets us release the weight of those things that have hardened, closed, or caused a heavy heart, while enabling our inner light to glow brightly with love, appreciation, and joy.

Unfinished business keeps the emotional circulatory system from running smoothly. *When our hearts and minds are closed as a result of unfinished emotional business, our energy is sapped, stuck, and refuses to flow—neither tears nor joy flow through us.*[7] People who die peacefully are those who have made peace with themselves, others, and their life. What does this mean? They have lightened their hearts by healing and letting go of resentment, jealousy, regret, and shame. They have allowed themselves to grieve losses, make amends, and move from dysfunctional relationships based on control and dependency to those that are giving, loving, and freeing.

Perhaps, much of the most important work hospice workers do is helping the dying deal with their unfinished business and open their hearts, which is key to finding peace. Befriending death and opening the heart helps us understand how to dive into the nothingness and emptiness that death appears to be. If we have learned to die our little deaths while alive, to grieve and work with sorrow and defeat, then death will no longer be a stranger or enemy, but an ally and friend. Not that we will seek it before its time, but it will exist as a constant measure of what matters, what is important, and how precious this moment, this breath, and this life is.

The most powerful way I know to befriend death, lighten the heart, and heal the past is the Death Lodge.

BEFRIENDING DEATH (OUR MORTALITY) AS AN ALLY HELPS US OPEN THE HEART AND FIND OUR WAY BACK TO THE OCEAN OF PEACE IN THE HERE AND NOW.

DEATH LODGE

I was introduced to the Death Lodge through my work with my friend, mentor, and teacher Bill Plotkin of Animas Valley Institute and author of many books on nature and the human soul, as well as Stephen Foster and Meredith Little of the School of Lost Borders. They have all been pioneers in the modern rites of passage movement. I recommend both schools, for they are excellent, long-standing programs in wilderness rites of passage. I completed the Death Lodge ceremony a number of times; however, it was clear to me during my dark time in 2004 that it was time to do another, once I regained enough strength and mental clarity.

I already felt as if I was dying. I had even contemplated suicide. It was an excellent time to do a Death Lodge, instead of actually taking my own life. As my teacher, Robert A. Johnson, would also say, if you can kill yourself without causing any bodily harm, please do so.[8] Of course, he was talking about letting go of ego identities, actually helping the ego move out of the self's center of gravity. Fundamentally, we couldn't kill the ego even if we wanted to, but we can see it demoted from ship captain to a worthy first mate. The Death Lodge is a powerful way to help facilitate this process.

The origins of the Death Lodge can be traced back to the Olmecs, a very early Mesoamerican civilization. Various versions of the ceremony and teaching can be found throughout the Americas.

One of the powers of the Death Lodge is its ability to help us learn to deal with the "little deaths" that come our way – the disappointments, losses, and illnesses. When we can see these experiences

The key to a good life is this: If you're not going to talk about something during the last hour of your life, then don't make it a top priority during your lifetime.

~ Richard Carlson

as preparing us or, even conditioning us, for death, we perceive a different, more powerful meaning in them. Remember, despair comes from suffering that is devoid of meaning. Ironically, when faced with an open heart, it is death that actually provides meaning to our lives.

The School of Lost Borders, and many other wilderness based rites of passage programs guide Death Lodges in a natural setting. There is no doubt that doing so can be a deeply moving experience, grounded in the vastness of nature. However, in 2004, when it was not possible for me to do my Death Lodge out in nature, I found doing one indoors to be equally powerful. Essentially, it is the sincerity and heart you bring to the ceremony that gives it transformative power.

I'll never forget the first time I enacted the Death Lodge: the sound of Bill Plotkin's voice, the look in his eyes, and the gravity with which he invited me to join the ceremony. He said, "I want you to imagine you're on your death bed. Reflect on what really matters to you as you find yourself lying there, knowing death will be come in a matter of hours, before the sun rises tomorrow morning."

My heart was in my throat as the question burned into my soul, stopping me in my tracks. I literally stopped breathing for a moment, then took a breath, as if for the first time. I let the question sink in. I was only 36 at the time, but I will never forget the answers that came to me that night.

That night I wrote in my Death Lodge journal on my imaginary death bed, "Did I become all of who I am? Did I share all of who I am? Did I let myself be seen, really seen? Did I unselfishly love people and life to my utmost? Did I make a difference and did my life make a difference on planet Earth?" Finally, I came to the deepest question that I was left with that fateful evening before sunrise. It felt as if all the other questions were beginning this most basic question I imagined God asking me as I took my last breaths, "How pure, genuine and authentic was the quality of love that lived in my heart while alive?"

You are loved, deeply cherished, forever. There is nothing you have to fear. You will always be loved, and there's nothing that you can do wrong.

~Eben Alexander

In addition to healing past relationships and wounds, the Death Lodge asks us to question what is unlived in our lives. What do we need to go back and complete so that when death arrives, we can meet it with gratitude and peace?

THE TWO LIGHTS

Keeping death over our shoulder at all times is a powerful way to live and reminds us to savor each moment to the fullest and give our full attention to what is before us.

Death is the ultimate stillness, silence, and emptiness. As such, it has the power to put everything in perspective. It renders life mysterious, and reminds us of the true miracle it is. With death in the visible background, life takes on great meaning. No matter your belief system, if you can get out of your head, let go of your beliefs about death, and simply be as curious about it as you are about sleep, life's infinite depths and essential mysteriousness will make themselves known to you.

Most Western culture is built upon a feeling profoundly expressed by Dylan Thomas as he rails against the imminent death of his father: "Do not go gently into that good night…Rage, rage against the dying of the light."[9] It is clear that Thomas could not see the light on the other side of life. Yes, there are two lights. To find deep peace, you must learn to befriend the deeper light of emptiness, death, and the beyond. This is the inner light.

You are not the body. You are the immensity and infinity of consciousness.

~Nisargadatta

To the ego, death is indeed an ending, just as in sleep, the ego disappears completely. While the ego experiences a dying of the light, the soul experiences a growing.

If we imagine awareness as a form of light (remember the flashlight and film projector examples) then any object of awareness, such as the ego, comes and goes. The ego is an object of awareness, but it is not awareness itself. As in our social feedback example in Diagram 10, Module 6 of *ego, self and soul*, this feedback creates the "I" we take ourselves to be. The body-self locates us in space and time, like an object the flashlight is shining on. It's like a prism.

If the body-self, or prism, dies, the light still shines. Thus, when the ego dies, it is painful, but we also touch something more essential. We experience the pure awareness that has been animating

10: PEACE WITHIN DEATH

the entire show of light and sound throughout our lives.

We realize we are not the movie on the screen. Instead, we are the light shining through. It is as if the fundamental ground of who we are is this pure awareness sparkling through each moment, giving rise to a multitude of possibilities in the shape of sound, light, and sensory appearance. The more we meditate, quiet the mind, and open the heart, the more we discern this miracle of pure awareness, and the less distracted we are by the drama on the screen. This enables us to sit back and simply enjoy the show.

Do you realize that it is not you who moves from dream to dream, but the dreams flow before you, and you are the immutable witness.

~Nisargadatta

INNER LIGHT

I have always loved the practice of sitting in silence as a way to access what the Quakers called the inner light. Pierre Lacout, a Swiss Quaker, in his book *God Is Silence*, describes how when people practice sitting in silence, their inner light begins to glow.[10] This is a beautiful belief, one with which most spiritual traditions would find some point of agreement.

WHEN WE PRACTICE DEEP STILLNESS AND SILENCE, OUR INNER LIGHT (PRESENCE AND AWARENESS) GLOWS.

Every spiritual tradition has acknowledged the understanding that within each human soul is a spark of the divine, the source, the Creator, God. These include the Hindu expression of *Namaste* (Sanskrit for, "I bow to the divine in you"), to the Hawaiian *Aloha* (meaning "the presence of breath/spirit"), the Jewish *Shalom* ("peace and well being"), and the Muslim *Salaam* ("peace" in Arabic). Each of these expressions recognizes the universal insight that within each of us lies a divine spark, one that connects us all and is the root of inner peace.

Deep stillness and silence bring us to a dissolving of the usual boundaries of self and other, body and space, which is the central experience of the ocean of peace. Our mind and logic work with duality: right/wrong, left/right, differentiating and judging everything perceived and experienced. The mind treats life and everything in it as a problem to be solved. In practicing mindfulness, meditation, and compassionate awareness, we move from the judging mind to the inner light of awareness, which is perhaps not so much a light as a space, field or clearing in which feelings, thoughts, and sensations flow. Awareness doesn't help us see; *it is what sees.*

Essentially, life is not a problem to be solved, but a beautiful journey to be experienced, a song to be sung, a mystery to behold!

DEEP GRATITUDE

One of the most lasting outcomes of performing the Death Lodge practice is deep gratitude. By appreciating the fragility of life and its fleeting nature, we awake more fully to the miracle of being here in each breath and moment. We begin to realize the preciousness of our life, and see that our ego, our social self, has been like a small boat on a river. While, who we really are is this vast river upon which that small boat floats. The river is our very soul. We become intimately aware of this river and the importance of honoring it. By taking care of ourselves, we are taking care of life, just as we do when we hold a precious infant, with a deep sense of concern, attentiveness, and a sense of preciousness.

The river we ride is so much more vaster than anything we could ever imagine. In this way: *deep peace = expecting nothing + appreciating everything!*

EXPECT NOTHING + APPRECIATE EVERYTHING
= DEEP PEACE

DEEP SLEEP PRACTICE

Most people imagine that the center of their existence resides in the impermanence of the exterior world. It might be a house, a person, a career, or an identity (social role). Some find their center in an online persona on Facebook or Twitter. There's no problem in having these in your life, as long as you remember that they are not who you really are. If you build your life around them and make them your center, it will only be a matter of time before you will have a major crash. Depending on something in the outside world to hold your center will always place you on the rocks in the end. Impermanence is the great teacher that reminds us that the external world of things is ever changing and fleeting at best. As the Blackfoot say, *"Life is a flash of a firefly at night, the breath of a buffalo in winter."*

Who you truly are is the pure awareness that witnesses everything that happens to you, appearing and dissolving in your consciousness, moment-to-moment. Remember the light bulb in the film projector of the mind in Module 4? You are that inner light.

With the suicide rate on the rise throughout the world, science has been unable to solve what ails us, living amidst the soulless institutions and corporations that dominate our world. Because our inner lights are not being nourished, we are dying on the inside. We are not being honored or loved, but snuffed out daily by the rush for profits, spawned by greed. The egomania that is evidenced in the hunger for power is ultimately nothing more than the result of people mistaking their egos for their true selves. One way we can offset these harsh influences is to orient our centers toward a nightly practice of dissolving the self into silence and stillness when we sleep.

In the following meditation, sleep is approached with great reverence, respect, curiosity, and even love. This meditation will take you on a journey into the ocean of deep peace and replenishment, a chance to return to your source.

Using this meditation will allow you to sleep more deeply and awake feeling more refreshed. You'll be able to fall asleep more swiftly, no matter where you are. You will also begin to sense the bodily sensations and feelings that accompany the deep relaxation of body and mind.

Love existed before heaven and earth.

~Hafiz

Take a moment before lying down to take one to three deep, cleansing breaths. Turn off the lights, and with great reverence and curiosity, climb into bed, anticipating the journey that awaits you in sleep.

MEDITATION FOR DEEP SLEEP

Say, "sleep" a few times, relishing the beauty of the word and how it calls to the part of you that knows the power and depth of peace that comes from deep slumber. Lie on your back, with your arms and feet a comfortable distance apart and palms facing downward.

Lying face down is best for preparing for sleep. Facing up is optimal for staying awake or doing your Peace Within meditation in the morning. Take three more deep, cleansing belly breaths. With each breath, imagine breathing out all of the tension, stress, and anxiety of your day…feel a wave of relaxation flowing over and through your body.

Now, allow yourself to let go physically into the plane of contact between your body and the bed. Imagine allowing all the physical, emotional, and mental tension to flow out of you, through the points of contact, down into the bed and even further down, into the Earth. As you let go, give your body up completely to the surface of the bed. Notice the points of contact between your body and the bed as you notice the subtle movements of energy and sensation throughout your body, deepened by each breath.

Become aware of the stillness and silence. Enjoy knowing you could move, but you are not moving. You are so overjoyed to have the day behind you and the opportunity to be deeply let go. You find yourself dropping into a deeper and deeper state of stillness…and peace…a very deep peace.

Continue with body scans and breath work to help encourage and nurture the two sleep states of dreaming and dreamless sleep.

PEACE WITHIN MORNING PRACTICE

Upon awakening, the following practice can be a wonderful, profound way to begin your day. This practice can help you start your morning feeling positive, energized, nourished, and centered. It is a great way to reconnect with your felt center before you head out into the world. If you sleep with someone, using your ear-buds will allow you to practice without disturbing anyone. Again, you may want to record this and play it back so you can simply relax and listen.

Take a deep, cleansing breath, feeling a sense of gratefulness for being alive. Now, slowly begin to feel your body as you lie comfortably on your back with trunk aligned and your feet and arms a comfortable distance apart, with palms turned upward, toward the sky, as if taking in the energy from the sun to awaken you fully.

Say silently to yourself, "Thank you for today…Thank you for this moment. Thank you for my eyes so I can see. Thank you for my ears so I can hear. Thank you for my legs so I can walk. Thank you for the air so I can breathe. Thank you for water to nourish my body. Thank you for…..(Continue being grateful for other personal gifts until you feel satisfied.)

Now, begin to breathe from the tip of your toes up to the top of your head, imagining every breath to be energizing and nurturing as you begin to feel yourself become more and more awake.

Imagine your attention like a beam of warm light. Imagine that when the light shines on a particular part of your body, it provides it with life energy that renews and readies you for the day. Light up your head…your eyes…your ears…your nose. Focus on lighting your arms and hands, your trunk, and your shoulders, and back. Light up and energize your pelvis, hips, and upper legs, your lower legs, and your knees. Now, focus on your entire body, bathing it with a radiance of light, energy, and sensation.

Breathe deeply, letting go of the past and the future. Just enjoy the joy of being embodied in this moment, with nowhere to go and nothing to be in this moment.

When you're ready, on your next breath, slowly open your eyes and take in the world around you. On the out breath, choose to open your eyes or close them again. As you open them on each breath, you will find them spontaneously wanting to remain open as you breathe in the light from outside of yourself. Your inner light is still lit and very much present, but now you are also connected to, and in touch with, the outer dimension of light and life outside. You are now grounded, centered and ready to start your day with energy, focus and clarity.

CREATIVE INFINITY

Those I work with often ask whether I believe in God or in life after death. What do I believe about the existence of a soul and an inner light? And if I do believe in them, where do they come from?

Of course, these answers are deeply personal. If we are working on letting go of expectations and beliefs, all these answers are of the mind; as such, they create ideas about the experience causing us to immediately leave it. As they say in the East, "The Tao that can be told is not the Tao."

How is it possible to talk about that which is always exceeding our ability to describe and define? As you can tell, I like metaphors. As a poet and musician, I find they help us hint at an experience that is beyond our descriptive powers. I also like the term *creative infinity,* which most people find hard to argue with— even a hard core Ph.D. physicist.

Not long ago, I was traveling to San Francisco for a workshop, and found myself seated next to a woman with a Ph.D. in physics. When she saw me reading a book about spirituality, she asked, "So do you believe in God?"

"I don't believe anything. I either have an experience of it and then know it, or I don't," I said.

It was clear she didn't expect this answer, so she pushed a bit further.

"So what are you saying? That you know God exists?"

I could see that it was going to be a very interesting plane ride. "No, I didn't say that. Why are you asking? Do you believe in God?"

She said, with some noticeable pride, "No, of course not. I'm a scientist, a physicist. I believe what can be proven through the scientific method, and there is no logical, rational proof of any kind of higher being."

I appreciated her candor and conviction. "I'm a scientist too, a social scientist, a psychologist. I have to admit I don't believe in an old man in the sky, with long white hair. But you have to admit there is something extraordinary about life and the Universe. I have had experiences I can't logically explain, events that question usual notions about cause and effect, space and time. Then, of course, there is the beauty of the sky at sunset, or the infinite expanse of stars in the night, to say nothing of the miracle of human love."

Looking curious, but also ready to pounce at any moment on a logical inconsistency, she said, "Go on."

Don't you know yet, it is your light that lights the worlds.

~Rumi

I looked at her to determine, whether she was really listening or was just judging me. There was a sincerity in the way she studied me, so I took a deep breath and responded, "When I play my flute, I feel some kind of energy flowing through me that makes my heart glide and sing. I love to improvise, and I've played things I had no idea how to play, no idea why I played them. For me, I know there is something greater than the human scale of life, and, although our minds are elegant, sophisticated, and amazing, I believe they grew from an intelligence greater than our own."

She looked at me, long and hard, as if trying to get behind my words to figure out who I was and what it was I was really saying. She obviously wasn't expecting my reply, and I could tell she wasn't sure how to respond.

After what seemed like an eternal silence filled with deep reflection and curious nodding, she finally said, "I will admit there is something about the creative infinity of the Universe that is awe inspiring."

The creative infinity of the Universe: That was exactly what I was trying to say. In a good-hearted way, I laughed at the beauty of her phrase. "Yes, the creative infinity of the Universe. That's exactly it. Thank you for that phrase."

A beautiful way to understand the creative infinity of the universe is through our human attempts at imagination. When we are deeply engaged in a creative process, time shifts to the timelessness of now, and we experience a sense of flow. It is almost as if our creativity is in communion with the invisible flow of nature and the Universe. Deep stillness and listening allow us to drop into this flow and ride it.

George Lucas had an insight into this dimension and truth with his penning of "the force" in the *Star Wars* epic, but he didn't quite get it right. As opposed to: "May the force be with you," he should have written, "May the *flow* be with you." To be in touch with the flow is to be a Jedi of our creative life. Of course, when you're in touch with the infinite creative flow of the Universe – you're much more interested in dancing, singing, and making love than blowing up Death Stars.

SONG OF THE SOUL

Over the years, I have played flute on occasion for those on their deathbeds. There is a long tradition throughout the world of combining music with the dying process. From ancient Egypt to Native America, music has often been used to calm the soul and help those who are riding the last waves of breath as they are ferried into the other world.

From my early experiences of using the piano to heal from my abdominal surgery to my self-healing with the Native American flute after Hurricane Ivan, I intuitively knew this truth. I always assumed, however, that there was more going on than I realized.

One experience was a profound reminder of this deeper connection between the soul of the dying and music. I had been asked to play the flute for a young mother dying of cancer. She was only in her late 30's and had been a surfer. She was a vibrant, good hearted, beautiful woman and soul. I did not know her before she'd became ill, but even when she was days from dying, she had a light and warmth about her.

A friend at hospice who knew about my work and music asked me to come play for her. The young mother said she didn't have a traditional religious affiliation, but she'd always had an affinity for Native American culture. I was touched by the request and was able to work it out in my schedule to be there. Unfortunately, the first day I arrived she went into a coma. The well-meaning nurses and doctors suggested I play anyway, which I did.

When I play the flute for healing I do my best to get out of my head and drop into compassionate awareness in my heart, to play what I feel moving through me. A particularly deep, touching song came out that day, one I'd never played before. I felt very connected to the song and the experience.

After I finished, I thanked the nurses, doctors, and counselors and left. The next day, I received a call from my friend to tell me that the woman, who we'll call Marie here, had come out of her coma and said she had the most amazing dream, that a man had come to her window and played the most beautiful song on his Native

American flute. They told her that this was no dream, because I really had been there, playing for her.

She asked if I could return, now that she was awake and conscious, so that she could meet me. Of course, I couldn't wait to get back and meet her.

It was a very special opportunity to share and connect. Her heart was so open, and her eyes just shone with such light, even though cancer had taken a great toll on her body.

"Would you play for me again?" she asked after we talked.

"Of course," I said.

I closed my eyes and played my flute, and my fingers began doing things they didn't usually do. I finished, kissed my flute as I always do, and opened my eyes.

Marie said, "Thank you so much. That song is just beautiful. What do you call it?"

"I don't know," I answered. "I have never played it before. It must be your song, Marie's Song."

Her eyes welled up with tears, and she said, "It reminds me of the wave I rode in on, and it gives me courage to ride the wave back out."

Both of our eyes welled up as we smiled affectionately at each other, with a gaze of deep inward knowing of the mysterious journey she was about to undertake.

Maria left her body a few days later, shedding it like a cocoon that had served its purpose. I know in my heart that her soul is free and dancing in the infinite expanse of spirit – surfing, swimming, and singing her soul song.

WITHIN YOUR HEART LIVES THE SONG OF YOUR SOUL. THIS SONG TELLS YOU WHO YOU ARE, WHERE YOU COME FROM AND WHAT YOU ARE HERE TO DO.

DEEP PEACE IN DEATH

When we lose our fear of death, we lose our fear of life. Most of us play it safe in life. We all exercise a certain degree of caution because of the risk of physical death, but what I am talking about is more subtle and insidious. We don't follow our hearts and live the life we are called to live out of fear of dying emotionally and psychologically and losing the ego needs of social acceptance. This includes fear of failure, of exposing ourselves to ridicule and embarrassment. Ironically, the only thing we lose are the very things that keep us imprisoned!

Once we transcend our need for acceptance and approval, there comes extraordinary freedom and the ability to follow our hearts without fear. We can then actually feel connected to our hearts and souls, and experience genuine connection to others, nature, and the cosmos.

What is death, really, but the unknown? We are like the 5-year-old before his first day of kindergarten, the freshman before his first day of high school, or the graduate who cries the night before leaving for college. Even these experiences, so normal and natural, create fear and anxiety, simply because we have never experienced them before.

What we truly fear in death is simply the unknown, the experience of nothingness, but the nothingness is not necessarily empty. It is something you can experience now, while you're alive, and that will take much of the sting and fear out of gazing at the undiscovered country. Exploring, welcoming, and befriending death as a natural, inevitable part of life (regardless of your beliefs about it), releases a tremendous amount of creative energy. We are then free to use this energy to express our creativity.

One day, each of us will take our last breath. To live under the illusion that this will never occur steals the preciousness of our current life from us. As odd as it may sound, death wakes us up to the life we are living here and now.

A good way to begin looking at your eventual death is to write down your feelings and fears about it. Following are some powerful journaling questions that can help you explore your beliefs and feelings about death. Remember, allow yourself to respond in an unedited, uncensored way without judgment. Just let the thoughts and feelings flow through you.

Find your Peace Within space and your Peace Within journal and explore these questions:

1. *If you fear death, why?*

2. *What do you believe will happen to you after your death?*

3. *Who (or what) do you believe dies? All of you? Your body? Your ego? Will you have a sense of yourself after death? If so, how do you think you'll experience yourself and life differently after death? If you believe there is 'nothing' in your belief system – then what do you feel will be your 'experience' of nothingness?*

4. *Imagine you are on your deathbed. Write down your last words to those you love.*

5. *Who comes to your deathbed?*

6. *Who would you want or need to see in order to make Peace Within yourself and the world before dying?*

7. *What would you regret not doing if you died today? This is often known as a bucket list.*

8. *Write down your bucket list and a timeframe for reaching everything included on it.*

9. *How old do you imagine you will be when you die?*

10. *If you want to have a long, healthy life, what do you need to do to stay healthy until that time comes?*

11. *What changes are you willing to make in your life in regard to diet, exercise, relationships, etc. in order to live till your target age?*

MODULE 10 – MAIN POINTS

To summarize, the main points contained in Module 10: *Peace Within Death* are:

1. *Death is a presence in our lives as well as an object of consciousness. Establishing a relationship with death is key to finding peace with it. When we realize that who we are at our essence is a wave and not a particle, our relationship with death changes radically.*

2. *When we explore deep meditation practices and begin to experience the fluidity of all phenomena, we are able to ground ourselves in the pure awareness of the present moment, with compassion, curiosity, and love.*

3. *It is when we lose our fear of death that we lose our fear of life and can get on with living from our hearts, letting go of the expectation of success or the fear of failure. We simply become who we were meant to be.*

4. *The practice of deep stillness and deep silence allows us to touch the still center, where the true dance of life exists.*

5. *When we open ourselves in this way, we can awake to who we truly*

are: the eyes, ears, hands of a wise, compassionate Universe, seeking once again to experience itself in all of beauty and compassion. We move from the Industrial and Information Revolution to the awareness and compassion revolution on the planet.

MODULE 10 - PEACE WITHIN DEATH PRACTICES

1. *Continue your mindfulness practice. Spend time exploring the subtle in between experience of the in breath and out breath – noticing how every ending is also a beginning. Pause particularly after the out breath (expiration) and notice the feeling of the end of a breath for a moment before feeling the natural flow into the next inhale of breath.*

2. *Journal on your relationship with death. If you choose, write a therapeutic letter to death or do a Death Lodge ceremony.*

3. *Write your epitaph and obituary. How do you feel about what you've written? How do you want to live your life from here forward so you can write an epitaph and obituary you feel good about.*

4. *Explore how a Heart Warrior faces death – through facing ending and loss with compassion, wisdom and grace. Journal on this.*

5. *Increase your fifteen minutes a day of sitting meditation to twenty minutes a day.*

6. *By now, you should have developed a meditative stance toward your day. Cultivate using each moment as an opportunity to wake up and be present, without judgment of what is.*

7. *Become an artist of life. Notice when your thoughts turn to death. What emotions arise? How do you deal with the anxiety of 'not being' and defend yourself against the unknown and uncertainty? Do you let yourself feel and breathe through it? Journal on your beliefs about death. What do you think happens when you die? If you continue, what part of you prevails? Your ego, your soul, your awareness? Explore this and notice how your feelings change. What happens when you go to sleep (hypnos) the son of death, (thanatos) in Greek mythology. We actually call Savasana, the pose you have been using for your meditations, as the corpse pose. What is the deeper meaning of this and how do you feel about it?*

8. *Continue with four thirty minute guided lying down meditation a week (You can always practice more – these are minimum.)*

POSTLUDE

Peace Within Death. While writing those words I found out my mother was dying. It was a cruel, yet appropriate irony that while writing this final chapter, I came face to face with the hardest death of my life. My mother was diagnosed with not one, but three terminal illnesses. During the next three years of editing and re-writing, I watched my precious, vibrant, beloved mother, who always looked twenty years younger than her age, steadily decline as she nobly fought multiple myeloma, cardiac amyloidosis, and congestive heart failure. During that time, she skated near death over and over again.

A mother is our first love, the body that grew us, held us, and carried us when we could not carry ourselves. For nine months, a mother and child are one. I knew my mother loved me in a way no one else ever would or could. Luckily, the two of us had already worked through much of the emotional baggage that all parents and children carry.

Still, when the body and soul that ushered you into life begins to depart, the pain can be intense and primal. As much as I'd lived with death over my shoulder; and had worked on my own fears of dying, I wasn't able to squarely face my mother's physical death, that is, until one particular Saturday evening, a year into her illness.

I had arrived to spend the night with her in the hospital, as I'd often done. She'd taken a terrible fall a few months earlier, one that required emergency surgery that nearly killed her. It was then that I began to perceive not just the flesh and blood mother I loved so dearly, but her soul, as it seemed to radiate through her flesh. She often leaned against me as we walked, arm in arm, to the infusion room, at times letting me hold her close as she gently wept.

We talked about death and she told me she wasn't afraid of dying. "I've lived a full life, Michael. I certainly want to fight these illnesses and last as long as I can, but I'm at peace. When the good Lord decides it's my time to go, I'm ready, but it seems like he's not quite ready to take me yet, and I'm not quite ready to go either."

That night at the hospital after months of chemo, and the emergency surgery, she developed serious heart problems. All at once, I realized that her heart had stopped beating. I pushed the code button as she lay in my arms, lifeless, her lips turning blue. I was unable to do anything but wait until the medical team arrived. After thirty years of meditation practice, I closed my eyes and tried my best to connect with her soul on the inner plane.

As I did, I was blinded by a golden, crystalline orb of light, which I knew, in my depths, was my mother's soul. The love I felt was unlike anything I'd ever experienced...it became so very clear to me the love that flowed between us had always been...and always would be...it was more fundamental and real that all of space and time...it was then that I knew that if she did not come back to her body, it would be okay...and I told her so.

As time and space continued to dissolve around us...I felt the quantum, ocean of peace...turn into an ocean of love flowing between the shorelines of our hearts...supporting this desperate, tragic moment with a sublime grace…I felt a strange calm in and amongst the chaos of the outer world that began to unfold around us…like birds flying through the eye of a hurricane…potential death all around… and yet, something more…an inner knowing.

I whispered in her ear, "Mom, whatever you need...whatever your heart and soul needs, is ok...if you need to go...or stay...it's okay. I'm here, and this love never dies…"

The medical team arrived, and although they were able to resuscitate her, they could not get an adequate heart rhythm, and so she was taken into emergency surgery for a pacemaker.

After that, she amazingly, lived two more years. We were able to celebrate her 60th wedding anniversary and her 80th birthday. Those two years were often painful, but alternatingly euphoric, as she slowly turned into an angel right before our eyes. Each time I saw her, I felt like such grace. I am deeply thankful for each of those moments, as our love continued to grow in ways I did not think possible. I did my best to hold onto that vision of her soul I witnessed that evening – so complete, whole and radiant. It became a constant reminder that her death could come at any moment.

In January of 2015, mom caught pneumonia and was placed in the hospital. After an agonizing week, her team of doctors said there was nothing more they could do and that she should be placed in hospice care. They thought she only had a few weeks left to live. Through our tears, our family agreed, and she was moved to the hospice room in a nursing home. Still, mom wasn't quite ready to depart.

Over the next nine months, there were miraculous rebounds and rallies. The medical staff weren't sure how she continued to stay alive, but she did. We celebrated the high school graduation of her youngest grandson, then Mother's Day, then various birthdays in that hospice room. Amazingly, she even was able to celebrate her 62nd wedding anniversary, two years past her last near-death experience. She continued to weaken, her body almost unrecognizable from the strong, vivacious, and animated woman who had once commanded any room she walked into with her beauty and childlike wonder. No matter how much she suffered, she always managed an "I love you" and smiled with a special radiance and love all her own – as if you were the only one in the world at that moment.

Finally, her pain and breathlessness could no longer be managed in the hospice room at the nursing home and she was transferred to a hospice residence that allowed us to create a beautiful space for her final days. There was a piano there that I played for her and other patients, along with my healing flutes.

Her first day there, Mom wanted to get out of bed one last time and go out, much to the surprise of the hospice team. Since her limbs had stiffened so, I carried her to a wheelchair and took her outside. The sun and wind made her face light up with pleasure, especially at the beautiful statue of Mary outside her room. DeMaria, our family name, means "of Mary", and we all had a special affinity for our beloved Mary, Mother of God. We wheeled her to a little Zen Buddhist garden and rang the bell of awakening and listened to the wind chimes.

She had begun talking to me about angels, "beings of light" who had been visiting her, telling her she no longer needed to eat or drink because she wasn't going to need it where she was going. She'd also begun to see her loved ones. She said she was excited about encountering her mother, brother, and others who were waiting for her. Still, the fighter in her, the one who loved life and us so much, still was not ready to let go.

It was difficult for some to accept it when she stopped drinking fluids and eating, but I'd spent extended periods of my life fasting in the wilderness, days without water and two weeks without food; I knew the sacred space that is created when one stops feeding the body. The soul grows as the body weakens. It's not unlike entering a dream state. Many of the most profound experiences of my life occurred through fasts. In wilderness survival, the rule of three is three weeks without food, three days without water, and three minutes without air. Once she stopped drinking water, the doctors felt she would survive four or five days at the most.

Five days came and went. Mom became unresponsive for the most part, with her eyes closed, but she still occasionally squeezed our hands and relaxed her face into a smile when we kissed her, told her we loved her, or when Danielle, my daughter, read to her from one of their favorite books. Danielle, a deeply intuitive soul, felt her death would be on September 22, Yom Kippur and the Autumnal Equinox, yet that was still three more days away.

We decided to perform a Yom Kippur ceremony at sunset on September 22. We created a beautiful altar in her room and opened the shades to the outdoors, turning her bed to face the windows and altar we had created for her. We gathered around her at sunset at the beginning of the Day of Atonement and the Autumnal Equinox, when light and darkness, day and night are in perfect balance. We held hands and recited a prayer, then said goodbye and let her know it was okay for her to go. We half expected her to leave at that moment, she would wait for the earth to turn one more time around its axis before taking her final breaths.

Our death vigil moved into its ninth day as the sun rose on the morning of September 23, the fulfillment of Yom Kippur and the Autumnal Equinox. Although it was difficult for some of her loved ones to be with her when she was so shriveled, weak, and struggling to breathe, for me, there was no more sacred place to be on the planet. As her body diminished, I felt her soul filling the entire room, preparing to go home.

As I played my flute, it vibrated my entire body and brought me back to the vision I'd had two years previously. I tried to comfort myself and her, to let her know she was going home and that she could still help all of us, even more from the other side of things. I told her that although we were losing the physical presence and pattern of connecting with our beloved Jacqueline — we were gaining the most special, precious angel one could imagine.

In between flute serenades, I massaged her body with frankincense, myrrh, rose oil, and cypress. I massaged her forehead and temples and cradled her head in the palms of my hands, kissing her forehead as I did. I sensed her preparing to leave her body, like a butterfly leaving a cocoon, to emerge into Spirit.

During her last hour of life, my father lay with her in her deathbed, lovingly whispering to her, recounting all of the precious highlights of their life together. He then did what was the hardest thing for him to do, what he had struggled so long to do, he let her know it was ok to go.

This took so much out of Dad that afterward, he simply collapsed on the couch. My brother held her hand, saying the rosary by her side, while I continued to massage her head. For the first time in a long while, her breathing became peaceful. Her eyes suddenly opened, and she looked upward and outward. Then there was a break in her breathing and a short gasp that sounded like a young child might upon seeing something so beautiful it took her breath away. Her heart was still lightly beating when she let out another gasp…this one deeper and more filled with awe…then silence… her heart barely beating…finally, there was a third great gasp as the door to the outside garden opened…and a beautiful breeze blew through the room…reminding us in the physical world of the profound mystery unfolding in the vast unseen realm my dear and most precious mother…had suddenly entered.

Sunlight and shadow shimmered through the room, and I sensed her soul releasing through her heart, as if a flock of doves had been freed. Suddenly, waves of emotion crashed through me… deep relief that she was free of suffering and profound grief over the loss of her tangible, physical presence in my life…Deep howls rose from my body, and a cascade of tears flowed down my face and anointed hers.

Ironically, with her death, my mother has, in many ways never been more present to me. Through her dying, I was able to become acquainted with her ageless, ancient, timeless soul.

Through this profound heart opening, I have often reflected on the tremendous love my mother gave me, where it comes from and where it has gone. I now feel this love braiding its way through each breath I take, pulsating through every cell of my body. Freed from its local home in my mother's physical body, it is now like an ocean in which I swim. The love she gave me helped me touch the Great Loving, which like the ocean of peace bathes all we see, feel, hear and touch. She was a deeply personal, individual, and unique expression of this ocean, a river of love that fed and nourished me, from the first moments the small cells that would become my body, while in her belly, to the decades she loved, guided and believed in me. This river of Jacqueline has now merged once again into that great ocean of divine love that is our source and destination.

I have begun to understand that the ocean of peace I encountered during my psychological and emotional death/rebirth after Hurricane Ivan prepared me to help my mother's soul to make the transition into spirit. There was a great similarity in these experiences. My tangible sense of that ocean of peace prepared me to hold, comfort, and support her soul's going into that ocean of love that bathes us all.

During her final days I spent a great deal of time in her room, syncing my breath with hers. It was a profound way to be with her, particularly when she was asleep or unresponsive at the end. As I tuned into her breath, my mind became so still and my heart so open. I felt at one with her. Even in the midst of her dying, I at times experienced such deep and lasting peace and grace. This only occurred when I encountered the process from a felt sense within my heart, instead of thinking about the process intellectually.

When I could be simply present without judgment or telling myself stories about what was happening, I could manage the impossible, and find grace in the tragic. I tuned into the light in the room, felt my feet on the floor and, my body against the chair, inhabiting my body and heart the best I could…In so doing, I could be present… feeling the full gravity of my sorrow…while honoring the full joy of my heart's deeper knowing of a connection that extends beyond the physical senses, into a vaster sphere that supported my love through that dark time.

Now, when I close my eyes, I see not just a crystalline, golden light, but something more. I see my mother's original face, her eyes closed, looking inward like a serene, tranquil, ancient yet youthful, wise woman who wears a gentle, blissful smile of inward knowing. I know she is with me; her love my roots and the trunk of the literal cells of my body. I also know she is home and at peace. Perhaps, she is having amazing adventures I can only dream of, here, on the other side. One thing I finally know tangibly and without question from deep within…is that peace…even in death…is only found…by turning…within.

NOTES

[1] This contract is adapted from Julia Cameron's book The Artist's Way which has been so beneficial to myself and so many of my clients and students over the years. An excellent resource for healing the inner artist in all of us.

MODULE 1 NOTES

[1] In fact, the original title of this book was Feeling Better, which referred to learning to deal with our feelings more skillfully, effectively and creatively. The entire Peace Within process and program is designed with this goal.

[2] The lungs oxygenate the blood while the heart pumps the oxygenated blood to all parts of the body. The heart then circulates blood that has been depleted of life giving oxygen and saturated with the toxic carbon dioxide back to the lungs to be expelled from the body.

[3] Ontosynthesis, a word I coined, is also my description of the process of turning life experience into wisdom and compassion. Where photosynthesis turns light into life, ontosynthesis occurs in the human heart and turns life into love.

[4] There are over 4,000 components of blood, but for the sake of simplicity we only look at these three components. There are also thousands of components to all experiences as well, but it helps to reduce the complexity by focusing on these three main categories; thoughts, feelings and sensations.

[5] Transpersonal Psychology with my mentor, teacher and friend, Dr. William Mikulas, author of The Way Beyond (Wheaton, IL: Theosophical Publishing, 1987) and Taming the Drunken Monkey: The Path to Mindfulness, Meditation, and Increased Concentration. (Minnesota: Llewellyn, 2014.)

[6] This mantra was introduced to me by poet, philosopher and wisdom teacher Mark Nepo in his beautiful work Reduced to Joy (audio program published by Sounds True 2015) which includes my music for the intros and outros to the program.

[7] Ellen Luders et al. "Shifting brain asymmetry: the link between meditation and structural lateralization. Soc Cogn Affect Neurosci 10 (2013): 55-61.

[8] R. Lutz & Richard Davidson. "Mind of the Meditator." Scientific America, Nov. 311 (2014): 5.

MODULE 2 NOTES

[1] In yoga, breathwork is known as pranayama, which comes from the Sanskrit word Prana, meaning breath or life force, and ayāma, meaning 'to extend or draw out.' I have chosen the word breathwork because this is the way I was taught by my teacher, Dr. William Mikulas, and also because I am not referring to many of the esoteric pranayama practices that have not been researched – and can be dangerous if practiced incorrectly.

[2] I learned this technique from my good friend and teacher, Grammy winner David Darling. It was a year into my recovery that I attended my first class with David in his famed Music For People school of improvisation and facilitation. I went on to study with him for 4 years and graduate from the program as a Certified Musical Improvisation Facilitator. My experience in MFP was a huge part of my own healing and recovery that I will always be grateful for.

[3] Exodus 3:5.

MODULE 3 NOTES

[1] The Drunken Monkey or 'Monkey Mind' is an often used phrase to describe the untrained mind before one has begun to practice mindfulness and meditation, which helps sober the monkey. This is one of my teacher's favorite phrases and the subject of his book, Taming the Drunken Monkey: The Path to Mindfulness, Meditation, and Increased Concentration (Woodbury, MN: 2014.)

[2] Although I have used a particular version of this for years with my clients and students it has become more mainstream with the excellent work on somatic mindfulness practices for healing trauma. In particular, I was thrilled to see a version of this in Peter Levine's excellent book, Healing Trauma. A Pioneering Program for Restoring the Wisdom of the Body. (Boulder, CO: Sounds True, 2005.)

³My healing/meditation music can be ideal for this. I particularly suggest my album Ocean for the healing shower experience.

⁴Studies on grounding and earthing illustrate how we become positively charged during the day, particularly from being near electronic devices. This positive electrical charge translates into stress on the mind and body. Showers are one way this charge is discharged; they can actually help induce a negative charge (negative ionization) in the body, which leads to a relaxation response in the mind/body.

⁵Othello, act 1, scene 3.

⁶My good friend and Peace Within process facilitator Tara Taylor, LMT shared this metaphor with me from her training with Yogi Vishvketu.

⁷Mikulas, Taming the Drunken Monkey, p. 73.

⁸EL Abel, ML Kruger, "Smile Intensity in Photographs Predicts Longevity," Psychological Science 21 (April 2010): 542-544.

⁹Madan Kataria, Laugh For No Reason (Mumbai, India: Madhuri International, 2002.)

¹⁰I'll always be thankful to Swami Jnaneshvara Bharati, a dear friend and teacher whose excellent CD *Yoga Nidra Meditation: Extreme Relaxation of Conscious Deep Sleep* was gifted to me during this time by Rusty Gasparian and it was another powerful part of my healing since it was one of the few meditations I could do in the physical and emotional pain I was in. I went on to study many different forms of laying down meditation including studying all I could find on the powerful pratice of yoga nidra including receiving training with Richard Miller and others. Swami Jnaneshvara's I still consider one of the best and his website www.swamij.com has excellent resources on understanding the subtler points of this profound practice.

MODULE 4 NOTES

¹Although there are plenty of reasons from a psychological and emotional level I struggled with suicidal feelings and thoughts during this time, from an integrative wellness perspective it is important to note I was eating a vegan diet during this time also, and I am now convinced

that it played a factor in this deep, dark suicidal depression I was in. On top of everything else, I had a severe serotonin deficiency due to lack of the essential amino acid L-Tryptophan only found in plentiful supplies in animal protein or with supplementation, neither of which I was receiving at the time. I highly recommend the book The Mood Cure by Julia Ross who I later trained with for more information on the importance of neuro-nutrition in regulating mood.

[2]Years later I discovered this mantra in a mindfulness and psychotherapy workshop with Ron Seigel, Ph.D. who also recommends this mantra to many of his clients and students and has found it extremely beneficial for quieting the mind.

[3]National Science Foundation. However, some like Deepak Chopra, believe that the average person may have as many as 60,000-80,000 thoughts a day. Although there is no current scientific consensus on the number, no one would dispute the fact that we all would benefit by quieting our minds substantially.

[4]Just as a smile creates a physiological positive feedback loop between the muscles of the face and the neurological pathways in the brain, so can a chronic frown accompanied by a negative internal story create self-reinforcing negative effects.

[5]Mantras are simple phrases repeated in order to facilitate spiritual or psychological growth. They can be thought of verbal meditations. The object of meditation in this case is the repeated phrase instead of the breath or a physical object.

[6]Both my albums on the Sounds True Label, In the Flow and Solace: Music for Emotional Healing, are excellent aids in this process.

MODULE 5 NOTES

[1]I was deeply comforted and validated years later when I came across this practice with many indigenous people – and, explicitly in the 'council work' practiced at the Animas Valley Institute. Dr. Bill Plotkin was the first to introduce this powerful formal practice of speaking from the heart and listening from the heart.

[2]Reinhold Niebuhr, The Serenity Prayer, The Essential Reinhold

Niebuhr: Selected Essays and Addresses, edited by Robert McAfee Brown. (New Haven: Yale University Press, 1987): 251

MODULE 6 NOTES

[1] For thousands of years, child-rearing practices have been based primarily on punishment. We are the inheritors of patria potesta, the Roman law that said that children (and women) were the property of the father. In ancient Rome, (and elsewhere around the world) children (and wives) were considered property that could be sold, traded or even put to death. It has only been in the last decades that children have begun to have legal protection from abuse by parents and adults.

[2] Mark 12: 31.

[3] Erich Fromm, The Art of Loving (New York: Harper & Row, 1956).

[4] Dr. Kristin Neff has developed a self-compassion scale that you can take online to explore how compassionate you are with yourself. It can be found at: http://www.self-compassion.org/test-your-self-compassion-level.html

[5] Kristin Neff, Self-Compassion: The Proven Power of Being Kind to Yourself (New York: William Morrow, 2011.)

[6] Ibid.

[7] For more on self-talk you might find my friend and colleague Shad Helmstetter's work in this area helpful.

[8] Neff, K. D.; Hseih, Y. and Dejitthirat, K. "Self-compassion, achievement goals, and coping with academic failure." Self and Identity 4 (2005): 263–287. Neff, K. D.; Kirkpatrick, K.; Rude, S. S. "Self-compassion and its link to adaptive psychological functioning," Journal of Research in Personality 41 (2007): 139–154. Neff, K. D.; Rude, S. S.; Kirkpatrick, K. "An examination of self-compassion in relation to positive psychological functioning and personality traits," Journal of Research in Personality 41 (2007).

[9] Ni, Hua-Ching, Attune Your Body With Dao-In: Taoist Exercise for a

Long and Happy Life. The Shrine of the Eternal Breath of Tao, College of Tao and Traditional Chinese Healing, 1990. Master Ni calls this Immortal Embracing of the Universe. I have adapted it over the years by having my student cross the ankles and rock gently instead of raising the shoulder blades and head above the ground.

MODULE 7 – NOTES

[1] I researched self-hate for my dissertation, which was later published as the book Horns and Halos: Toward the Blessing of Darkness (Peter Lang Press, 1992.)

[2] One of the reasons I became a certified instructor in Yoga was because of the injury I suffered in a yoga class and my desire to help prevent this with others. Yoga as practiced in the West has focused too much on competition and perfecting the body. Yoga is primarily a spiritual path of awakening and not about competition, ego or perfecting the physical body. It is designed to support people connecting to the here and now, and allowing them to experience a unity between their inner nature and the outer nature of the cosmos. In fact, the asanas (postures) are only one small part of the traditional practice of yoga.

[3] Stephen Covey and Anais Nin both used this phrase, although the origin is the Talmud and comes from an ancient Jewish Proverb.

[4] Matthew 18:3

[5] Linda Kramer, Sudevi of Blue Lotus Yoga at the time. She had also cured herself from a serious back injury through yoga. She taught me the finer points of listening to my body and learning what worked best for me as well as how to experience my body as energy and not simply a physical collection of muscle, sinew and bone.

[6] Marty Klein, LMT, was a true gift to me for the next five years. He taught me a great deal about caring and healing myself, while helping my body, mind and spirit heal in his amazing space. Marty is not only a gifted massage therapist, but extremely gifted in working with chi in his many year practicing Tai Chi. I remain deeply grateful for the role he played in my healing and transformation.

[7] Pranic Healing and Reiki.

[8] I wrote about some of this experience in my second book, Ever Flowing On: On Being and Becoming Oneself (Terra Nova Press, 2001.)

[9] Bill Plotkin is one of the world authorities on contemporary wilderness rites of passage. In addition to being the founder AVI (Animas Valley Institute) he has written three seminal books on the subject, Soulcraft, Nature and the Human Soul, and Wildmind, all published by New World Library. He remains a dear teacher, mentor, colleague and friend.

[10] The acorn theory of the soul was popularized by James Hillman, the archetypal psychologist in his book The Soul's Code. It was Hillman's belief that nature and nurture could not account for the fullness of human development. For him, psyche, the Greek word for soul, was a third kind of energy that contributed to individual development as seen in one's character, aspiration and achievement. James Hillman, The Soul's Code: In Search of Character and Calling (New York: Grand Central Publishing, 1997)

[11] Peter moved to Boulder, Colorado when a young man to pursue improvisational music and found himself playing music while Alan Ginsberg read his poetry, listening to Chogram Trungpa Rinpoche and becoming one of the early pioneers of healing, meditative music. The two of us recently created the album Heart of Silence: Meditations for Piano and Flute on the Sounds True Label.

[12] I learned this method from Steve Pavlina, on his blog, stevepavlina.com, who gave permission to share it here. When I asked him where he first come across the exercise he could not remember where it originated. I've adapted it here and came up with the title, "Writing Yourself to Tears."

[13] This exercise is adapted from one of Julia Cameron in The Artist's Way (New York: Jeremy Tarcher, 1992.)

[14] This is meant only as a metaphor. It is less a map or a scientific schema, and more of a poetic way of understanding the Peace Within process. I find in my own life and with those I work with, using nature metaphors for working with the body, mind, heart and soul

is tremendously beneficial. It is helpful to realize that we each are not only part and parcel of the earth, sky, ocean and sun, but that these forces have been etched into our being during billions of years of evolution.

[15] Once again these are metaphors and as such are not stating a scientific fact, but a metaphorical and poetic way of exploring an inner world that can be very fruitful. Essentially, awareness arises from the fundamental ground that is numinous (superordinate to sensory phenomena) and not phenomenal (known by the five senses) as such can never be known or described. Whatever we say about it won't be it.

MODULE 8 – NOTES

[1] Letters to a Young Poet, Rainer Maria Rilke, Herter Norton (translator). (New York: W.W. Norton & Co., 1993).

[2] Kahlil Gibran, The Prophet. (New York: Alfred A. Knopf, 1923.)

[3] Sam Keen, Fire in the Belly: On Being a Man. (New York: Bantam, 1992).

[4] It's important to note that it's healthy to show concern for a partner who is not feeling well, but if you are in possession of your sense of self when doing so, you can reach out to them out of compassion and not fear and anxiety. If they respond negatively you don't take it personally and continue on with your day and let them work it out for themselves. This example, illustrates what happens when we reach out to others out of fear and insecurity, instead of from strength and love.

[5] I first heard this term from James Hollis in his book, The Eden Project: The Search for the Magical Other (Inner City Books, 1998).

[6] Shared with me by my good friend and colleague, hypnotherapist Carol Hicks, who studied with Erickson.

MODULE 9 – NOTES

[1] Mark 12:30-31.

[2] I was introduced to this phrase and term by Bill Plotkin, Ph.D. of

Animas Valley Institute during my studying and training with him.

[3]Carl Rogers, On Becoming a Person: A Therapist's View of Psychotherapy (London: Constable, 1961.)

[4]I will always be grateful to Ed Hrebec of Spirit of the Wood Flutes who helped me tremendously in rebuilding my collection for a very reasonable price.

[5]Eckart Tolle, Music for Inner Stillness (Sounds True, 2012.)

[6]Carl Rogers, On Becoming a Person.

[7]Gallup Corporation, Forgiveness poll.

[8]Van Oyen, C. Witvilet, T.E. Ludwig and K. L. Vander Lann, "Granting Forgiveness or Harboring Grudges: Implications for Emotions, Physiology and Health," Psychological Science 12 (2001): 117-23

[9]S. Sarinopoulos, "Forgiveness and Physical Health: A Doctoral Dissertation Summary," World of Forgiveness 2 (2000): 16-18. There is an extensive collection of 46 innovative research projects at www.forgiving.org funded by A Campaign for Forgiveness Research, the results of which are available to review online. Also Learningtoforgive.com and Fred Luskin, Forgive for Good: A Proven Prescription for Health and Happiness (New York: Harper, 2002.)

[10]Jack Canfield, The Success Principles (New York: William Morrow, 2004.)

[11]Merle A. Fossum, & Marilyn J. Mason, Facing Shame: Families in Recovery (New York: W.W. Norton, 1986.)

[12]Chata'ah is the Hebrew word most often translated as sin in English Christian Bibles. Its literal meaning is "missing the mark," as an archer might miss a bull's eye when shooting an arrow. Even when it was translated into the Greek word Hamartia, the English remains sin, although the Greeks also use it to mean "missing the mark." Both terms suggest that we would all be served by referring to what we usually call 'bad behavior' as 'unskillful' instead.

[13] Brene Brown, The Gifts of Imperfection: Let Go of Who You're Supposed to Be and Embrace Who You Are (Center City MN: Hazelden, 2010.); Brene Brown, Daring Greatly: How the Courage to Be Vulnerable Transforms the Way We Live, Love, Parent, and Lead (New York: Avery, 2015.)

[14] Brene Brown, The Power of Vulnerability, https://www.ted.com/talks/brene_brown_on_vulnerability?language=en

[15] Martin Luther King Jr. "Forgiveness is not an occasional act, it is a constant attitude."

[16] Richard Lazarus, Emotion and Adaptation (New York: Oxford University Press, 1991.)

[17] Ibid.

MODULE 10 – NOTES

[1] It is important to remember I am using the ocean of peace as a metaphor. Everyone experiences these transcendent states in their own way, and ultimately the experience is always going to exceed the words we use to describe it. It is a poetic metaphor to express what the experience has been like for me and many others. Ocean here simply means all pervasive, ever present, and healing. My experiences of these states continue to most closely resemble a sense of being bathed in an extremely subtle energy, where thoughts cease and any normal bodily sensations give way to a sense of floating in an extremely subtle fluid like state. Any pain I am having drops away – physical or emotional. I only invite the reader to explore their own experiences. In this way, we are each pioneers and explorers in the world of consciousness and compassionate awareness.

[2] Bruce Lee, The Tao of Gung Fu: A Study in the Way of Martial Art, (Osaki: Tuttle Publishing, 1997).

[3] Richard Carlson, Don't Sweat the Small Stuff—and It's All Small Stuff: Simple Ways to Keep the Little Things from Taking Over Your Life (New York: Hyperion, 1997).

[4] Raymond O. Faulkner (translator) and Eva von Dassow (ed.) The

Egyptian Book of the Dead, The Book of Going forth by Day. The First Authentic Presentation of the Complete Papyrus of Ani (San Francisco: Chronicle Books, 1994.) The feather used was a peacock feather; Anubis was the measurer, and Ammat was the one who devoured the heart. According to the authors, a better translation of the Book of the Dead would be The Book of Emerging Forth into the Light.

[5] Psychology made the same reductionistic mistake regarding emotions when John B. Watson defined the psychological as only that which could be observed and measured.

[6] A Caregiver's Guide to the Dying Process. (Washington, D.C.: Hospice Foundation of America, 2011.)

[7] This is similar to what Eckhart Tolle calls the Pain Body in his book The Power of Now (New World Library, 1999) and spiritual leader A.H. Almaas calls 'Holes.'

[8] Robert A. Johnson, author of the books We, Inner Work, Owning Your Own Shadow and Balancing Heaven and Earth, wrote the introduction to my book Ever Flowing On: On Being and Becoming Oneself. (Terra Nova, 2001.) Robert has been one of the most articulate authors in Jungian psychology and integrating the soul back into life.

[9] Dylan Thomas, The Poems of Dylan Thomas (New York: New Directions, 2003.)

[10] Pierre Lacout, God is Silence (Quaker Books, 1994.) 16

Made in the USA
Middletown, DE
12 February 2020

84614860R00199